Affirming Limits

Affirming Limits

ESSAYS ON MORTALITY, CHOICE, AND POETIC FORM

❦

ROBERT PACK

The University of Massachusetts Press

Amherst, 1985

LC 85–2768
ISBN 0–87023–483–8
Designed by Barbara Werden
Set in Linoterm Trump at the University
of Massachusetts Press
Printed and bound by Edwards Brothers

Library of Congress Cataloging in Publication Data

Pack, Robert, 1929–
Affirming limits.

Includes index.
1. Literature—Addresses, essays, lectures.
2. Poetry—Addresses, essays, lectures. 3. English
poetry—History and criticism—Addresses, essays,
lectures. I. Title.
PN45.P26   1985   809.1   85–2768
ISBN 0–87023–483–8

Some of the chapters of this book were first published in the following:
Robert Frost: Lectures on the Centennial of His Birth, Library of Congress,
Washington, 1975; *Middlebury Alumni Magazine; Southern Review; New
England Review; Kenyon Review; Hudson Review; Yale Preview; Tendril
Magazine; Denver Quarterly; Selected Letters of John Keats*, edited by
Robert Pack, New American Library.

Acknowledgments for permission to reprint material under copyright appear
on the last printed page of this book.

CONTENTS

PREFACE

EACH CHAPTER of this book was written to be an essay complete unto itself, and so the reader is invited to skip around if he or she so pleases. Yet, I have always had in mind the themes of how the idea of death is related to the idea of literary art, and, more generally, how human beings resist or accommodate themselves to their own mortality. These central themes have provided the book with its unity and structure which the reader may wish to consider.

A serious artist can hope for nothing more than to be read with care for detail and nuance, as well as for the sweep of passion and psychological or philosophical meaning. This book is my partial attempt to give thanks to the master artists whose work is here examined by reading them with sustained attention. I take their works to be their best inheritance. What I have learned about the demanding craft of poetry over the years, I have learned mainly from them; and what I have taken to heart about cherishing the little life we are given to live, that, too, has been their gift. As Stevens said: "In the last analysis, [poetry has] something to do with our self-preservation." The pleasure that poetry offers, I believe, must augment our troubled will to survive.

For the convenience of my readers, I have included within my own text the poems that are being discussed—when they are relatively short. It is assumed that the reader will have access to such longer works as *King Lear, Paradise Lost,* and *The Prelude* even in a time in America of the dominance of television and popular culture. I trust that this always will be so.

I wish to record my gratitude to Harold Bloom, John Elder, Paul Mariani, Gary Margolis, John Bertolini, Syd Lea, and Jay Parini—for their insights which have helped me test my own, for their detailed editorial suggestions, and, especially, for their friendship. Patty, my wife, listened and advised from beginning to end. Above all, I have tried for clarity and directness, assuming my reader to be a companion in the fellowship of art.

PART ONE

ONE

Art and Unhappiness

❦

HAPPY FAMILIES are all alike; every unhappy family is unhappy in its own way." So Tolstoy begins *Anna Karenina*, choosing unhappiness as his primary theme, for only in unhappiness does human identity and uniqueness seem to reside. Happiness is anonymous, and therefore it may appear inherently uninteresting to the contemplative artist. It is an emotion to be lived, to be experienced, an end in itself with no need or compulsion to examine itself. Happiness is essentially wordless, or so the logic of Tolstoy's statement would imply. "And so they lived happily ever after." The happy lovers vanish into their happiness, and we, as readers or writers, return to our true medium, our suffering, where, in Keats's words, "to think is to be full of sorrow / And leaden-eyed despairs." The inexorable dialectic of the thinking artist, to alter Descartes, would read: "I suffer, therefore I am." Or as Byron says: "Knowledge is sorrow." And as Denis De Rougemont claims in his study *Love in the Western World*, "Happy love has no history."

Theoretically, there is no aspect of reality that the gifted artist cannot describe or dramatize. Does the theme of happiness, then, present the artist with some special problem? Is

3

there something in the very nature of literary art that mili-
tates against choosing happiness as a theme? In paradise, or in
a social utopia, would there be little motivation for the creating of art? If, in choosing to become a literary artist, one
henceforth depends upon the world's unhappiness for one's
creative substance, how can one oppose that unhappiness
upon which one's identity depends? Is the project of art in
some way tied to the sickness of man's loving the very affliction out of which his art arises? The fact that one sets out to
be an artist may affect the way one looks at the world by
tempting one to focus on violence and pain because such
themes are more exciting than those of tranquility or contentment. If, as W. B. Yeats says, "art is but a vision of reality," how can artists hold to that model of objectivity if they
wish to compete for an audience whose bias is to be told of
anguish and terror, of human failure?

We all can recognize in ourselves the perverse pride that
we take in talking about our own troubles, as well as the perverse pleasure we take in gossiping about the failures of
others. This is the universal principle of malicious joy,
Schadenfreude, from which artists also suffer and in which
they delight; it has been described as "the bearable sorrow
one artist feels when a fellow artist receives a bad review." To
be told by a friend that he understands your troubles is to be
accepted as human, to be embraced for your endearing frailty.
To be told by a friend that you have not suffered is to be dismissed condescendingly, to be banished from the human
circle. "I suffer, therefore I am; I suffer more than you do,
therefore I am more human"—such is the logic of perverse
pride that worships pain and can make of art the temple in
which pain is exalted.

The romantic fascination with and adulation of pain has
come to dominate and perhaps even determine almost all
contemporary poetry, novels, drama, and film. Violence,
sadism, rape, suicide—these are our themes. Hatred and
anger—these are our voices. It is routine to find a movie ad-
vertised with such words as "shocking" or "brutal" because
these are "qualities" that will attract an audience. Imagine
a book jacket that claims a novel to be about "a serene and
peaceful marriage." Who would buy it? The most difficult

achievement for an artist is to present suffering so that its main effect is not entertainment (attention and profit for the artist), and to present what is good in such a way that the spectacle of goodness, as in human kindness, is as compelling as the spectacle of degradation and destruction. "Evil, be thou my good," says Milton's Satan. "Evil, be thou my source of power" is the unspoken principle at the heart of much contemporary artistic endeavor.

There is an alternative view of the artist's relation to evil that argues that all art is affirmative because it is the creation of order, no matter what its theme or its attitude toward evil. In this view, there is no nihilistic art, there is only good or bad art according to the coherence or power of its own order. The hidden assumption here, however, is that human life is fundamentally chaotic and without purpose. The order that the artist creates replaces the sorrow of chaos, even as chaos remains the theme. This paradox suggests that art is joyous simply by being art, no matter how gloomy its vision is of the human condition. The artist is thus the happy bringer of bad news.

Art is joyous in that it transforms cruelty and chaos into order and meaning, but in so doing it places art above life and loses touch with the very evil that it purports to confront. Auden reminds us that "No metaphor, remember, can express / A real historical unhappiness. / Our words have value if they make us gay. / O happy grief, is all sad art can say." But if art can only be happy and if life itself is sad, then the happiness we enjoy in art is merely fantasy, a holiday from reality, and such happiness is all too fragile and vulnerable. The art in love with its own "happiness" can never help to guide us in our own lives. In our struggle to survive with purpose, what we need is an art in which the indigenous happiness of art, its order-giving power, is wedded to an idea of goodness—a goodness that is attainable in daily life. When this idea of goodness is passionately held, the theme and spectacle of evil may be treated without exploitation, for the deprivation or loss of good feelings (as in friendship or love) will be powerfully felt, and the power of the longing for their restoration will replace the increasing need for shocking stimulation that the imagery of violence generates. This desire to evoke and restore good feelings is what Wordsworth calls "tranquilizing power," and it possesses the "wondrous influence of power gently used."

The temptation of valuing art more than daily life is that it indulges the fantasy of existing beyond limits, for artists have greater control of their own created worlds than they do over the historical and cultural conditions of their births. The wish for omnipotence and the desire for immortality are manifest in our oldest myths, and they are undoubtedly primal forces in the human imagination. All artistic creation partakes of the wish for power and control, which in its fullest fantasy is the wish for immortality, to exist beyond the bonds of nature. Since artists' creations are always themselves, their own substance, they are both creator and creature in one, they are parents unto themselves, and they survive in the form of their own offspring, which is also themselves. The fundamental rebellion against nature and its absolute limit, mortality, is completed in the fantasy of creation, and, as Freud argues, all our instincts are galvanized in the enactment of this fantasy: "All the instincts, the loving, the grateful, the sensual, the defiant, the self-assertive and independent—all are gratified in the wish to be the *father of himself.*" But such a wish, persistent as it has been throughout human history, is doomed to failure. We must return to our lives, to the limits of our aging bodies; we must return from the realms of our creation, from our imaginings, to the circumstances of time and place. Our invented worlds cannot replace the world that is given us prior to any choosing. As Wallace Stevens says, "we live in a place / that is not our own." If we build our creations out of hatred for the world we have, since it is not the world we would have made or chosen, then we merely add to the hatred and ugliness that is there already. And since we cannot create anything truly alive except through the natural process of childbirth, we must necessarily survey what our art has wrought and cry out with Keats: "Cold pastoral." Art is the creation of dead things. All art is epitaph.

"We had fed the heart on fantasies," says Yeats, "the heart's grown brutal from the fare." When violence is the

theme of that creation, the energy that goes into artistic creation exploits that violence by directing it against mortality
itself in the fantasy that the work of art can overcome the
necessity of one's own death. But this fantasy must fail, and
any art grounded in this fantasy is finally a pathetic rebellion
against the inexorable facts of decay and death. Rather than
relieving us of violent passion that rebels against our mortal
condition, the energy of art in the fantasy of creating its own
order exacerbates that feeling of violence out of the primary
frustration of all art: it cannot prevent death, nor can it give
life. Frustration compounds frustration, anger compounds
anger, and the hatred of life for what it denies and what
it takes away continues to build so that the given world
comes to be seen as adversary. Yeats's lines go on to define
precisely the brutality that derives from the nurturing of
one's fantasies. He asserts that there is "More substance in
our enmities / Than in our love." Where, then, is the art that
can proclaim our love and find in it a happiness that is equal
to our hatreds? On what premise might an art be based that
would free it from a dependence on violence as its primary
source of energy and thus lead the artist from the maker's
happiness back into his life? In that return, the artist might
become a model, adding a tranquil perspective out of his
ordering power, and thus freeing his voice from dependence
on irony or cynicism.

For all Yeats's fascination with violence, there is a longing
for an alternative power, an intense peacefulness, that is "by
quiet natures understood." This peacefulness, potent in its
achieved equipoise, is given intermittent expression in his
writing, but nowhere is it more lucidly described than in his
Autobiography: "We artists suffer in our art if we do not love
most of all life at peace with itself." I believe that Yeats
means that the artist without a vision of life at peace with itself suffers as a human being, but suffers equally *as an artist*.
He suffers as an artist because his depiction of violence, his
moral perspective of human suffering caused by human vi-
ciousness or injustice, is merely the thematic excuse for his
art unless he possesses a heartfelt belief in a genuine alternative to such corruption. Without such a belief, he is an aes-

thetic hypocrite, for there can be no true moral horror in the face of violence if violence is the only possible mode of human interaction or the primary source of artistic power. The challenge the artist must confront is to realize the "drama," the quiet intensity, of life at peace with itself, so that all the imagery of violence will be felt, not as vicarious sadism, but as a deprivation of peaceful goodness.

Peaceful goodness can only mean the harmony of man with the conditions of his life, knowing what is within his power to change, and knowing as well what is merely in his power to accept. What every man must accept is his own history, his one life, his particular body, and finally his death which may be mitigated only by the survival of others, his children. For a little while his memory endures. For a while, perhaps, his work endures. But within a finite span everything is lost. The human mind cannot avoid this thought. As Yeats says: "Everything that man esteems / Endures a moment or a day." The knowledge of final and absolute loss is inescapable. Yeats continues: "Man is in love and loves what vanishes." If this condition, the vanishing of all things, cannot be accepted, there can be no harmony, only the fantasy of an afterlife or the illusion of a kind of immortality through art. Neither the creation of art, the power of the tyrant, nor the murdering of rivals can confer immortality. People die. If artists consider artistic creation as primary to the meaning or purpose of their lives, inevitably they enact the fantasy of giving birth to themselves that is at heart the manifestation of their deepest despair—the wish for omnipotence. Until they can outgrow this wish and reject it, cast it out, artists live and work as adversaries of nature, for limitation and finitude are their enemies, and they must necessarily find their voices in the violence of opposition. Their inescapable theme, seemingly beyond choice, must be unhappiness.

II

The only way to create life is through the sexual coming together of man and woman in the making of a child. Incredible as it may seem, this is the limiting fact that the artist is prone to suppress or forget. The artist dreams that his mind is androgynous and can generate living things, like Athena's springing from the head of Zeus or like Shakespeare's imprisoned King Richard who imagines: "My brain I'll prove the female to my soul; / My soul the father: and these two beget / A generation of still-breeding thoughts." But they are only thoughts, and Richard is not free to escape his fate. He is not the omnipotent creator. His world of thoughts is a mockery of his condition; it is a marred imitation of true begetting. The artist must take natural begetting and generation as his primary model, but he can never hope to emulate nature's model, for he cannot bring forth a truly living thing. Yet, this knowledge can serve him, for it can combat the essential pride within his wish to be omnipotent and bring about humility which will allow him to place his art in the service of life. This humility is the fundamental acceptance of limitation and the parent's knowledge that his or her life must be given over to the life of the child. Acceptance of the fact that one generation replaces another is the very trial of parental love. As Blake says, "The most sublime act is to set another before you," and this act of achieved harmony through renunciation and acceptance must be the artist's model as well, as he humbles himself before the natural order of inevitable change. If there is no happiness in the creating and nurturing of children because the despair of relinquishing oneself for another is too great, then there is no image of life at peace with itself, of life's accepting its own passing; thus the artist will have no theme but his unhappiness. A happy art necessarily celebrates biological creation and mortality; it is an art in praise of parental acceptance and parental love, either directly or in surrogate form, finding its power in what it serves.

The suppression or replacement of biological creation as the primary model for creation with the model of the creative human mind results in the repression of the fact of mortality. Such repressive thinking resembles the magical thinking of childhood and of dreams, for it places mind over nature, and it dwells in an unsustainable holiday from reality. On the other hand, to affirm the idea of having and nurturing children as the true model for creation—woman and man together—reminds us that neither we nor our works are immortal, and we can then begin to seek what is good in our lives within this knowledge, free of the despair of longing to be other than what we are, of longing to become divine. Freud says: "as for the great necessities of fate, against which there is no remedy, these [man] will simply learn to endure with resignation." Art cannot cure us of our mortality, nor can it remove "the slings and arrows of outrageous fortune." Art cannot even cure the world of man-made evil ("We have no gift to set a statesman right," says Yeats); it can only aid the individual artist, and his reader, in relieving despair in the face of death and injustice. No matter how great the artist's satirical powers and his ability to shame us; no matter how compelling the artist's vision of suffering caused by human cruelty, the world goes on as it always has. If Shakespeare's *King Lear* could not and cannot humanize us collectively, then what can? We leave the theater, this "two hours' traffic of our stage," a time apart from our lives, having been made happy by a spectacle of evil transformed by the poet's art into a play. Momentarily, we enjoy the illusion that we are safe, that we live in an order created by the mind. But we are not safe, fantastic play comes to an end. What has the play added to the reality to which we must return? Is the violence that we must confront on our "awakening" intensified as a source of our unhappiness, so that our seemingly happy art, inevitably at its conclusion, speaks again of sorrow?

For art not to be unbearably sad, it must return us to a source of happiness that precedes the artist's "rage for order," as Stevens describes the basic human wish for power and control. That source of happiness, life at peace with itself, is the only theme that can rescue art from solipsism, the fantasy that its own order controls anything other than its own material, which is not human events, but only language. Satan's *"non serviam"* (I will not serve) is equivalent to the artist's refusal to put his art at the service of natural creation seen as natural goodness, and to make, in effect, a religion of art by regarding it as the highest of human values. Rather than serving in time, the rebellious artist seeks to perpetuate himself through his art as if he could control the future, and this "will-to-self-immortalization," as Otto Rank calls it, "arises from the fear of life." But to set another before you, to be at peace with that act of renunciation, and to affirm it in its sublimity is finally to accept one's replacement in life. We owe nature a death, and to be at peace with the future, even to love one's children, is willingly to give over the gift of life. Not to do so is to desire one's own perpetuation through a denial of natural generation. This is "desire," as Stevens tells us, that is "too difficult to tell from despair." We are "sick with desire," according to Yeats, when we wish to be "out of nature" and take on immortal form, to become, as it were, a golden work of art, to become our own progenitors. The cure for such desire, which is the violent rebellion against nature, can only be achieved by the artist when he puts himself again in the service of nature, when he affirms the very conditions of his own death, and when he chooses the model of nurturing parenthood as his guide to achieve peace within what is possible. Stevens describes this possible peace, free from the sickness of desire for the unattainable, when he says: "the health of the world might be enough."

The artist who puts himself in the service of life becomes the artist as celebrator, but this can only be achieved when he overcomes his fear of life which is inseparable from the denial of limits. Only then does his art cease to be a retreat into a fantasy of power or of self-immortalization. Knowing that he can neither control the future nor change the course of history with his art, he may become free of the curse of pride and need not cry out with Hamlet: "O cursed spite, / That ever I was born to set it right!" Rather, he becomes Erik Erikson's aged man who has achieved the peace of "integrity" through the "aceptance of one's one and only life cycle and of the people who have become significant to it as something that had to be and that, by necessity, permitted of no substitutions." Or he becomes the ecstatic Yeatsian artist who collectively finds in "creative joy an acceptance of what life brings," so that "we laugh aloud and mock, in the terror or the sweetness of our exaltation, at death and oblivion." This is the sublime extreme of life at peace with itself, at peace with its own nec-

essary limits, in celebration of its own mortality. Choosing
to be only what he is, the artist leaves his inheritance: the
dramatization in his poems of the power to make such a
choice. The choice changes nothing except his attitude toward necessity, but therein lies his freedom, and with that
freedom an ecstatic peace becomes possible. In freely affirming the limits of his one and singular life, the artist may
achieve harmony with his own mortality, find his own
unique history infinitely precious for all its disappointments,
and thus remake the choice to be exactly what he has become. Contained in that choice, which must continually be
remade as the dynamic of daily life, is the vision that human
happiness, what Wordsworth calls the "little unremembered
acts of kindness and of love," is a higher value than the happiness that art can bring. If art is to serve human happiness, it
must choose to remember our acts of kindness and of love,
even within the spectacle of violence and of loss, and celebrate their goodness.

III

Historically, the primary function of art was to praise God
and his works, his manifestation in nature, or, as in Milton,
to "justify the ways of God to men." Art was not its own end,
for human creation served the purpose of extolling divine creativity and was totally dependent upon God as the creative
model. The acknowledgment of this dependency was crucial
for the artist in defining his humility before God's power and
thus in accepting the limited scope of his art. In this spirit
Gerard Manley Hopkins enjoins us: "long before death /
Give beauty . . . back to God, / Beauty's self and beauty's
giver." The origin of art was the ritualistic celebration of
power and beauty beyond the fabricating strength of man's
greatest efforts. The role of the artist was to serve and glorify
divine power that "doth not need / Either man's work or his
own gifts," as Milton exclaims. The modern artist, sick with
alienation from the world and thus from himself, speaking
mainly in the sardonic tone of irony, retreats to his art as if
it were a world in which he might live, though its only sub-

stance is his own unhappiness feeding upon itself. He has nothing to serve but his own creation, and thus his art becomes a monument to his own solipsism. Even in an age deprived of the supporting belief in a benevolent God whose presence in the world makes all things holy, the artist still needs to place himself in the service of nature. In spite of nature's indifference and man's historical inhumanity to man, the artist must continue to serve the simple power to enjoy what our senses engage in daily life, to enjoy the demands and consolations of family love as if those pleasures were all the meaning we needed and all the fulfillment that we desired. In such service to a power outside and beyond his art, the artist, as Wordsworth says, would embody an "homage paid to the native and naked dignity of man, to the grand elementary principle of pleasure, by which he knows, and feels, and lives, and moves." We must learn again in our time of collective despair and pervasive apocalyptic imaginings to take pleasure in pleasure.

If we think of affirmed pleasure as the source of human meaning and thus the source of human happiness, we must return to the artist's fascination with sorrow and the peculiar problem that happiness itself may create. The fear of happiness taken as a human end derives from the fact that affirmed pleasure brings us to a limit, forces the awareness of that limit upon us, and thus reminds us of our mortality. The instinct to rebel against our condition may arise in us most potently when, in happiness, we reach the border of human possibility. The greed for *more* is most threatening and dangerous when we have achieved what we have wanted. Unlike accepted happiness, however, sorrow projects us wishfully into infinite possibility, and secretly we may prefer this sorrow since it nourishes our fantasies in which no limits need be confronted. In this way, even happiness may be converted into sorrow so that our fantasies need not be abandoned, and in that sorrow the artist again may find his theme, seeming to oppose what inwardly he perversely nurtures. The difficulty of loving a real woman and real children is the same as the difficulty of accepting the conditions of one's life and one's mortality. All require choosing the actual; all require affirmation

of limits and renunciation of the desire for something beyond. The power of the affirming artist is the power to celebrate those limits, to see in finite happiness an image not of
deprivation but of human fulfillment. The banishment of
fantasy returns the artist to himself as friend, lover, and parent, to his one life in whose service he places his art.

To allow oneself to be happy, to accept what one is, does
not mean that one becomes passive in one's relationships or
unfeeling toward the suffering of others. Rather, to know
clearly the goodness that those who suffer are deprived of
may become part of the energy that seeks to better their condition. The artist with a vision of happiness, life at peace with
itself, is compelled to enhance the desire for that happiness in
his readers at the same time that he seeks to exorcise the
reader's desire for power beyond human possibility. The vision of possible happiness, happiness that comes from the
acceptance of limits, enables the artist to place evil and suffering in their proper perspective: they are seen as the deprivation of goodness. Without a vision of goodness as a possibility residing in ordinary experience, the artist is compromised
by depending on the very suffering that is the source of his
creative powers. With such dependency, the artist serves the
devil, the father of the lie, the father of the fantasy of power,
under whose aegis, as Isaiah proclaims, "we have made lies
our refuge." The test of honesty in the face of the temptation
of power necessarily must be confronted in the attitude an
artist takes toward his material. It is not enough to hate what
is hateful, for one cannot hate hatred away through satire or
outrage, which only adds to the sum of hatred already in the
world. The artist must love what is lovable, he must name it
and glorify it, and his depiction of life in its simple and essential goodness must be the theme that brings forth the power
that resides in his love of language and verbal order.

Nothing comes more readily to man than self-deception.
The artist in his pride is particularly susceptible to this vice.
Yet we all need to dream at night; adult and child alike require a time to play; no one can endure without periodically
taking a holiday from reality. Art can provide such play and
such "feigning." Through art we can enjoy a respite from our

own lives and enter into the lives of others. But it is the peculiar burden of artistic dreaming and artistic play that they must return us to reality, freshened and strengthened. This is the vast difference between serious art and the many forms of entertainment. It is easy for entertainment to drive out serious art, for entertainment demands little of us; it encourages fantasy and self-forgetfulness. Pornography and violence are the predominant modes of contemporary entertainment, often presuming to be art. The lie inherent in the kind of fantasy that pornography inevitably evokes is that through sexual passion one can escape from oneself into a freedom from bodily limits. Pornography is the dream of anonymity whose motive, derived from fear, is to be unburdened of responsibility and commitment. Its pretense is that repressiveness can be overcome by destroying inhibition, but what is lost is tenderness, the freedom to show restraint in behalf of the other. When the other is regarded as an object, as anonymous, the defense of anonymity in the mind of the fantasizer tightens its grip and the illusion of freedom becomes a substitute for personality. As Freud has argued, "To ensure a fully normal attitude in love, two currents of feeling have to unite—we may describe them as the tender affectionate feelings and the sensual feelings." In pornography, this essential tenderness has undergone repression, leaving us with a mockery of liberation in the form of uninhibited sensuality. Rather, as Rank says: "it is the willed affirmation of inhibitive family ties that is the creative and at the same time liberating factor." The pornographic "artist" is the exemplar of the lie of self-denial in the guise of self-indulgence; for the rejection of family ties, of family intimacy, and of shared history is again the rejection of limits and the rebellion against mortality. Both the anonymous love object and the anonymous lover, who in fantasy can be anyone, are, in reality, no one at all.

The illusion that the depiction of violence most easily encourages is that someone else is the victim, that we, the audience (or the artist), are the survivors. The extreme model of this illusion, ironically, may be found in the poetry of suicide. The fantasy of suicide enacts a death in which the dreaming

author witnesses his own cessation and thus, in effect, becomes his own survivor. Although the absoluteness of death
appears to be the source of mourning, the inherent lie of the
suicidal artist surviving himself as witness reveals that the
proud wish for immortality has been repressed but not exorcised. The willed removal of that wish can be accomplished
only by the parental imagination which sees not itself but the
child as survivor. The continuity of life exacts the replacement of life. The liberation from the unexposed wish to survive oneself in turn liberates one from the wish to survive
others, and thus the vicious cycle of violent imaginings may
be broken, as Freud says: "No neurotic harbors thoughts of
suicide which are not murderous impulses against others re-
directed upon himself."

The parental imagination, willing the necessary fate of its
own replacement, nevertheless finds in the continuity of life
a sufficient substitute for immortality. The bond that makes
possible and protects that continuity is the willed acceptance
of the finite self and the finite other in marriage. What is
chosen is then endowed with the spirit of an absolute, so that
the mutual and equal commitment to the raising of children
is likewise taken as an absolute and thus made holy. In this
spirit, the parents are at peace with their finitude, for they
have willed it, and they celebrate continuity in their extended bond to their children, which in time involves relinquishing them to their own lives. Without the marital and
parental bond that creates the context of love, sensual pleasure is merely repetitive, for such pleasure does not lead to
a feeling of worth. The need for the continuous repetition of
pleasure may be experienced as the feeling of being perpetual-
ly empty. Only within the bond of a continuing and chosen
love can sensuality breed affection, so that the accumulating
sum of one's life, one's shared history, may be seen as one's
accrued identity and the earned source of a sense of worthiness. In the face of inexorable time and final loss, this is the
happiness, built from pleasure, that the artist must celebrate,
as Stevens says of the pineapple that is his symbol for the
natural source of pleasure, "This is everybody's world."

Beyond purgative lament, lament that is inevitable as the

artist beholds the repeating sorrows of human history, what
the artist adds to the world is the order of celebration. Celebration imposes itself, its own energy, its own forms, upon an
order that is already there—the immemorial order of generation in the form of parental love. The culmination of celebration is achieved in the artist's power finally to celebrate his
own power of celebration; thus every work of art, in this
respect, takes itself as its own subject, demonstrating the
power of the human mind to will itself to perform an act of
will. The pessimistic art that takes unhappiness as its central
theme, as if unhappiness were the inescapable condition of
human life, dooms itself through its own self-fulfilling
prophecy and thus destroys the mind's freedom. Yeats said in
the fullness of old age, "I thought my problem was to face
death with gaiety, now I have learned it is to face life."

The artist returns to his source, life's possible happiness,
and chooses himself as the celebrator of that gaiety. This
model of the chosen self, which, paradoxically, is a choice of
what one has already become as circumstances of time and
place have shaped one's life, transforms the passivity of acceptance into something new. That something new is what
choice has added, what Erikson calls "acceptance of the fact
that one's life is one's own responsibility," as if one had
willed to be what one necessarily has become, as if one were
the author of the story of one's own life. This power of choice
is what the artist may earn for himself and offer his readers as
a guide leading from imaginary realms back into actual life.
This power is the same gift that the parent leaves the child as
blessing and inheritance: the gift to choose to accept one's
own life. The passing on of this blessing, the renewing of the
will to live and thus to die, is the holiness of tradition and the
only immortality of which we may partake.

I V

The creation of a work of art is an intensified model of the
human will making choices. Although it is a dogma of the
modern tradition that poetry must imitate natural speech, no
good poem, in fact, is identical to modern speech. What is es-

sential to the poem as such is not what it imitates but what it adds as design or pattern. Poems are fabricated, usually slowly, and they are revised, embodying care, enhancing nature (what is already there) with their new presence. Though poems cannot reform society or deflect our fates, they can make possible feelings of happiness that otherwise would be lost to us, by affirming the mind's power, through patterned language, to remake itself. Stevens calls this power the "gaiety of language," and this gaiety is inherent in the human mind as a continuous source of possible happiness. When language is made to flourish through willed pattern, the feeling it brings forth is one of spontaneous pleasure, yet this is paradoxical, since the feeling of spontaneity is achieved only with the completion of the work of art, only *after* the necessary choices have been made. The making of the choices is what brings forth the feeling of freedom. Spontaneity and freedom come last: they are the achievements that result from mastery; they are the triumph of willed happiness. The willed happiness of art returns the artist and his readers to the source of that happiness, the power of language that is the power of choice, and, in turn, the power of choice returns him to the power of affirming the one life that he must live and lose. Even the artist's contentment, his palpable sense of the goodness of life at peace with itself, does not yield the full feeling of completion until he can celebrate that happiness. He renews himself, choosing himself again, through the ongoing process of continuing to give praise. As Auden says, "There is only one thing that all poetry must do; it must praise all it can for being and for happening." In the absence of praise, the devil reigns, making evil his good, whispering his oldest lie: that "ye shall be as gods."

   To receive the world in the spirit of celebration, of giving praise, the artist confronts his most fundamental temptation: an engagement with the theme of unhappiness. Since happiness does not have the immediate dramatic power that sorrow does, and since conflict is more compelling to the viewer than peacefulness, it is as if happiness were beyond distinction and ineffable, not a theme for the artist. Tolstoy is right—happiness is essentially anonymous. But the anonymity of happiness differs profoundly from the anonymity of the artist who rejects his own life by replacing it with a world of his own making, by making art its own end, by living in a fantasy of power as if he were a god. To affirm one's happiness is to be unique in the fact that it is *you* who experience it and *you* who choose to celebrate that experience, not because you are unusual or different. "How beauteous mankind is! O brave new world that has such people in it," exclaims Miranda to her father. And Prospero replies: " 'tis new to thee." The newness is the refreshing of immemorial human delight in others. It is as old as human history and belongs potentially to everyone. Only in that sense is it anonymous. Earlier, when Prospero overhears Miranda and Ferdinand exchange vows of love "with a heart as willing / As bondage e'er of freedom," he remarks to himself: "So glad of this as they, I cannot be, . . . but my rejoicing / At nothing can be more." There is really nothing new in the young lovers' happiness, nothing idiosyncratic, but it possesses a power that is great for its quiet modesty. Such moments of life at peace with itself, and the artist's (like Prospero's) participation in their happiness, inevitably evoke this paradoxical power of quietude. The lovers are models of harmony against which evil, as in Milton's Satan, may be comprehended as the deprivation of good; they are models of the power of peacefulness.

Before Lady Macbeth's words to her husband, "look like the innocent flower / But be the serpent under 't," have been realized, Banquo and King Duncan are returning to Duncan's castle. The good king says, "the air / Nimbly and sweetly recommends itself / Unto our gentle senses," to which Banquo replies:

> This guest of summer,
> The temple-haunting martlet, does approve
> By his lov'd mansionry that the heaven's breath
> Smells wooingly here: no jutty, frieze,
> Buttress, nor coign of vantage, but this bird
> Hath made his pendant bed and procreant cradle:
> Where they most breed and haunt, I have observ'd
> The air is delicate.

The sum of the play's corruption, the breeding of destruction ("Unnatural deeds / do breed unnatural troubles"), must be measured against the grace of naturally generative life of which the martlet is the embodiment and symbol. In the image of the martlet, building and breeding even in the walls of a human temple, man, too, is seen approvingly as a creature of fleeting time, a "guest of summer." Merely to observe this scene is to be happy, delighting in one's senses so intensely that "heaven's breath / Smells wooingly here." To perceive nature as a "procreant cradle" is not to be unique, but merely to partake of a blessing available to all human beings. These are Banquo's words while he is still everyman, before he, like Macbeth, has become less than he was by seeking to become more. This moment, experienced in the same way by both Duncan and Banquo, in which the senses are "gentle" and the air is "delicate," is Shakespeare's model of life at peace with itself, and to seek more is to violate what nature allows. This quiet power of intense gentleness is the human utmost, beyond which we must will ourselves not to desire.

In Wordsworth's poem "Michael," before Michael's son, Luke, must leave the family farm for the city with the hope of helping to repay his father's indebtedness, Michael says to his son:

> —Even to the utmost I have been to thee
> A kind and good Father: and herein
> I but repay a gift which I myself
> Received at others' hands; for, though now old
> Beyond the common life of man, I still
> Remember them who loved me in my youth.

Michael is speaking in the voice of all parents, in the voice of all children who have been loved by their parents, and, becoming parents themselves, pass along the gift of love to their own children. It is an immemorial voice, accepting its indebtedness and transforming that indebtedness into the gift of generation and continuing love. Michael desires to feel nothing more than what he already feels in the parental love for his child. The failure of Luke to return in the poem (and sustain the covenant of memory by which love is renewed and passed on) must be understood in terms of Michael's utmost achievement, his kindness and goodness as a father. There is nothing more powerful to be felt beyond what Michael has experienced in the universal roles of son and father, merged into one; and the power of Michael's voice, at the human utmost, resides in its quiet restraint. To be able to say with Michael to his son, "whatever fate / Befall thee, I shall love thee to the last," is to come to the end of human possibility beyond whose happiness there is no further power. Such happiness sets the measure for all loss and betrayal. It is passionate in desiring only what it already possesses, so that its energy is to be seen as if in repose or resolution.

The essence of paradise before the Fall, as Milton shows it to us, is simply Adam and Eve's contentment with one another, desiring no more than what they have. In this spirit, everything they do is a source of pleasure, as is the passage of time itself, and thus each moment has the quality of eternity. The completed bond between them, a bond language makes possible, allows them to celebrate what they possess, and their consciousness of shared pleasure raises pleasure into happiness. Eve says:

> With thee conversing, I forget all time,
> All seasons, and their change, all please alike.
> Sweet is the breath of morn, her rising sweet,
> With charm of earliest birds; pleasant the Sun,
> When first on this delightful land he spreads
> His orient beams, on herb, tree, fruit, and flower,
> Glistering with dew; fragrant the fertile Earth
> After soft showers; and sweet the coming on
> Of grateful Evening mild; then silent Night,
> With this her solemn bird, and this fair Moon,
> And these the gems of Heaven, her starry train:
> But neither breath of Morn, when she ascends
> With charm of earliest birds; nor rising Sun
> On this delightful land; nor herb, fruit, flower,
> Glistering with dew; nor fragrance after showers;

Nor grateful Evening mild, nor silent Night,
With this her solemn bird, nor walk by Moon,
Or glittering starlight, without thee is sweet.

The symmetry of the passage embodies the spirit of celebration: returning to what is already there, "all seasons, and
their change," with conscious and willed thankfulness. The
limits of Adam and Eve's world are set by what they have, the
"fertile Earth" and each other. Their power, for this moment,
is to choose to ask for no further power. This moment of life
at peace with itself receives the benediction of Milton's most
musical language. Adam and Eve are the potentiality of all
men and women, anonymous in the simplicity of their
human happiness. All loss is measured against this measured
happiness: "[nothing] without thee is sweet." All violence
reduces to such loss and flourishes bitterly in the fantasy of
impossible power, of something more than a parent's love for
a child, a man's and a woman's love for each other, friendship,
the pleasure the senses may take in a fertile and generative
world. These experiences are the utmost, and they are possible. "The utmost must be good and is," says Stevens.
Though all stories, fully told, must end in death, the artist, to
be true to his sorrow, the inescapable theme of unhappiness,
must equally be true to what he loves, and celebrate, beyond
the desire for something more, what Stevens calls "the full of
fortune and the full of fate."

Lyric Narration: The Chameleon Poet

❦

O NCE UPON a time, having just given a reading of
my own poems, I was delighted when a woman
from the audience came to the podium and took
my hand in both of hers, in what I assumed was
a warm gesture of appreciation and approval. "I feel so sorry
for you," she said; "believe me, I understand." At first I
thought she was commiserating with me for an unsuccessful
performance, and then I realized that she must be referring to
a poem I had read about the death of "my brother" in a hunt-
ing accident. The poem contains the lines: "But at his funeral
I would not cry, / Certain that I was not to blame for it." I
apologized to her, explaining that I never had a brother, that
I invented the brother for the sake of my poem. If my hand
could have been detached at the wrist, she would have
thrown it on the floor, so violent was her disgust with me.
"You mean you lied," she said; "you took advantage of my
sympathy."

I didn't have the wit then to say that is exactly what poems
ought to do. Poems tell personal lies in order to express impersonal truths. And even if I had so replied, I doubt that she
would have been convinced and not felt cheated. The inti-

our awareness of having a single sexual identity. We are not complete, and it is the poet's artistic fate to yearn to heal the wound of being merely a vulnerable and dependent part of a larger unity. Self-love without the supporting love of others is a desperate passion. Like Plato's descriptions in the *Symposium* of how originally the sexes were one, and of how they got split in half, Freud expresses the idea of man's wounded consciousness, his sense that he is not complete, in *Civilization and Its Discontents*:

> Man is an animal with an unmistakably bisexual disposition. The individual represents a fusion of two symmetrical halves, of which, according to many authorities, one is purely male, the other female. It is equally possible that each half was originally hermaphroditic. . . . We are accustomed to say that every human being displays both male and female instinctual impulses, needs and attributes, but the characteristics of what is male and female can only be demonstrated in anatomy, not in psychology.

There seems to be a fundamental human need, which becomes heightened in the poet, to envision oneself as part of a larger unity, both male and female. Virginia Woolf, in "A Room of One's Own," articulates this directly:

> It is fatal for anyone who writes to think of their sex. It is fatal to be a man or a woman pure and simple; one must be woman-manly or man-womanly. It is fatal for a woman to lay the least stress on any grievance; to plead even with justice any cause; in any way to speak consciously as a woman. And fatal is no figure of speech; for anything written with that conscious bias is doomed to death. It ceases to be fertilized. . . . Some collaboration has to take place in the mind between the woman and the man where the act of creation can be accomplished. Some marriage of opposites has to be consummated.

The wish for completeness—to be both male and female, both parent and child, to be all possible selves throughout all time, and thus to be whole—a wish that Freud also described as "the wish to be father of oneself," is enacted by the artist in his projection of himself into others. Thus, in fantasy, he relieves himself and his readers through story and illusion of the burden of their essential nothingness. Yet, unlike the dreamer and the madman, the artist must return his readers to the actuality of their mortal singularity and to their own lives. It follows that an effective poem must be a dream—a convincing illusion—and a waking return, as Keats says, to "one's sole self." In this return, the poem becomes an act of celebration of the mind's fecund power of identification with others, and, finally, a celebration of the finite and the limited self from which imaginative art may spring.

Freud emphasizes that the need for artistic illusion must be based in conscious awareness: "The artist, like the neurotic, withdraws from an unsatisfying reality into this world of imagination; but unlike the neurotic, he knows how to find a way back from it, and once more gets a firm foothold in reality." And Wallace Stevens asserts the same idea—that fictional belief must be contained by the rational mind which recognizes the need for human dreaming: "The final belief is to believe in a fiction, which you know to be a fiction, there being nothing else. The exquisite truth is to know that it is a fiction and that you believe in it willingly."

The lyric poet fictionalizes himself, projects himself into others and thus into a fuller life, dreaming, yet returning to the reality of his limited body, his instant in cosmic time. Yet he must also acknowledge the reality of his central need—the need to dream, to take on other lives and selves in his art.

II

It is apparent that the novelist and the dramatist project themselves into the characters they create, but the lyric poet—even when speaking as "I" and thus appearing to be only his own self—also may be re-creating himself as something other than what he is in fact. As Yeats proclaims: "Myself I must create."

In Yeats's poem, "Father and Child," for example, a father recounts an exchange he has had with his daughter:

> She hears me strike the board and say
> That she is under ban
> Of all good men and women,
> Being mentioned with a man
> That has the worst of all bad names;
> And thereupon replies
> That his hair is beautiful,
> Cold as the March wind his eyes.

The father speaks as if he is listening to himself from his daughter's perspective. There are two aspects of his single sensibility, for his daughter has become an extension of himself, even though he only half understands himself by seeing himself through her eyes. The reader hears the father as a biased narrator with a particular point to make. Like Yeats himself, the reader understands more than the narrator does, for he perceives the narrator's uncertainty and confusion as the father's lips tremble over the *M* sounds when he mumbles the line "of all good *m*en and wo*m*en being *m*entioned with a *m*an." The reader is aware of the father's unintentional parody of himself: his language is pompous, and he is uncomfortable playing the role of the authoritarian father.

Yeats's parody of the father continues when he describes the man his daughter fancies as having "the worst of all bad names." This is a verbal gesture of repression, for the father cannot speak that name and probably does not even know what it is. The poem is resolved when the father takes into his own voice the voice of his daughter who speaks the last lines of the poem through him: "his hair is beautiful, / Cold as the March wind his eyes." What happens, wonderfully, at this point in the poem is that the rhythm radically changes from a regular iambic to a more highly stressed, irregular rhythm. The stunning last line begins with a stressed syllable on the word "Cold," which is followed by a double stress on "March wind." The troubled rhythm reflects what the father feels—a chill of anxiety in the *I* sounds: "h*i*s," "*i*s," "beaut*i*-ful," "w*i*nd." Perhaps what prevents the father from being able to reply to his daughter's statement is that she has told him something for which there can be no fatherly reply: the reason she finds the man attractive is suggested by the hint of cruelty in him, as in the cold March wind. The father recognizes the truth of this romantic attraction and knows that it is a force greater than parental persuasion. In speaking his daughter's words, the father has become other than himself for the moment of the poem, although the complexity of the father's character is realized only through the poet's double awareness which the father cannot share.

In Theodore Roethke's "My Papa's Waltz," we see again a double narrator: a child and a man combined. In the course of the poem we hear the intermingling of their two vocabularies. The title suggests that we are listening to the poem from the son's—the child's—perspective. It would be a very different poem if the title were "My Father's Waltz."

> The whiskey on your breath
> Could make a small boy dizzy;
> But I hung on like death:
> Such waltzing was not easy.
>
> We romped until the pans
> Slid from the kitchen shelf;
> My mother's countenance
> Could not unfrown itself.
>
> The hand that held my wrist
> Was battered on one knuckle;
> At every step you missed
> My right ear scraped a buckle.
>
> You beat time on my head
> With a palm caked hard by dirt,
> Then waltzed me off to bed
> Still clinging to your shirt.

We enter the poem through the son's memory of his drunken father dancing with him, but as we move into the poem it becomes clear the perspective is that of the child having grown up, remembering this occasion after the father has died. The phrase "But I hung on like death" is not spoken in a child's voice—it is the voice of the child, grown into an adult, having become a poet, looking back and trying to re-enter that scene. The waltz in this poem, from the narrator's and the reader's perspective, thus becomes both a dance of life and a dance of death, which only can be understood through the adult's perspective looking back, not from the child's perspective. All the child understands at the time is that he feels danger and excitement. "We romped until the pans / Slid from the kitchen shelf" expresses the child's sensibility through verbs of action, but the phrase "My mother's countenance" belongs to another vocabulary—that of the grown poet who is capable of using abstractions as well as images.

The frowning mother is excluded as the son experiences the passion of being roughly wooed by his father at the moment when the bond of their love seems complete. With the phrase "The hand that held my wrist / Was battered on one knuckle" there is a growing sense of danger and of damage, reinforced by actual pain: "At every step you missed / My right ear scraped a buckle." From the child's perspective, this is a moment of intense happiness, but it contains pain— pain that the child can endure because it brings him closer to his father. "You beat time on my head / With a palm caked hard by dirt" continues the near violence of the dance, and the image of "dirt" returns the reader to the earlier simile, "like death."

The father, in retrospect, has become an emblem of death for the grown son, the poet; he is now seen as being of the earth, of the dust to which he has in fact returned. The father had waltzed his son off to sleep and has, himself, been waltzed off to death. Looking back, the adult son remembers resisting being put to bed, and this moment has become also his resistance to the pain he feels on confronting the memory of the father's death. At the poem's end, the adult narrator is clinging to the memory of his father in the waltz. The narrating voice that speaks this poem is enriched by the merging of the child's voice and the adult's voice as suggested by Wordsworth's phrase, "The Child is father of the Man." Roethke's identity as poet has been enlarged to include both his present and past self in the three-beat waltz of his poem, which gives new embodiment to the historical waltz of his childhood.

In Robert Frost's " 'Out! Out—' " we hear a narrator who
is outside the story he is telling, but who wishes to enter into
the scene as one of the characters. As narrator, however, he
has only one role to play—the role of witness; essentially,
what he will witness is the absence of divine meaning or purpose in nature and in human affairs. The title of the poem is
an allusion to Macbeth's soliloquy that ends with the phrase,
"signifying nothing." This poem, like many of Frost's poems,
is a confrontation with *nothingness*. Toward the end of it, the
words, "little, less, nothing," complete the echo from Shakespeare's play:

The buzz saw snarled and rattled in the yard
And made dust and dropped stove-length sticks of wood,
Sweet-scented stuff when the breeze drew across it.
And from there those that lifted eyes could count
Five mountain ranges one behind the other
Under the sunset far into Vermont.
And the saw snarled and rattled, snarled and rattled,
As it ran light, or had to bear a load.
And nothing happened: day was all but done.
Call it a day, I wish they might have said
To please the boy by giving him the half hour
That a boy counts so much when saved from work.
His sister stood beside them in her apron
To tell them 'Supper.' At the word, the saw,
As if to prove saws knew what supper meant,
Leaped out at the boy's hand, or seemed to leap—
He must have given the hand. However it was,
Neither refused the meeting. But the hand!
The boy's first outcry was a rueful laugh,
As he swung toward them holding up the hand
Half in appeal, but half as if to keep
The life from spilling. Then the boy saw all—
Since he was old enough to know, big boy
Doing a man's work, though a child at heart—
He saw all spoiled. 'Don't let him cut my hand off—
The doctor, when he comes. Don't let him, sister!'
So. But the hand was gone already.

The doctor put him in the dark of ether.
He lay and puffed his lips out with his breath.
And then—the watcher at his pulse took fright.
No one believed. They listened at his heart.
Little—less—nothing!—and that ended it.
No more to build on there. And they, since they
Were not the one dead, turned to their affairs.

The confrontation with the meaninglessness of death is
anticipated early in the poem with the image of dust: "The
buzz saw snarled and rattled in the yard / And made dust."
The poem's narrative arc is of "dust" returning to "dusty
death" (Shakespeare's phrase), although the narrator and
reader are at first misled by the "sweet-scented" odor of the
cut wood in the breeze. The narrator, along with those who
have "lifted eyes," appears to be enjoying a vision of great
depth into nature itself—the "Five mountain ranges one behind the other / Under the sunset, far into Vermont"—as if
nature were beautiful and benign. But the narrator subsequently will realize that he has had a vision of nature's beautiful indifference which he can describe but cannot affect. He
says, "day was all but done. / Call it a day, I wish they might
have said." In that "I wish" we hear the narrator seeking to
intrude into the story, to become simultaneously both actor
and narrator. Until now, we have seen him as the seemingly
omniscient narrator, the removed narrator, but now we see
him as a man wanting to enter into the scene, to join these
people, to help. But he cannot control the world of the story;
all he can do is tell the story and contain his own grief to the
best of his ability as a witness.

We hear the narrator's human voice intrude again in two
other places. When he says "However it was," describing the
meeting of the saw and the boy's hand, he expresses his reluctance to complete his story of the boy's needless death in that
beautiful Vermont landscape. He, however, is not the one
who can cry out, because he is not in the story. The boy gives
voice directly to his terror, but the narrator can cry out only
as storyteller, by implication, in partial identification with
the boy whose tale he is relating: "The boy's first outcry was

a rueful laugh, / As he swung toward them holding up the hand." The boy's horrible laughing cry seems to bring him to a final vision which replaces the earlier vision of the five mountain ranges: "Then the boy saw all." But the boy did not see all. The most his terror could imagine was that he was going to lose his hand; he was not able to take that terrible imagining to its finality of nothingness—his own death: "Don't let him cut my hand off— / The doctor, when he comes." His vision of *nothing* is not complete.

Yet for the narrator, there will be, ironically, an increase of "less," until less becomes "nothing," and there is nothing he can do. For a moment, his narration is reduced to the impotent word "So," and in that minimal word all his restrained grief is held. In effect, Frost's poem contains exactly what the narrator cannot express. That "So" is the narrator's cry of bearing witness to a story that must be what it is in a scene he cannot enter. He cannot rescue or protect the boy: "the hand was gone already." Yet there is still more *nothing* to perceive: "the watcher at his pulse took fright." In the poem's sense of human helplessness in an indifferent universe, we are all "watchers," and what we see is death without redemption, "signifying nothing." So. So? So! How shall we read that enigmatic word? But the story is not over yet; the boy will die, and someone must tell of it: "And they, since they / Were not the one dead, turned to their affairs." There is a strange coldness in those last lines, a sorrow spoken in the guise of indifference. The characters of Frost's poem continue their lives in the spirit of necessity; all the narrator can do, holding in his personal grief, is express it through the telling of the tale that itself becomes an extension of his own identity. He has become—beyond the uncertain "So" of his own voice—the characters to whose lives he has borne witness.

The poems above may be described as having a limited narrator, or a self-deceiving narrator. There are really two voices in the poems—the voice of the character speaking, and the voice of the poet who is speaking through the voice of the character, so that we, as readers, know something about the speakers of these poems that they do not fully realize about themselves. What we know—that they do not know—is what the narrators have repressed because of the circumstances in which they find themselves. We, as readers, sharing the poet's perspective, are not blinded or confused by the narrator's particular situation. But we cannot act; we can only observe. These are the two existential aspects of our lives: we are both actors and watchers. We bear witness to the lives we live—sometimes as if they were someone else's life or a story we have read—yet we must make our personal choices as best we can; we must turn to our "affairs."

The poet may clarify or enlarge himself through the creation of a self-deceiving narrator or a narrator who is a reduction of himself. The lyric poet may present himself as a character with a partial or diminished self, and yet a larger "I," with full awareness, will be implied by the poem in its entirety by virtue of the context it creates. Blake's poem "The Poison Tree," for example, appears to be set physically in the Garden of Eden, but the poem (except for the title which belongs to the poet) literally takes place in the mind of the speaker. The speaker's mind is a corrupted garden, and the whole poem is a nightmare with a false awakening at the end. The context of the poem is the speaker's self-deceiving mind.

> I was angry with my friend:
> I told my wrath, my wrath did end.
> I was angry with my foe:
> I told it not, my wrath did grow.
>
> And I watered it in fears
> Night and morning with my tears,
> And I sunned it with smiles
> And with soft deceitful wiles.
>
> And it grew both day and night,
> Till it bore an apple bright,
> And my foe beheld it shine,
> And he knew that it was mine,—
>
> And into my garden stole
> When the night had veiled the pole;
> In the morning, glad, I see
> My foe outstretched beneath the tree.

We see the narrator at the poem's beginning as possessing the ability to understand his own wrath, as having sufficient knowledge to free himself from his resentful anger. As the first two lines reveal, the narrator understands that the expression of wrath can liberate one from one's wrath, and the result of this psychologically achieved freedom is friendship. What we next see, however, in lines three and four, is a foe distinguished from the friend only by the way in which the speaker chooses to regard the foe. He is angry at both of them, but when the speaker fails to exorcise his anger through expression, that anger dominates his mind and usurps his soul. His mind then becomes a perverted garden; his thinking becomes paranoid and twisted: night is mistaken for day; fantasy, for reality; lies, for truth. Things that should nurture have a poisonous effect. In his mind, the speaker re-creates himself as a Satanic figure, perverting God's natural benevolence in the forms of water and sun into destructive forces. And the apple, which is his own poisoned sensibility, his lie to himself, begins to grow, extending the effect and influence of false knowledge. Throughout the poem, we do not see an objective garden—nature as it is—we see only the speaker's projection of his own wrath and jealousy. The speaker comes to mistake his own lying for reality; therefore, the foe exists as foe only because the speaker fears him as a projection of his own wrathful self. Although he does not understand this—for the understanding of the first two lines has been repressed—the speaker suffers from the dread of his own wrath.

Blake's ingenious parallel to the biblical story reveals that the speaker blasphemously is comparing himself to God, the true creator of the garden. It follows then that the foe who eats the apple is Adam, for Blake is parodying the concept of a jealous God (elsewhere Blake calls him "Nobodaddy") who takes delight in poisoning mankind, his foe, Adam. Through the depiction of the narrator's repressed and poisoned mind, Blake's satire dramatizes his belief that it is a failed imagining on our part to conceive of God as being jealous. Blake shows how people can become corrupted when their imaginations become corrupted and when their religious institutions are founded on repression and false mythology.

As the poem proceeds, everything the speaker sees is distorted by the darkness of his own mind. In effect, the poem is the speaker's nightmare. The snake of false knowledge is implied in the poem through the image of the "pole"—since the medical insignia for cure is a pole with a snake wrapped around it, an emblem of a curative force, evil overcome. But Blake diagnoses the cause of the failure of the mind's curative force as the failure of the imagination to overcome repression.

At the end of the poem, the speaker seems to wake up happily; his wrath appears to have triumphed. But there is little reason to trust anything that this speaker says by this point in the poem. He has proclaimed himself as a liar, and to admit that he is lying does not make him truthful; it merely reveals to the reader that the admission itself is a kind of lie, since no repentance follows. We cannot trust the speaker of this poem; we only can trust the poem itself. What is being repressed, and its consequences, are revealed to the reader beyond the narrator in the context of understanding provided by the poem's structure. The poem reveals exactly what the speaker is lying about even to himself—that he feels good. In the statement "In the morning, glad I see / My foe outstretched beneath the tree," the reader perceives a dreamlike repressed distortion of the speaker's natural impulse to *mourn* the death of his foe who could have been his friend if he had expressed his wrath. But his poisoned mind no longer is free to acknowledge this possibility. The speaker's denial of his guilt, his repressed *mourning* (as suggested by his unintentional pun on "morning"), holds him fixed in his own lie.

The figure of Adam at the end of the poem as the murdered foe—seemingly God's enemy since the speaker has fantasized himself as God—is extended into the figure of Christ (the second Adam) in the image of his crucifixion, "outstretched beneath the tree." The tree of life, through repression and denial, has become the tree of death, and the speaker awakens to his own mistaken nightmare of reality. It is not, however, truly an awakening, for the narrator is trapped in

his own guilty mind, his poisoned garden. The nightmare
will continue. The reader realizes this self-deception from
a perspective opposite to that which the speaker possesses.
The reader is aware of what the speaker has falsified, and
through his doubling of visions, false and true, Blake presents
an image of the mind with its capacity of imaginative understanding—a mind vulnerable in its inclination to deceive
both itself and others. With the dramatization of the divided
self, Blake provides us with the necessary knowledge that can
make the healing of the mind possible so that Christian For-
bearance (Blake's earlier title for the poem) may be awakened
and become an actuality.

The need for unity within all people to complete themselves out of their limited sexual identity into a larger human
identity, an androgynous identity, can be seen again in
Yeats's poem "Three Things":

> 'O cruel Death, give three things back,'
> *Sang a bone upon the shore;*
> 'A child found all a child can lack,
> Whether of pleasure or of rest,
> Upon the abundance of my breast':
> *A bone wave-whitened and dried in the wind.*
>
> 'Three dear things that women know,'
> *Sang a bone upon the shore;*
> 'A man if I but held him so
> When my body was alive
> Found all the pleasure that life gave':
> *A bone wave-whitened and dried in the wind.*
>
> 'The third thing that I think of yet,'
> *Sang a bone upon the shore,*
> 'Is that morning when I met
> Face to face my rightful man
> And did after stretch and yawn':
> *A bone wave-whitened and dried in the wind.*

The coming together and merging of the male self and the
female self is suggested by Yeats through his use of a double
narrator in this poem: a woman, after death, remembering

the three great pleasures of her life, and a disembodied voice that speaks the poem's refrain. The central figure of the poem is Eve who, having once been taken from Adam's rib, has now turned back into the bone that was her original form, the creative essence of Adam's body. What remains of Adam now that his created self, Eve, has been reduced by death to a bone, is the depersonalized voice of the poem's refrain. Images of mortal limitation and mortal fullness—the bone and the breast—establish the emotional polarities of the poem. Between these two narrators, the poem unites thought absorbed in memory and the refrain's consciousness of loss. The mind's begetting of itself in the double-voice structure of the poem extends awareness into the consciousness of consciousness.

Within the refrain of the narrator—Yeats's abstraction of Adam—the bone-woman recalls the three basic pleasures of life: nursing a child, enjoying sexual love, and, after impersonal sexual pleasure, determining her "rightful man." The poem reenacts an archetypal story of three wishes, but the underlying irony of the poem is that all the woman's wishes, granted in her life, have been taken away by "cruel death." Yet the bone's memory of life's pleasures and abundance is so powerful that the sense of loss seems to dissolve in the memory of those fulfilled wishes. The awareness of death's cruelty almost disappears in the intensity of remembered pleasure so that the poem in its wholeness unifies Yeats's sense of the vanishing of all things with his sense of the imagination's power to restore and contain them in song. The unification of life and death, body and thought, male and female, takes place momentarily, for Yeats, in sexual love and, more lastingly, in song or art.

Consciousness of self and the imaginative projection of self as other, enhanced and complete, survive in the art of the storyteller. The bone, Adam's extension of himself as Eve, returns to the sea, the origin of life, but a song survives that disappearance, its measured rhythm like the waves advancing and receding from the shore. In imagining his otherness, first in the figure of a woman, but finally in the form of the poem itself, Yeats, as Adam, can meet "cruel death" like a lover, "face to face," assuaging the dread of his singular life, his mortal identity.

I I I

Yeats tells his readers: "The heroes of Shakespeare convey to us through their looks, or through the metaphorical patterns of their speech, the sudden enlargement of their vision, their ecstasy at the approach of death. . . . They have become God or Mother Goddess." In that image Yeats unifies male and female—God or Mother Goddess—for, ultimately, the poet must be not merely himself, but a storyteller, a larger self, both male and female, both young and old, both blind and consciously aware. Thus, the poet should not assume that he must speak only in his own beliefs and history. Though we die in a single body, covered easily by a little earth, the imagination, facing the abyss of ancient *nothing*, has its visionary countertruth: the power to identify with lives other than our own and to give those lives embodiment in poetic form. That power is the bone within us, the seed, the creative germ. In the words of Erik Erikson: "I am what survives me."

I V

Last year I was teaching a writing class in which we were discussing what autobiographical events cannot be used in one's poems because they would not seem true to the reader, even though they actually had occurred in the poet's life. I tried to make the point that the only criterion that matters in artistic choices is what convinces the reader, what enables the reader to believe the poem. I told the class a story about what happened to me in New York City about ten years ago. It was pouring, and I couldn't get a cab, so I walked to the nearest subway even though crowds make me anxious. I entered the train, and halfway down the car I saw the profile of my high-school friend Frankie, whom I had not been in touch with for twenty-five years. I pushed my way through the crowd and tapped him on the shoulder. When he turned toward me, I realized that I had been mistaken. It was not Frankie. "Pardon

me," I said, "I thought you were someone else." At the next
subway stop the doors slid apart, and Frankie walked into the
train.

I asked my class if they would believe this story if I told it
in a poem. What point could it make? Would it show that the
speaker is clairvoyant? Would it suggest that indeed the
supernatural does exist? Since I was there in the room, and
since my students trusted me even though they were trained
in perceiving literary ironies, they assumed that the story
I told must have been true. Just as the class ended, I shocked
them when I asked if any of them thought I might have made
up the story. They pleaded with me after class to tell them if
it really happened: "Is it true? Tell me, is it really true?" But,
of course, it is possible I invented this story about my class,
dear reader, only to make my point to you.

THREE

Silences, Sighs, Caesuras, Ellipses, Ohs and Ahs

❦

I N H I S line "As if we saw our feeling in the object seen," Wallace Stevens succinctly describes two essential aspects of metaphorical language. First, there is a perceived correspondence between an inner, subjective feeling and some physical reality out there. And, second, the perceiver is aware that this correspondence does not exist except in his "as if" assertion of its existence. Metaphorical seeing always involves making believe and the awareness—somewhere on the fine line between consciousness and subconsciousness—that one is making believe, so that the projection of a feeling onto an object can take place.

When one sees a beautiful sunset, for example, one sees the beauty of the sunset as if the beauty were inherent in the sunset itself. Thus the phrase "a beautiful sunset" is in effect a metaphorical statement. Metaphorical language is so natural to ordinary speech that usually one is not aware of it as such. When one says, "She is a cold woman," or when Grandma says to Grandson, "You are so sweet that I could eat you," the listener knows, without being warned, that "cold"

and "sweet" are not to be taken literally. They describe subjective feelings about people that are assumed to correspond
to physical experience.

Robert Frost's description of metaphor, like Stevens's,
emphasizes the connection of inner and outer: "It is just saying one thing in terms of another . . . matter in terms of spirit,
or spirit in terms of matter, to make the final unity." This
unity may be further described as one of place and person, or
of world and mind, and it cannot exist without its expression
in language, so that the felt (experienced) correspondence of
feeling and object depends on the metaphor that brings the
two together. Frost calls this unifying effect of language a
"gathering metaphor." For the "gathering" power of a poem
is its design, a sort of megametaphor that holds the whole together and extends in complexity and nuance the various and
discrete metaphors the poem contains. Yet as a structure
of words, the poem is metaphorical in another way. The
words themselves on the page become an object, and, to vary
Stevens's line, it is as if in reading them we hear our feelings
in the sounds a human voice would make in speaking them.
Every poem creates the illusion of a speaking human voice,
and the reader may choose to think of that voice as belonging
to an invented character or to the poet himself. But even if the
latter assumption is made, the poet, through selection, has
represented only an aspect of himself—one mood among
many—and thus has fictionalized himself.

The feelings that the poem as verbal structure invites the
reader to project upon the poem are never only the feelings
appropriate to the subject of the poem itself—feelings such as
sorrow, regret, sympathy. Inseparable from such subjective
emotions is the pleasure the poem must always provide as
a poem. No matter how sorrowful the subject matter of a
poem, a good poem will not make a reader feel sad. The reader
does not experience sorrow but rather the poem of sorrow and
the pleasure of the poem of sorrow, even though the reader is
reminded that, indeed, real sorrow exists in the world. The
reader experiences the illusion of a human voice, knowing
that it is an illusion, and therefore experiences this voice
as a metaphor. The implied vocal qualities of the written
words—tone, pitch, speed, roughness, or melodic ease—are

an essential part of the poem's gathering design and they can evoke the sense of human presence.

The essence of metaphor, then, is not merely the correspondence between inner and outer, between subject and object, but rather the verbal design itself, embodied as voice, which holds the two together, for the design is always more than the connections that it makes. Metaphorical design always evokes a sense of mystery—the mystery of connectedness and connection—and in particular the mystery of language, without which the connections of inner and outer do not exist. The essence of metaphor, seen in this way, is innuendo, implication, and the awareness of possibility. Preceding language and idea is the human cry—the body's voice of sounds without words. For both our cries and our words are preceded and followed by silence. Yet silence, too, may become articulate because of the context in which it is placed— as with a musical rest note. We hear the silence of a rest note because it is contained within a musical phrase. In this sense, the mystery of the evocative power of metaphor may be compared to the delineated silences, the pauses within a poem, that are suggested by a shift in rhythm, for example, or a line break, or a missing syllable when two syllables are expected to complete a foot. In fact, the metaphorical center of a poem may be found in the implications of its silences.

II

In Robert Frost's "Hyla Brook," for example, we are listening to a brook that has lost its song:

> By June our brook's run out of song and speed.
> Sought for much after that, it will be found
> Either to have gone groping underground
> (And taken with it all the Hyla breed
> That shouted in the mist a month ago,
> Like ghost of sleigh bells in a ghost of snow)—
> Or flourished and come up in jewelweed,
> Weak foliage that is blown upon and bent,
> Even against the way its waters went.
> Its bed is left a faded paper sheet

Of dead leaves stuck together by the heat—
A brook to none but who remember long.
This as it will be seen is other far
Than with brooks taken otherwhere in song.
We love the things we love for what they are.

The poem, in effect, is a response to and a celebration of the silence of the brook. The poem opens with the implication that there is a specific listener for this poem, since the speaker refers to "our brook," and that intimate "our" suggests the auditor may be his wife. By the end of the poem it has become clear that this is indeed a poem about the strengthening of the bond of love through the mutual metaphorical viewing of an object in nature, just as the woman says in "West-Running Brook": "As you and I are married to each other, / We'll both be married to the brook. We'll build / Our bridge across it, and the bridge shall be / Our arm thrown over it asleep beside it." Hyla Brook possesses two qualities that are named as "song and speed." But while the brook's speed is literal, a material quality, the quality of song is not inherent in the brook itself and thus necessarily implies a subjective beholder who thinks it sings.

The poem moves backward in time, for it is a poem, after all, about seeing the past, the signs of which have physically vanished, so that a present absence gives way here to a past presence. Paradoxically, the brook's absence is seen and heard again in the poem as if it were once again early spring when the Hyla frogs were there, and, even further back, to a ghostlier winter, with its "ghost of sleigh-bells in a ghost of snow." The brook moves one way and the weeds another, just as the speaker's mind both remembers and looks ahead to the future. Again, as in "West-Running Brook," love is defined as having the power to embody and affirm contraries, male and female, past and present: "It must be the brook / Can trust itself to go by contraries / The way I can with you—and you with me."

All the speaker actually sees in "Hyla Brook," from June on, is a bed of dry leaves, so that someone not familiar with this landscape would not see a brook at all and would not know the Hyla frogs ever lived there. Only by virtue of memory, by cherishing what has been there before, can the mind bring to the eye what is now gone and thus give body to absence: "A brook to none but who remember long." Filling the silence, seeing into the past, are then projected into the future as a bond of understanding between the speaker and his wife. Frost gives the reader a lesson on how to surpass literal sight as he assures us: "This as it will be seen is other far / Than with brooks taken otherwhere in song." The bond between the man and the woman in this poem requires that the past be contained even in the radically changed present and continued into the future. This is precisely what ongoing love must accomplish. Frost is teasing his reader with a subtle boast, saying in effect that any other poet would write a poem about a brook that is a brook, while he has the wit to write a poem about a brook that is not a brook, except to someone who knows the landscape well enough to remember that a brook was there.

In order to love a brook that is no longer a brook, the speaker must incorporate the past, as if it still existed, into the way he now sees "dead leaves stuck together by the heat," so that the absent brook can become a metaphor for the continuity of love despite the passage of time. The poem's final line, "We love the things we love for what they are," which at first reading seems so solidly committed to a literal and factual reality, can now be seen as reverberant with innuendo and implication. For the brook is both what it once was—a brook—and what it is now—merely dead leaves stuck together. To love things for what they *are* must include loving them as well for what they are not now but once were, and for what they still may be. Reality will not be fixed in a simple, declarative "they are." What things are for Frost is what the mind can make of them—as if this sonnet-song itself were written on a faded paper sheet. Frost transforms his brook that is no more into a metaphorical brook, which continues to flow in the speaker's memory, the mind's "underground," so that the poem's last line reads as a promise to continue loving, a promise flowing even into the silence that follows speech.

Wallace Stevens's "The Snow Man" is another poem about beholding what "is not there":

One must have a mind of winter
To regard the frost and the boughs
Of the pine-trees crusted with snow;

And have been cold a long time
To behold the junipers shagged with ice,
The spruces rough in the distant glitter

Of the January sun; and not to think
Of any misery in the sound of the wind,
In the sound of a few leaves,

Which is the sound of the land
Full of the same wind
That is blowing in the same bare place

For the listener, who listens in the snow,
And, nothing himself, beholds
Nothing that is not there and the nothing that is.

Unlike Frost's speaker who tries to remember spring in June, Stevens's snow man attempts to see only winter images in the winter landscape. As if the world could be observed objectively as a purely physical fact, the snow man resists all metaphorical thinking. He will not allow himself to hear the wind as if it were expressing any human feeling like "misery." This speaker wants to behold the landscape as *it* is, adding nothing of himself to what he sees. When Blake says: "We are led to believe a lie / When we see with not through the eye," he defines, in wholly negative terms, the "winter mind" of Stevens's snow man who sees "with" the eye, for to see "with" the eye is to perceive the world as an object apart from the beholding self. To see "through" the eye, however, is to perceive the world with one's mind—to associate objects with feelings and ideas, to behold the landscape as metaphor. Like Blake, Stevens is a celebrator of the imagination, seeing through the eye, yet he also knows how easily metaphor passes over into fantasy or illusion. For this reason, seeing with the eye, with the winter mind, is a necessary corrective or balance for the imagination, since the literal eye provides the mind with a constant reminder of external reality.

Just as there are two ways of perceiving reality, with and

through the eye, so there are two observers in Stevens's poem: a snow man who sees only what is objectively present, and a narrator-observer who regards the snow man and is keenly aware of what the snow man is *not* thinking. This subjective narrator-observer beholds not only the visible, but the invisible as well. For him, the *idea* of absence and silence has its own being and content, so that his language approximates winter stillness in the steadily repeating sibilants that hiss like dried leaves across the floor of this poem. Although "The Snow Man" seems to be a poem about total winter desolation, it is of particular significance that the scene is filled with evergreens and that it has its own pristine beauty, free of the mind's association of "misery" with wind and coldness. Furthermore, the month is January, the commencement of a new year and the turning toward spring. In effect, Stevens suggests that this is not a poem merely about the diminished mind of the snow man who can no longer make any human connections with the landscape, but about a beginning as well. In order for the mind to begin again, however, to perceive the landscape in a metaphorical way, it must imagine energetically the ending of the imaginative effort that preceded it.

For the poem's narrator, imagining the snow man's winter mind involves imagining the absence of imagination. The snow man hears monotonous sound, almost like silence itself, but from the narrator's point of view there is a paradoxical fullness to this description of emptiness in which a winter scene is "full of the same wind." The snow man sees things as things, facts as facts, but to the more imaginative mind of the narrator, objects may also be seen as metaphors, and therefore, for him to perceive winter as an objective, physical fact, and not as a symbol of misery, betokens a failure of the imagination. Still, he realizes, there is the intractable sound of the wind which is merely itself, only one step removed from silence. The snow man is the best perceiver of a nothingness that does indeed exist. As close as we can get to the sense of silence in the repetitions of the sounds of sameness and monotony, so, too, do we approach unmediated reality as we postulate its independent existence prior to any metaphorical imposition upon it. Nevertheless, Stevens's whole poem becomes a metaphor, since absence, when well imagined, encompasses its opposite—the presence of the *idea* of absence, the idea of nonbeing.

The poem's narrator, beholding the snow man, realizes by implication that perception is nothing—it is empty—until human associative thought (of things that are not there) transforms objects into metaphors. But this nothing does exist as "the nothing that is," though only the narrator and not the snow man can know this. What the snow man *sees* is what the narrator *knows*, for the narrator confronts the *idea* of nothing, and that idea quickens his desire for the renewal of metaphorical perception. As Stevens says in a later poem: "And not to have is the beginning of desire, / To have what is not in its ancient cycle." This renewal of the desire for metaphor is suggested by the approach of the distant sun as the year turns toward spring. With the realization that "nothing" must be confronted, we hear a kind of gasp—a flash of silence one might say—in the penultimate line, the only line in the poem that ends with an enjambment: "nothing himself, [the snow man] beholds / Nothing that is not there and the nothing that is." Only through metaphor can the absence of metaphor be imagined. A world without metaphor is nothing, yet this is true for Stevens in both a literal and metaphorical sense; and thus the poem both partakes of silence and is about silence—silence as natural fact and silence as possibility.

Human reality—emotion, mood, need—cannot be expressed denotatively as fact because it is always changing, fluid, open to further possibility. So human love, for example, is composed as much of memory and hope as it is of physical desire. Love is an idea of obligation and responsibility wedded to, inseparable from, a bodily need for touch and sexual release. As Yeats said: "love would be [no] more than an animal hunger but for the poet."

In William Blake's poem "Never Seek to Tell Thy Love," we have a story about a traveler's amorous, wooing sigh, and the poem itself expresses the sigh of the rejected narrator after he has failed to win the lady with the direct declaration of his love:

Never seek to tell thy love,
Love that never told can be;
For the gentle wind does move
Silently, invisibly.

I told my love, I told my love,
I told her all my heart;
Trembling, cold, in ghastly fears,
Ah! she doth depart.

Soon as she was gone from me,
A traveller came by,
Silently, invisibly:
He took her with a sigh.

In contrast to the blunt and forthright narrator, the traveler's sigh is the epitome of language as suggestion and connotation. Blake implicitly compares human breathing with nature's breathing, the "gentle wind," and thus conveys to the reader the emotions of the narrator and the traveler in terms of how the poem breathes evenly or catches its breath through rhythmical shifts. The radical metrical interruption in the refrain line, "Silently, invisibly," for example, characterizes the interrupted breathing, the sigh, the anxiety of the narrator, and also suggests his subconscious identification with the traveler.

The narrator begins urgently—almost all his lines start with stressed syllables, "Never seek to tell thy love," and a strong rhythmic pattern quickly is established. But that pattern breaks abruptly in the fourth line: "Silently, // invisibly." The two missing stresses in this poem of four beats per line must be read into the caesura in the middle of the line. In the comma, like a musical rest note, we hear a doubly stressed pause—a sigh, an intake and exhalation of breath, invisible and approaching silence. The traveler is compared to the easy movement of nature itself in the figure of the gentle wind, open and ongoing in contrast to the narrator who seeks to limit love by thinking to tell "all his heart." Love is destroyed, Blake implies, by placing it within mental boundaries, as though one could ever capture it. Blake says elsewhere: "He who binds to himself a joy, / Does the winged life destroy, / But he who kisses the joy as it flies, / Lives in eternity's sunrise." The woman who hears the narrator's declaration of love is aghast because love has been limited in its unmetaphorical telling, and we hear her dismay echoed in the extended sigh, the outcry of the narrator: "Ah, she doth depart." Better to speak, like the wind, the language of innuendo and suggestion. Unlike the narrator's sigh of despair and defeat, the traveler's sigh is one of pleasure and of promise, love's opening the senses and the mind to natural mystery.

If the traveler's sigh corresponds to the "gentle wind," nature's benevolent power, then the gasping, anxious sigh of the narrator corresponds to a failed imagining of nature and thus a constricted sense of bodily desire and of love. These opposing sighs constitute the central metaphor of Blake's poem, and they remind us of the nature of metaphor itself, the language that enables us to see things, not merely as they are, but in the fullness of their open possibilities, always there to be realized through the marriage of inner and outer, mind and nature. In "The Marriage of Heaven and Hell," Blake reminds us that "If the doors of perception were cleansed everything would appear to man as it is, infinite."

Another of Frost's poems, "The Road Not Taken," can be read as a series of sighs for one's self, divided into the life one lives and the life one might have lived:

> Two roads diverged in a yellow wood,
> And sorry I could not travel both
> And be one traveler, long I stood
> And looked down one as far as I could
> To where it bent in the undergrowth;
>
> Then took the other, as just as fair,
> And having perhaps the better claim,
> Because it was grassy and wanted wear;
> Though as for that, the passing there
> Had worn them really about the same,
>
> And both that morning equally lay
> In leaves no step had trodden black.
> Oh, I kept the first for another day!
> Yet knowing how way leads on to way,
> I doubted if I should ever come back.

> I shall be telling this with a sigh
> Somewhere ages and ages hence:
> Two roads diverged in a wood, and I—
> I took the one less traveled by,
> And that has made all the difference.

The impossible wish for more than one life leads the speaker to seek consolation in the belief that the choice of his actual life at least has had some positive significance. The speaker's first palpable sigh for the recognition of mortal limitation can be heard in the line, "And be one traveler, long I stood," where the heavy pause after the comma carries over into the stress on the word "long." A sigh of regret is unmistakable in the speaker's voice, whose varying intonations constitute the fundamental metaphor of the poem. For that voice is far more complex and self-revealing than the relatively simple allegorical image of the two roads would suggest. In fact, the speaker tries to persuade himself that the two roads can be distinguished, that a real choice was made, but he soon catches himself and corrects that rationalization. Actually, both roads turn out to have been the same: "And both that morning equally lay / In leaves no step had trodden black." The speaker cannot convince himself that a meaningful choice took place, and there is an extended sigh in that recognition in the stressed "Oh" that opens the subsequent line against the flow of the iambic meter: "Oh, I kept the first for another day!" The "first" road is kept by the poem itself, surprisingly, in its title, despite the later claim that the road he *did* take has made "all the difference." After all, the poem itself is what he will sigh for in the future when he will again look back, for he tells us that "I shall be telling this with a sigh." In effect, the telling has already been told, but here the poem is projected into an indefinite future. When and where is "Somewhere ages and ages hence"? Is the speaker imagining that he might be reciting this poem perhaps to his grandchildren as an intentionally misleading and therefore subtly comic parable about looking for meaning in life where none is to be found because choice was, after all, an illusion? Or is the speaker imagining an afterlife in which the purpose of the journey of life, even in distant retrospect, will still be obscure to him? If so, will his sigh then express eternal uncertainty? The reader only can follow the speaker's meaning here in speculation. The speaker, however, returns to the objective fact, "Two roads diverged in a wood," though now even the detail "yellow" has dropped away, suggesting the increased remoteness of his perspective. The line break places another pause, another sigh, between the double self: "And I—I took," separating one "I" from the other, reinforcing the reader's sense of the sorrow of the speaker's divided consciousness. We hear his melancholy tone for being limited to "one" life in the breaking of his voice. His sighs, his troubled breathing, however we interpret them, are more concrete than any meaning the speaker can impose upon his experience.

The apparently affirmative and individualistic claim, "I took the road less traveled by," then, is contradicted by the facts of the poem. The two roads which "equally lay" are indistinguishable except for the historical fact that he took one and not the other. He cannot know what another life might have been, nor can he make a useful comparison. His statement, as he fully recognizes, is ironic, and that perhaps accounts for the prolonged sigh that is the very "telling" of this poem—for it is a sigh that must go unrelieved in any future retellings wherever "ages hence" they may take place.

As in many of Frost's poems, the experience presented here is one of nonrevelation. The wish for a revealed meaning or a proven significance, as in the making of a choice, is disappointed, and the reader can hear that disappointment in the speaker's voice in the constrained ironic bitterness of the last line. Frost once described irony this way: "A good sentence does double duty: it conveys one meaning by word and syntax and another by the tone of voice it indicates." So, while the words of the final line, "And that has made all the difference," denote that a meaningful and positive choice has been made, the very tone of voice undermines that assertion. In this steadily iambic poem with only few variations, the final two metrical feet are reversed; they are troches which give a falling effect—"all the difference"—and in them the reader can hear the diminishing of the speaker's voice. The last line is the only one in the entire poem to end on an unstressed syllable, an exhalation of breath, a sigh fading into silence. The voice that speaks this poem, filled with the mysterious inflections of a sigh, is the true metaphor corresponding to the narrator's experience of nostalgia for a revelation that never took place.

I I I

The voice that speaks a poem, as implied by the written words, is itself a metaphor; what the reader learns or surmises from that voice may provide the crucial information of the poem. Voice inflections, like pitch and speed, and voice qualities, like harshness or mellifluousness, may be suggested, for example, by rhythm, rhyme, or the emphasis on vowel or consonantal patterns. Yet there is nothing more expressive in a poem than its pauses, its silences, for they evoke the bodily sense of breathing, easy or hard, and they may correspond to the *idea* of silence as absence or, at the other extreme, to an *idea* of silence as mental or spiritual inwardness. Howard Nemerov's exquisite and poignant lyric, for example, "During a Solar Eclipse," relates the silence of reflective thought, "we stand bemused," to the silence of the cessation of individual life in the light of cosmic change:

> The darkening disk of the moon before the sun
> All morning moves, turning our common day
> A deep and iris blue, daylight of dream
> In which we stand bemused and looking on
> Backward at shadow and reflected light,
>
> While the two great wanderers among the worlds
> Enter their transit with our third, a thing
> So rare that in his time upon the earth
> A man may see, as I have done, but four,
> In childhood two, a third in youth, and this
>
> In likelihood my last. We stand bemused
> While grass and rock darken, and stillness grows,
> Until the sun and moon slide out of phase
> And light returns us to the common life
> That is so long to do and so soon done.

Nemerov speaks his poem in the collective "we," since watching a solar eclipse is a public and communal event which unites us for a moment in "our common day." His individual voice enters only in the second stanza, "A man may see, as I have done," and quickly passes back into the indistinguishable "we." The speaker, observing a cosmic event beyond himself, turns inward as his thought deepens and becomes still with the repetition of "We stand be- mused," which leads immediately to the image of the dark- ening "grass and rock" and to the increased heaviness of meditative silence as the "stillness grows."

Within this silence, however, there is a pause, a breathful sigh, in which the individual self, Nemerov speaking as "I," holds to this reflective instant of his own life as he watches in quiet inspiration ("bemused") the "reflected light" beyond him. The pause is felt profoundly in the stressed word "this," enjambed doubly by line and stanza. Nemerov dwells on "this" rare moment of sight as if his life somehow could be prolonged a little in its contemplation of the eclipse. If this pause is heard as a sigh, it is a sigh of possession and at the same time an acknowledgment of loss in the inexorable "turning" of time. The phrase "as I have done," suggesting the recapitulation of his individual life, passes over into the final phrase, "and so soon done," making more precious "the common life" whose shared light the speaker will cherish for whatever time remains to him. Finally, the sigh of the poem is released in the subdued lament of predominating O sounds, "so long to do and so soon done," whose melancholy is equaled by its loveliness.

In the following passage from *The Prelude* (bk 5), Words- worth evokes silence, not as a metaphor of nothingness or ab- sence, but of psychological and spiritual inwardness.

> There was a Boy: ye knew him well, ye cliffs
> And islands of Winander! —many a time
> At Evening, when the earliest stars began
> To move along the edges of the hills,
> Rising or setting, would he stand alone
> Beneath the trees or by the glimmering lake,
> And there, with fingers interwoven, both hands

Pressed closely palm to palm, and to his mouth
Uplifted, he, as through an instrument,
Blew mimic hootings to the silent owls,
That they might answer him; and they would shout
Across the watery vale, and shout again—
Responsive to his call, with quivering peals,
And long halloos and screams, and echoes loud,
Redoubled and redoubled, concourse wild
Of jocund din; and, when a lengthened pause
Of silence came and baffled his best skill,
Then sometimes, in that silence while he hung
Listening, a gentle shock of mild surprise
Has carried far into his heart the voice
Of mountain torrents; or the visible scene
Would enter unawares into his mind,
With all its solemn imagery, its rocks,
Its woods, and that uncertain heaven, received
Into the bosom of the steady lake.
   This Boy was taken from his mates, and died
In childhood, ere he was full twelve years old.
Fair is the spot, most beautiful the vale
Where he was born; the grassy churchyard hangs
Upon a slope above the village school,
And through that churchyard when my way has led
On summer evenings, I believe that there
A long half hour together I have stood
Mute, looking at the grave in which he lies!
Even now appears before the mind's clear eye
That self-same village church; I see her sit
(The thronèd Lady whom erewhile we hailed)
On her green hill, forgetful of this Boy
Who slumbers at her feet, —forgetful, too,
Of all her silent neighbourhood of graves,
And listening only to the gladsome sounds
That, from the rural school ascending, play
Beneath her and about her.

Silence is experienced as having presence and *being* as if,
paradoxically, it were the essence of human speech in its
capacity to respond to the divinity inherent in natural ob-

jects. As so often in Wordsworth, the circumstance in which
silence is experienced as meaningful silence requires that the
speaker be alone. The boy in this passage, as if seeking some
answer from nature, some reply to his own need for connection, calls out to the owls in a gesture of unconscious prayer.
We sense this from the image of his pressing his palms together: "with fingers interwoven, both hands / Pressed closely palm to palm." For a moment, the owls are silent, and then
the boy seems able to win from them an answer. An answer
comes in the sound of the owls' "halloos and screams," but
this is not the deep, inward answer the further experience of
silence will provide later for the boy when a "lengthened
pause / Of silence" follows. This extended silence will pass
over to the speaker and become his own, and it will be further
extended and internalized even after the boy has died. The
breaking of the phrase to end the line adds duration and emphasis to the crucial word, "pause." There are other instances
in this passage where Wordsworth radically breaks his line,
and silence is felt in the very voice of the speaker, but none
more telling than the powerful enjambment: "in that silence
while he hung / Listening." In that "hung," suspended moment, containing the opposites of gentleness and shock, the
boy experiences subconsciously, "unawares," the "voice"
inherent in nature through the "mountain torrents." This
pause of silence, which the reader also is given to hear in the
text itself, leads the boy into the depths of his own mind and
activates a power of intelligence within him which the par-
ticipating speaker subsequently will employ.

The boy dies, and the poet-narrator survives him as if
adulthood were born out of the death of childhood in the natural process of growth, preparing adult consciousness for the
actual bodily death yet to come. The speaker's adult intelligence brings the boy's subconscious experience of divine
silence into the full light of consciousness and thereby repeats it, giving silence new embodiment. This silence has
worked so powerfully on the speaker's mind that the whole
process of mourning the boy's death seems instantly completed. This episode is remarkable in that we are given no immediate and direct expression of grief: "Fair is the spot, most
beautiful the vale," says the speaker of the boy's origin, juxta-

posing the boy's birthplace with his grave. What accounts for the speaker's tonal serenity is that the message he receives from silence suggests the possibility of life's continuity after death. Silence becomes the language of visionary faith—linking the visible with the invisible—which sees through death, though it also necessarily remains the language of poetic metaphor.

In the enjambed line, "A long half hour I have stood / Mute," the speaker reenacts the boy's experience of silence, his "lengthened pause," and that pause actually becomes the speaker's deep inhalation between the words "stood" and "Mute" and gives expression to his meditative, visionary silence. The image of the silent statue of the Madonna, "The thronèd Lady," returns the speaker through the earned power of forgetfulness that comes from the completion of mourning, "forgetful of this Boy / Who slumbers at her feet, —forgetful, too, / Of all her silent neighbourhood of graves," from the silence of death back to the living world of ordinary "gladsome sounds" of playing school children. The normal medium of linguistic life is sound, and thus the sense of sound surviving silence is also the sense of life surviving nothingness and death. Yet it is the silence within speech that provides for Wordsworth the metaphor expressing the continuity between life and death and their mysterious reconciliation as a divine unity.

I V

Life emerges from silence and stillness and returns to them. The connecting interim is composed of sound and movement, and Stevens's "Life Is Motion" may be read as a little parable on this theme:

> In Oklahoma
> Bonnie and Josie
> Dressed in calico,
> Danced around a stump.
> They cried,
> "Ohoyaho,
> Ohoo" . . .

> Celebrating the marriage
> Of flesh and air.

Stevens employs and distinguishes here two aspects of language: language as image and language as abstraction, which correspond to physical presence and conceptual thought—the word as sound-object and the word as idea. The letter *O* and the sound *O* are introduced doubled in the word "Motion." Person, dress, and place are related by having a prominent *O* letter and their implied sounds. Bonnie's and Josie's names have their O; their state, Oklahoma, is filled with Os; they are dressed in calico; and their cry, "Ohoyaho," which sounds perhaps like a caveman's version of Oklahoma, is a primitive warbling on the variants of the vowel *O*.

The first two words of the title, "Life Is," prepare the reader for an abstract and general proposition, and the word "Motion" completes the concept. Although "Motion" as a word evokes only an idea, not an image, it directs the reader's attention to the physical world of concrete, moving things, and Stevens will not return to abstract language until the poem's concluding two lines. For Stevens, every poem contains by implication the origin of language itself—the physical cry of the human voice not yet shaped into a word. He says in "The Man with the Blue Guitar," "The poem is the cry of its occasion"; inherent in the words and the design of the poem is the sound made by a rush of breath from the lungs, through the throat, directed by the tongue, against the teeth or the lips. This is the breathing voice that cries out "O" either in pleasure or in pain. The letter *O* presents the idea of this sound and, in essence, makes manifest what Stevens calls "the poem of the idea within the poem of words," to which we might add, in Stevens's behalf, "within the poem of sounds." Stevens says in his essay, "The Noble Rider and the Sound of Words": "above everything else, poetry is words; and words, above everything else, are, in poetry, sounds."

The setting of the poem, suggested by the calico clothing, is the nineteenth-century American frontier. A farming family has taken time out from work for a celebration, probably a wedding. The expansion of the country westward and the clearing of the land for farming suggest life-affirming activity and energy, yet the image of the stump which appears at the dead center of the poem (eleven words before and after), produces a countereffect. The reader hears and witnesses a physical dance accompanied by a primal, incantatory poetry around the central "stump" of death. Creation and destruction are thus seen as inseparable. The cry, "Ohoyaho, / Ohoo," is breath itself, pure voice unmediated by linguistic meaning. An emphatic breath pause is indicated by the ellipses, and in that moment, as cry trails off into silence, the reader-listener is invited to make the connection between the expressiveness of bodily voice sounds and the mind's power to conceptualize, to articulate ideas such as the idea of "marriage." The poem thus presents the idea of celebration and *is itself a celebration* of the idea of marriage: the marriage of person and place, life and death, body and mind, and, above all, sound and poem. The poem celebrates itself, wedding the body's cry with the mind's linguistic design; it is a metaphor for the literal human voice transformed into poetic speech. One might imagine that in the beginning was the letter O and its breathful sound. The poem is itself the unified and musical cry (as in the pun on "air") of the body and the mind-spirit, truly a "marriage of flesh and air."

William Carlos Williams's "Sea-Elephant" is a poem spoken by a variety of voices. We hear the voice of a circus barker, an animal trainer, a lady at the circus, the sea-elephant, the poet-narrator, and the partially remembered voice of an anonymous poet returning from the distant past. The two primary voices, however, are those of the sea-elephant who cries out in frustration, hunger, and desire, and the poet-narrator who in effect translates the sea-elephant's expressive sounds into the language of conceptual speech, as when the poet as circus trainer says, "Speak!" and the sea-elephant replies "Blouaugh," which the poet then interprets as "feed / me."

> Trundled from
> the strangeness of the sea—
> a kind of
> heaven—

Ladies and Gentlemen!
the greatest
sea-monster ever exhibited
alive

the gigantic
sea-elephant! O wallow
of flesh where
are

there fish enough for
that
appetite stupidity
cannot lessen?

Sick
of April's smallness
the little
leaves—

Flesh has lief of you
enormous sea—
Speak!
Blouaugh! (feed

me) my
flesh is riven—
fish after fish into his maw
unswallowing

to let them glide down
gulching back
half spittle half
brine

the
troubled eyes—torn
from the sea.
(In

a practical voice) They
ought
to put it back where
it came from.

Gape.
Strange head—
told by old sailors—
rising

bearded
to the surface—and
the only
sense out of them

is that woman's
Yes
it's wonderful but they
ought to

put it
back into the sea where
it came from.
Blouaugh!

Swing—ride
walk
on wires—toss balls
stoop and

contort yourselves—
But I
am love. I am
from the sea—

Blouaugh!
there is no crime save
the too-heavy
body

the sea
held playfully—comes
to the surface
the water

boiling
about the head the cows
scattering
fish dripping from

>the bounty
>of. . . . and spring
>they say
>Spring is icummen in—

The sea-elephant's "Blouaugh" suggests the primal cry out of which, eventually, all speech will come. We hear an echoing resemblance of its sliding *O* vowel in the poet's exclamation, "O wallow / of flesh," even before the sea-elephant speaks in the poem. The sea-elephant is on show, but so, too, is Williams in composing his poem; both in a sense are out of their element and have to struggle to perform in a new medium, the sea-elephant on land, the poet in language. For the poet, identifying himself with the sea-elephant as a fellow creature, only language heightened into poetic design can lighten the weight of the "too heavy / body." The "crime" of flesh, its voracious hungers, requires relief through the expression of itself in voice and, finally, in poetry.

Like the sea-elephant out of the sea which has been for him "a kind of heaven" because it gives buoyancy to his body, human consciousness alienates us from the demands of our bodies, our unappeasable "appetite." For the poet that alienation may be overcome through his sympathetic and accepting identification with the sea-elephant, an emblem of his bodily desires. So, too, their languages must merge into one, equally concrete and abstract. The poet's declarative statement, "But I / am love," speaks both for himself and the sea-elephant. This identification becomes explicit in the following line, "I am / from the sea," and reminds the reader of the common evolutionary heritage of all creatures. Thus the repeated cry "Blouaugh!" also belongs both to the sea-elephant and to the poet as it exists simultaneously as bodily cry and metaphorical word. Expressing the carnal and the mental need for satisfaction and love, the poet's human language is both voice and meaning, both physical gesture and idea.

At the end of the poem, the poet-narrator describes the sea-elephant in his natural element, water, evoking again the imagery of his appetite for food and love as he "comes / to the surface / the water / boiling about the head the cows / scattering / fish dripping." This power of appetite and desire is the creature's "bounty," as the variety of conjured voices, gathered together by the poem, have been the poet's bounty, his circus performance of verbal images as if he were balancing "on wires" or "toss[ing] balls." This final description, "fish dripping from / the bounty / of . . ." breaks off into a sigh or a deep pause, a silence. At that moment the cultural past of poetic tradition floods back into his mind so that the poet speaks not only in a creature's voice, not only in his own voice, but in a voice realizing the long history of poetry and desire.

The poem, however, cannot end by drifting off into silence as the ellipses suggests, for as Williams says in "Asphodel that Greeny Flower," "Silence can be complex too, / but you do not get far / with silence. / Begin again." So Williams begins again at the end, out of silence, returning to the thought of spring and an early memory of the tradition of poetry in English. His own contemporary voice merges with a voice from the past, just as his human voice merged with the animal voice of the sea-elephant. The design of the poem, gathering these separate voices together, is itself a single metaphor, both making connections and expressing the idea of continuity. The human voice of words and sounds, surrounding and giving shape to silence, fixed in the poem's design, is the metaphor that also creates the continuity between nature and art, as if nature had found a voice in which she could express herself.

V

Although the "rest is silence" into which our lives will vanish, the moment of art may realize and thus make real the illusion of life as extended and intensified, an illusion in which we see ourselves truly as our own metaphorical creation. A poem is of the body as much as of the mind; a poem is physical as the human voice is physical. It comes from the chest and the throat and the lips and the tongue and the teeth. It is fast or slow, loud or soft, steady or wavering; it embodies sobs and sighs and laughter. Stevens says that the poem of the mind "is a violence from within that protects us from a violence without. It is the imagination pressing back against the pressure of reality. It seems, in the last analysis, to have something to do with our self-preservation; and that, no doubt, is why the expression of it, the sound of its words, helps us to live our lives." It is not just the words that help, but also the *sound* of the words, the words as voice, the voice as physical utterance.

When Gerard Manley Hopkins envisions the descent of the Holy Ghost in the image of the dawn, figured as a dove, his ecstasy is given voice, beyond intellectual formation, in the prolonged, breathful cry of an "Ah!" breaking into the midst of the final phrase of the poem: "Because the holy ghost over the bent / World broods with warm breast, and with Ah! bright wings." And at the end, at the edge of a final silence, when King Lear kneels over the body of hanged Cordelia, even though his reason knows that she is dead—"And thou no breath at all? Thou'lt come no more"—Lear mercifully has the illusion that he sees her lips stir, and his outcry then constitutes his final lines in the play: "Look on her! look! her lips / Look there, look there! O. O. O. O." We, as audience, cannot tell whether it is joy or grief or some inscrutable combination that breaks his heart and releases him from the rack of the world—just as Gloucester died, "his flawed heart . . . Twixt two extremes of passion, joy and grief, / Burst smilingly."

Lear moves beyond us into some ultimate emotion; so, too, his language moves beyond words into pure sounds and silence—silence that is both the end and the beginning of speech. Silence here both is nothing and also is replete with emotional implication, just as the fool had insinuated to Lear early in act 1, "Now thou art an O without a figure. I am better than thou art now. I am a fool, thou art nothing." Having borne witness to Lear's emerging from the O of nothing into the mysterious fullness of his final "O. O. O. O.," we are left behind, with Edgar, to console ourselves, to find the words to live by—not merely the meaning of the words, but the sounds of their emotions, the voice and cry of the human heart. Edgar says: "The weight of this sad time we must obey; / Speak what we feel, not what we ought to say." This plea for the merging of feeling and language is a plea, finally, for the expressiveness of metaphorical speech.

PART TWO

FOUR

Macbeth: The Anatomy of Loss

❦

MACBETH, the character, differs from Hamlet, Othello, and Lear in that he is a good man whose intention is to do evil and who succeeds, while the others are all good men whose intentions are to do good and who, for the most part, fail. In compensation for their failure, Hamlet, Othello, and Lear all learn something in the course of their plays, but Macbeth is only confirmed in what he already knew, that "We still have judgment here." To call Macbeth a good man is perhaps merely to call him a man, for Shakespeare's understanding of human nature is that it is essentially moral, and that all contain within themselves their own heaven and hell, with virtue its own reward and evil its own punishment: Macbeth suffers not simply because he is evil, but because he is a good man doing evil. Why, then, does Macbeth, or anyone, if all are of such a moral nature, commit evil deeds, succumbing to pride or ambition? Evil is mysterious, beyond prediction or explanation; it follows no psychological laws that make it inevitable; it is the product of a free will. Shakespeare knows that good may come from evil—indeed, this is the wisdom we learn from all tragedy, but though Shakespeare accepts this paradox, he also embraces the further paradox that, though evil may be necessary in a world of free men, it must be opposed as if this necessity did not exist.

In Shakespeare's plays, the world, the state, and the individual are interrelated, macrocosm to microcosm. Any influence on one affects the others. A broken law in the affairs of men will be felt throughout the cosmos. The morning after Duncan's murder, Ross says:

> Thou seest the heavens, as troubled with man's act,
> Threatens his bloody stage: by the clock 'tis day,
> And yet dark night strangles the travelling lamp.
> (2.4.5–7)

Animals no longer act according to their kind, but become strangely violent: a falcon is killed by a mousing owl, and Duncan's horses, "turn'd wild in nature," attack and eat each other. The world is in turmoil, the state is disrupted with the killing of the king, and, metaphorically, Macbeth has also killed the king within himself.

Hamlet both accepts and doubts this universal moral structure. He knows that by his action Denmark can be cured of its ills, when he says: "The time is out of joint. O cursed spite, / That ever I was born to set it right!" and yet he finds that reason alone will not suffice in the rendering of justice in a corrupt state. His apparent unwillingness to believe the truth about his uncle's crime conceals his innate repulsion against the convention of revenge and impedes all significant action. Hamlet is trying to commit justice in a world he fears may not be moral and may not sanction moral action. Hamlet's problem is not that he is unable to act, but that he is unable to do *the significant* act for fear that it will not prove significant in this world. Hamlet wants to do the right thing, in the right way, for the right reasons, and since he finds this impossible, he questions all existence. Finally he acts, and there is momentary joy in the knowledge that life must go on, that his story will serve as a parable for those to come. Hamlet snatches the cup of poison from Horatio's lips and exhorts him:

> If thou did'st ever hold me in thy heart,
> Absent thee from felicity awhile,
> And in this harsh world draw thy breath in pain,
> To tell my story. (5.2.349–52)

The world is harsh, but it is, all in all, a good world, one in which Hamlet desires to have his story told. By contrast, at the end, life for Macbeth seemed "a tale / Told by an idiot, full of sound and fury, / Signifying nothing." For Hamlet, his own tale became the tale of man's moral struggle, and Hamlet's tragic ecstasy was that he came to know that it had *signified everything*. The play ends with Horatio's effort to tell Hamlet's story, "And let me speak to the yet unknowing world / How these things came about," although it is Shakespeare's irony that Horatio reduced the story to its melodramatic components.

Othello also learns that the world is better than he had ever really believed. What was his jealousy but a deep skepticism about love? It is not until the very end that Othello fully realizes the world *can* include a faithful love. Like Hamlet, Othello feels called upon to commit justice and purge the world, and when Othello learns how he has been deceived by Iago, this instinct still does not leave him, and he kills himself. He does this for the sake of the state, as if still acting in an official capacity, and Othello is elated as he plunges the knife into himself. He loves Desdemona more fully in the wisdom of that moment than he had before, and he knows that his tale will be told and that it will benefit all to hear it. He says to his audience before he dies:

> ... I pray you, in your letters,
> When you shall these unlucky deeds relate,
> Speak of them as they are. Nothing extenuate,
> Nor set down aught in malice. Then must you speak
> Of one that lov'd not wisely but too well. (5.2.340–44)

Only Macbeth feels in the end that life is worthless and that its story is not worth telling. He fights his last battles, not because he desires to win, not to achieve or gain something, but out of blind defiance. Even Lear, who undergoes the greatest suffering of these four tragic figures, does not renounce life, but desires it more intensely than ever. He has passed through madness, forgiveness, and self-forgiveness, and has learned, at last, to love, and in this love Lear is redeemed. Lear's final illusion of Cordelia's breathing expresses the spiritual truth of his existence. It is not pain, but joy in love, that breaks his heart and frees him from the rack of the world. Lear's grief, like Macduff's, is more consoling than Macbeth's lack of feeling on learning of the death of his wife. Nature's ironic blessing is to make Lear's love most strongly felt in its loss, and, in the final moment of loss, Lear experiences the ecstasy of affirmation. Just as the tragedy in *King Lear* begins with the hypocritical declarations of faith by Goneril and Regan, it closes with the statement by Edgar that this story must be told truly, sad as it is, by speaking "what we feel."

I I

In Shakespeare's plays, all reward, retribution, and punishment take place on earth and within the sphere of mortal life. Tragedy requires a world that is complete unto itself, its own end, not a means to another world. Reward, therefore, is not transcendence to a beatific state, nor is punishment merely something that is imposed upon one like physical torture. The assuming of a burden or a responsibility must, in part, be its own reward: wisdom acquired through suffering, joy in right action, affirmation of moral values. And like reward, punishment, too, will be a state of conscience.

Macbeth is a play about a man who violates the moral order within himself and is punished for it. No torture is imposed upon him to fit his crimes, but, rather, the blessings of Macbeth's natural humanity fall from him one by one until he is deprived of all human ties, even concern for himself. Macbeth's punishment is to lose those things that made up his "milk of human kindness" humanity.

Macbeth is his own antagonist. The entire moral order is reflected within his conscience as the functioning of his imagination. The conflict of the play is primarily interior. Hamlet is opposed by Claudius, Othello by Iago, Lear by Regan, Goneril, and Edmund; their fates are partially determined by hostile, external forces. But Macbeth, more than any other tragic hero, can anticipate and calculate the results of his actions—he is free to choose—and so he is most the master of his fate. He falls, not out of ignorance, foible, or weakness, but, like Satan, out of defiance and ambition, willingly embraced. Conscience, in all its vivid imagery of warning, Macbeth willfully rejects.

Once Macbeth has killed the king, the entire natural and moral order is disrupted, and, in this chaos, results can no longer be calculated from causes. Macbeth is unable to read the signs of nature and is misled by appearances. Shakespeare describes this disorder by showing us storms, winds, wild seas, thunder, war, and witches, or in subtle ways as in the banquet scene when everybody enters in proper order (Macbeth says: "You know your own degrees; sit down: at first and last"), but exits in confusion (Lady Macbeth says: "You have displac'd the mirth, broke the good meeting, / With most admir'd disorder"). The "breach in nature" imagery is continuous: blood, sickness, predatory animals, dark overcoming light:

> Light thickens, and the crow
> Makes wing to the rooky wood;
> Good things of day begin to droop and drowse,
> Whiles night's black agents to their preys do rouse.
> (3.2.50–53)

Macbeth is pictured as a man enveloped in a coat too large for him. He cannot properly wear the clothing of his usurped positions:

> Now does he feel his title
> Hang loose about him, like a giant's robe
> Upon a dwarfish thief. (5.2.20–23)

The reverberation of sounds echoing over vast regions, filling all of space, suggests the incalculable and boundless effect and spread of evil issuing from a single source. But perhaps the most important of all the play's imagery is that of the child. The child is the symbol of Macbeth's ambition to defy the laws of nature, redirect fate, and shape the future according to his own anarchic order. Macbeth's free and proper choice was, in a sense, to stand still, to accept his role, his place in society, the natural order. But in choosing otherwise, Macbeth determines his personal doom, although control of the future, which the child represents, is beyond him. The witches can predict the future, not because they control it, but because they see into the heart of Macbeth's character and therefore know the fate that will result from it. In their first speech, the witches speak the words that will come independently into Macbeth's mind. "Fair is foul, and foul is fair," and, likewise, Macbeth's first words are "So foul and fair a day."

The order of Shakespeare's cosmos is never interrupted by miracle. Every extraordinary event takes place nonetheless within the limits of natural law, for Shakespeare's natural law includes spiritual as well as material reality. The witches, therefore, should not be regarded as supernatural beings. They are objectifications of Macbeth's imagination, like the bloody dagger and Banquo's ghost, neither of which can be seen by anybody else. The objection that Banquo also sees the witches is overcome by the fact that his mind has become tainted with exactly the same evil that has corrupted Macbeth. Banquo's ambition, too, is willing to seek its fulfillment by illegal or dubious means, so that the witches have the same relation to Banquo as they do to Macbeth; they must be considered imaginative projections from both of their corrupted minds. Before he gets murdered, Banquo has decided not to expose Macbeth as Duncan's murderer because he believes that Macbeth's advancement is the herald of his own familial enthronement:

> BANQUO: Thou hast it now: King, Cawdor, Glamis, all,
> As the weird women promised; and, I fear,
> Thou play'dst most foully for't; yet it was said
> It should not stand in thy posterity,
> But that myself should be the root and father

> Of many kings. If there come truth from
> them,—
> As upon thee, Macbeth, their speeches
> shine,—
> Why, by the verities on thee made good,
> May they not be my oracles as well,
> And set me up in hope?
> (3.1.1–10)

Shakespeare shows us the likeness between Macbeth and Banquo even before the above scene. Banquo's corruption is intimated when, earlier, he says to Fleance:

> BANQUO: A heavy summons lies like lead upon me,
> And yet I would not sleep: Merciful
> powers!
> Restrain in me the cursed thoughts that
> nature
> Gives way to in repose.
> (2.1.6–9)

Banquo is sensitive to Macbeth's state of mind. Immediately after the witches' first prophesy that Macbeth will become king, Banquo says: "Good sir, why do you start, and seem to fear / Things that do sound so fair?" This, in addition to Lady Macbeth's question to her husband, "What made you break this enterprise to me?" makes it clear that Macbeth, not Lady Macbeth, initially conceived the idea of murdering for the crown. Banquo is not duped by the temptations of evil any more than is Macbeth, and yet he, too, succumbs in conscience and through his lack of action:

> BANQUO: But 'tis strange:
> And oftentimes, to win us to our harm,
> The instruments of darkness tell us truths,
> Win us with honest trifles, to betray's
> In deepest consequence.
> (1.3.122–26)

Banquo might have saved his own life, if he had acted according to this knowledge and opposed Macbeth after Duncan's murder, rather than hoping to ride to power by the forces that had prognosticated Macbeth's ascension to the throne.

This kind of betrayal of one's wisest self also describes Macbeth's personal history. Macbeth conceives the crime, knows the ultimate folly of committing it, yet plunges into the ways of blood so that there is no return. To assume that Macbeth is seduced into crime by Lady Macbeth when she argues that his reluctance is cowardice and that he is bound to a promise (that Lady Macbeth probably invented) is to underestimate his intelligence. Lady Macbeth, in the fervor of ambition, is entirely duped by her own false reasoning; she does not see the sword's other edge, as does her husband. Her convictions become Macbeth's rationalizations, for, inwardly, he has already committed the crime of regicide.

Before Macbeth begins his career in crime, he knows with certainty—unlike Lady Macbeth—that punishment and judgment must follow. But what he does not fully realize (and here lies his tragic foible) is the means by which this punishment will be executed. The means are nature's means—nature working through Macbeth in the forms taken by his imagination. Macbeth ceases to be able to tell the false from the true, the real from the illusory, and he is brought to his death as if nature—like the gods in classical mythology—could be consciously active in the affairs of men.

I I I

At the play's commencement, Macbeth exhibits a balance of hard and soft virtues: courage, bravery, strength, defiance, pride, and ambition; but also kindness and conscience. In the play's unfolding, he loses the soft virtues, and we cease to feel sympathy for him, but he retains throughout his hard virtues. When we are in his presence, we are struck with awe; he is a spectacle of horror from which we cannot take our eyes. Because his strength is admirable, he is doubly dangerous, both for doing evil and for making evil secretly appealing. Like Satan, he is a fallen angel, and there is something within all of us that feels the temptation to join the devil's party. Shakespeare's art does not deny that there is something attractive about evil—for why else would so much evil flourish in the world?—but he wants to show how a human devil like Macbeth is destroyed, not merely by punishment, but through the acting out of his own evil.

Satan, it has been wittily suggested, was the first romantic. His evil was the result of his energy's lacking a creative goal of its own and thus becoming perversely misdirected in opposition to God's moral order. Macbeth, seen as such a romantic, is not the creator, but the destroyer, not the reformer, but the anarchist. Because of an excess of selfish energy, Macbeth attempts to exploit even the forbidden possibilities of his life, and he tries to shape the order of nature to fit his own demands. The idea of Macbeth as Satan is suggested within the play in many forms and guises. There is much talk about rebels; there are references to hell and images of hell; and there are numerous illusions to the devil himself. Lady Macbeth says to her husband before Duncan arrives: "look like the innocent flower, / But be the serpent under 't." Malcolm, speaking of Macbeth, remarks, "Angels are bright still, though the brightest fell"; and a little later in the conversation, Macduff replies: "Not in the legions / Of horrid hell can come a devil more damn'd / In evils to top Macbeth." Macbeth's evil, like Satan's, is entirely self-generated. Hamlet, Othello, and Lear are provoked from without; they are trapped by extreme and extenuating circumstances. Out of ignorance, they are tempted into acting wrongly, and they suffer for it. They sin like Adam, who in the course of being tested was still being created, but Macbeth sins as Satan—without any provocation except his own inexplicable pride and ambition. Macbeth's crime is treason.

The most important analogy between Satan and Macbeth is that they are both fully aware they are opposing an ultimately indestructible moral order, so that—absurd as it may seem—they enter into crime aware of the inevitability of their punishment. Macbeth knows fully, even before the murder of Duncan, that crime has its fitting consequences, but nevertheless he proceeds, and directly after the murder, he exclaims: "Will all great Neptune's ocean wash this blood / Clean from my hand? No, this my hand will rather / The multitudinous seas incarnadine, / Making the green one red." Macbeth defies the repeated warnings of conscience and of his own knowledge and suffers a series of punishments, all consisting of deprivations, until he has lost what the poorest have—that most precious gift of all, his humanity.

He loses the ability to pray:

MACBETH: Listening their fear, I could not say 'Amen,'
          When they did say 'God bless us!'
LADY M: Consider it not so deeply.
          But wherefore could I not pronounce
             'Amen'?
          I had most need of blessing, and 'Amen'
          Stuck in my throat.
          (2.2.29–33)

He loses the blessing of sleep:

MACBETH: Methought I heard a voice cry 'Sleep no
             more!
          Macbeth does murder sleep,' the inno-
             cent sleep . . .
          Balm of hurt minds, great nature's second
             course,
          Chief nourisher in life's feast,—
          (2.2.35–39)

He loses his sense of the seriousness of life, making of his own ambition an ironic mockery:

MACBETH: Had I but died an hour before this chance,
          I had liv'd a blessed time; for, from this
             instant,
          There's nothing serious in mortality:
          All is but toys; renown and grace is dead,
          The wine of life is drawn, and the mere
             lees
          Is left this vault to brag of.
          (2.3.98–103)

He loses his trust in even the men who work for him and sends a third murderer to watch after the first two:

SECOND
MURDERER: He needs not our mistrust, since he
                delivers
             Our offices and what we have to do
             To the direction just.
             (3.3.2–4)

He loses the power of rational thought and is trapped
within his own fears and emotions:

MURDERER: Most royal sir,
             Fleance is 'scaped.
MACBETH: Then comes my fit again: I had else been
                perfect;
             Whole as the marble, founded as the rock,
             As broad and general as the casing air:
             But now I am cabin'd, cribb'd, confin'd,
                bound in
             To saucy doubts and fears.
             (3.4.19–25)

He loses trust in his senses and is seized by madness.
Banquo's ghost is not like the witches, but like the imaginary
dagger, which can be seen only by Macbeth. Like distrust,
madness separates men from their society:

LENNOX: What is't that moves your
                highness?
MACBETH: Which of you have done this?
LORDS: What, my good lord?
MACBETH: (To Banquo's ghost who is sitting in Mac-
                beth's chair.)
             Thou can'st not say I did it: never shake
             Thy gory locks at me.
ROSS: Gentlemen, rise; his highness is not well.
             (3.4.48–52)

He loses all companionship, the comfort of family and society, and falls into complete loneliness and isolation:

MACBETH: I have liv'd long enough: my way of life
             Is fallen into the sear, the yellow leaf;

And that which should accompany old
  age,
As honour, love, obedience, troops of
  friends,
I must not look to have.
(5.3.22–26)

He loses the power of compassionate feeling and cannot
even grieve at the death of his wife:

SEYTON: The queen, my lord, is dead.
MACBETH: She should have died hereafter;
         There would have been a time for such a
           word.
         (5.5.16–18)

Macbeth loses love for everything and can take pleasure in
nothing:

MACBETH: Life's but a walking shadow, a poor player
         That struts and frets his hour upon the
           stage,
         And then is heard no more; it is a tale
         Told by an idiot, full of sound and fury,
         Signifying nothing.
         (5.5.24–28)

Macbeth, stripped of his humanity, is left only with blind
animal defiance, fitting to the beast that he has become. His
early knowledge in act 1:

MACBETH: I dare do all that may become a man;
         Who dares do more is none.
LADY M: What beast was't, then,
         That made you break this enterprise to me?
         (1.7.46–48)

becomes a fact in act 5:

MACBETH: They have tied me to a stake: I cannot fly,
         But bear-like I must fight the course.
         (5.7.1–2)

Macbeth has violated nature's moral order and has thus become estranged from it, so that to him the face of nature becomes a false one whose smiles are deceitful and whose warnings are misleading. As Macbeth has acted falsely to his nature, so nature equivocates in its appearances, rendering Macbeth's punishment, the deprivation step by step of his humanity, to its culmination by means of Birnam Wood and Macduff's premature birth—whereby Macbeth is defeated in battle and destroyed. From hopeless defiance to the hopelessness of solitary and loveless death, there is little space.

By the end of the play, the spectator has lost compassion and sympathy for Macbeth, so that our feelings for him have been completely reversed. Now he evokes in us only fear and horror. Since Macbeth has, in effect, ceased to be human, the most we can feel for him is an abstract pity; we are not sorry for *him* because of the fate he suffers, but we are sorry that in *our* world such corruption does take place, and that such power, of potential good, can release what is terrible and dark in human affairs.

Our pity and sympathy for Hamlet, for Othello, and for Lear increase as their tragedy directs them to their inevitable end. It is the necessity of their suffering that holds our fascination and makes us love them. For with our knowledge of their loss, we recognize the inevitability of our loss; and since to understand loss, to feel the weight of suffering through it, is also to understand *that which has been lost*, we recognize that through the suffering of loss our affirmation of life is expressed and strengthened. This is the knowledge by which, at the time of their deaths, Hamlet, Othello, and Lear accept their own fates while affirming the goodness of life, and feel love most strongly out of the depths of their losses.

Macbeth does not make such an affirmation; in dying, he does not affirm the moral order, nor spiritual love, nor any force of life, but the moral world *affirms itself* in the way it has punished and destroyed him. For natural morality, according to Shakespeare, is an order by means of which its opponents are punished by the very fact of their opposition, so that Macbeth suffers commensurately with his power to defy moral laws. Out of the same necessity that makes suffering a means to the recognition of the good, comes the reestablishment of harmony after the hour of evil.

IV

If, in the course of the play, our feelings for Macbeth move from sympathy and admiration to horror and awe, our feelings for Lady Macbeth move in an opposite way: from horror and revulsion to pity and sympathy. At the beginning, she is unable to understand Macbeth, mistaking conscience for cowardice, and she is therefore unable to help him; and at the end, Macbeth—having opposed and rejected his own conscience—can no longer sympathize with his wife or help her when she suffers the extreme recriminations of her conscience. Macbeth knows before he acts that the rhythm that leads from deed to consequence is a rhythm established in the stars, not to be changed by human choice: "If it were done when 'tis done then 'twere well / It were done quickly." But Lady Macbeth does not learn this lesson until temptation is chronicled in action: "What's done cannot be undone." Shakespeare's repetition of the words "done" and "do" throughout the play, like waves upon a shore, reveals an inevitability that leads Macbeth to his fate as a necessary result of his initiating choices.

Macbeth's greatness, Shakespeare shows, is opposed to his goodness: he is able to accomplish feats beyond the powers of ordinary men. His greatness of will enables him to detach himself from his own character and act against the dictates of his own knowledge and his own conscience. Macbeth refuses to be himself, maintaining this position no matter what the outcome and without self-pity or regret. This is a fantastic feat, one that Lady Macbeth thinks she can execute, but at which she fails miserably. Macbeth, by his success, wins our hatred. Lady Macbeth, by her failure, wins our pity. It is a paradoxical ascent that Lady Macbeth travels, for she is destroyed by the goodness of her moral nature, by her conscience. Not by strength of will does she repent; her nature repents for her.

Lady Macbeth undertakes the murder of Duncan because she thinks that any resulting consequences will be entirely social, and her ambition is willing to assume this calculated risk. She does not realize what the consequences of crimes and conscience will be. But she is wrong to think that "A little water clears us of this deed." Her inability to act on discovering that Duncan resembles her father ironically reverses her disavowal of parental feeling, "I have given suck, and know / How tender 'tis to love the babe that milks me: / I would, while it was smiling in my face, / Have plucked my nipple from his boneless gums, / And dashed the brains out," and so her weakness to act derives, though unwillingly, from natural goodness.

It becomes increasingly obvious that Lady Macbeth's repentance, as well as her guilt, is instinctual and not considered. Because of this dichotomy in her personality, she sinks into madness in which she acts out her symbolic penances, and in such a way is her humanity stated. In this madness she attempts to shut out the darkness of her corrupted rational mind, so that the light of her innermost being can reveal her in those gestures of submission to the natural order that she has violated. Her own darkness has corrupted her, and she must pitifully seek for the light that will redeem her:

DOCTOR: How came she by the light?
GENT.:   Why, it stood by her: she has light by her
         continually; 'tis her command.
         (5.1.24–26)

This is the darkness of blood and of dirt and of the grave, so that her gesture of repentance is one of washing to remove the blackness that is upon her:

DOCTOR: Look, how she rubs her hands.
GENT.:   It is an accustomed action with her, to seem
         thus washing her hands. I have known her
         to continue this a quarter of an hour.
LADY M: Yet here's a spot.
         (5.1.29–34)

At her death, Lady Macbeth has lost all will to oppose the will

of nature as its exists in society and in its manifestation as her
guilt and her conscience. She ends in the weakness of utter
submission to this greater will, and the doctor who has
tended her has no prescription for her but forgiveness:

> DOCTOR: Unnatural deeds
>   Do breed unnatural troubles; infected
>   minds
>   To their deaf pillows will discharge their
>   secrets;
>   More needs she the divine than the
>   physician.
>   God, God forgive us all!
>   (5.1.72–82)

That the doctor should ask "all" to be forgiven suggests that,
in some secret way, there is something in himself that he
identifies in Lady Macbeth, so that Lady Macbeth receives
a response that returns her to the fellowship of human
sympathy.

                                    V

Greatness is an attribute of will. Goodness, as Shakespeare
portrays it in this play, is an attribute of the natural heart.
Will either may be in opposition to goodness or may embrace
it, so that moral action exists in this freedom of choice: sin is
opposition to the natural order, and virtue is acceptance of its
limits. Though greatness in itself is not virtue, greatness always is fascinating because it reveals the power of will by
which people are capable of destroying themselves. People
are alike in their instinctual goodness; but they are unique in
their greatness. Thus goodness is a social and moral force,
while greatness primarily makes itself manifest through
anarchic defiance.

The heroes of Shakespearean tragedy are romantics, men
who first desire an order that their selfish wishes would impose upon the world. Ultimately, their greatness and their
goodness may be reconciled if they accept the natural order as
one imposed by a greater power than their own. Macbeth is

Shakespeare's exception; he is a romantic to the end, unwilling to bow himself to an order other than his own. The penalties follow; for him there is not any recovery, no pardon, no tender memory.

The will opens the final door to action as one steps from the threshold of moral contemplation into the arena of social action. Causality, then, operates in this way in the Shakespearean universe: there is free choice of action in the world, but the consequences following from action are fixed. The punishments our moral nature imposes on us are implicit in the sinful actions that violate this order, so that the very violation contains within itself the means by which the harmony of moral order may be restored. Ambition always exceeds satisfaction. The most potent meaning of peace is as a goal that never may be permanently reached, and, if attained for the moment, must be again sought, and again attained. Thus success is a kind of failure, for it is always partial, and so failure is a kind of success, for it speaks most truly of the limitations of what men can achieve. We accept Lady Macbeth in her failure. Macbeth succeeds to the end in remaining willfully defiant in the face of natural limits, but at the total price of his humanity.

>   ... the silent mind
> Has her own treasures, and I think of these;
> Love what I see, and honour human kind.
>   *—The Recluse*

FIVE

Wordsworth and the Voice of Silence

ORDSWORTH chose his own mental growth as his epic theme, but it was not sufficient for him to begin tracing his mental history from his infancy; he postulated a "heavenly" influence which the child received as his inheritance at birth. Wordsworth sought to evoke both his personal and his racial past out of silence as God had created the world out of nothing.

The "blessing" in the "gentle breeze" that opens *The Prelude* is a presence, and it evokes thoughts from Wordsworth as if that were its intent. When nature speaks most profoundly to him, it speaks silently, and these silences contain "intimations" of life before his life and of immortality. Such silences possess the "calmness of eternity" as Wordsworth says in his essay "The Sublime and the Beautiful." As a poet whose theme is growth, Wordsworth undertakes to explore both what the mind remembers and what it forgets; what it can know and what is concealed from it; what it half creates and what it perceives.

Wordsworth had no fear greater than that of solitude when solitude is felt as loneliness. In his twenties, he began preparing himself for his old age as if his mental powers soon would fail him. Solitariness, loneliness, and failure were linked in his mind. One is truly alone, for Wordsworth, when there is no honest communication of feeling, "greetings where no kindness is," or when memory fails. Wordsworth's adult sense of the past includes an earlier sense of nature as home. Loneliness and homesickness are virtually one in Wordsworth's writing. When he feels cut off from those he loves, or when he feels out of touch with his own "genial nature," he is fearful and lonely; in both cases the symptom of loneliness is the result of a fault that lies within him. One need not feel lonely just because one is alone. The person who feels lonely suffers from a kind of disease: the inevitable disease of separation and loss for which, nevertheless, the silent mind can find a cure—in silence.

I I

"Tintern Abbey" is a meditation about the recollection of youthful, spontaneous delight in nature—delight that is now gone; and yet the power of recollection that has been gained in adulthood becomes a greater means toward affirmation than the power of spontaneous joy that has been lost. When Wordsworth wrote the poem he was twenty-eight, and his sense of having grown past early manhood includes the fresh realization that there is a "burthen" to the mystery of life. The poem expresses a fear of further change—intimated in the change from boyhood to adulthood—and warns of the need to prepare for new difficulties and the "dreary intercourse of daily life." He meets this threat by strengthening and reaffirming his belief in a universal bond of love: his changed love for nature modulates to embody his unchanging love for his sister. And the theme, which Wordsworth will never abandon, fully emerges: How does a young man prepare himself for the aging of his imagination?

"Tintern Abbey" begins with the poet moved by the fact that five years have passed and now, having returned to a particular place, he finds that familiarity and all its associated feelings have not left him. His first impression is that nothing

has changed; he uses the word "again" four times in the first
fourteen lines. The atmosphere is one of silence and isolation, and the question—When is a man lonely?—implicitly
pervades the whole paragraph. The crucial point of this thematic repetition, "again I hear. . . . Once again do I behold,"
is that things are the same as they were, and yet different. The
waters are still rolling from their mountain springs, but the
cliffs impress him with the deeper seclusion of thought itself.
Although heaven and earth still seem to be part of one landscape, the unchanging scene intensifies Wordsworth's awareness of his changed mind. No longer is he simply and undivid-
edly at home in this setting. Despite their familiarity, both
the quiet of the sky and the smoke sent up in silence from
among the trees create an atmosphere of loneliness, a "sad
perplexity" that troubles his repose, as if Wordsworth himself were a "vagrant dweller." That the scene seems just as
beautiful as before makes the loneliness he feels even more
troubling; perhaps this is a place where only a hermit can feel
at home.

With the phrase "These beauteous forms," Wordsworth's
attention shifts from the visible scene to speculation on the
salubrious effects of remembered pleasure. Memory has provided him with something permanent: the presence of past
beauty. When this past is evoked presently in the mind, the
possibility of overcoming loneliness exists even though one
is alone. Through retrospection, when the goodness of past
experience is recalled, the burden of the world may be eased:
the body slumbers, and a clairvoyance of the spirit sees into
the joy of all created things. But Wordsworth's consciousness
constantly confronts itself, and he questions "If this be but
a vain belief?" only to turn to the physical scene before him
for renewed consolation: "Yet, oh! how oft . . . have I turned
to thee, O Sylvan Wye!" Here the poem reaches its first resolution, with Wordsworth convinced that nature includes a
health-giving power that can be silently stored within the
human memory. This power, he feels, will enable him to face
a threatening future with hope—a hope that is nevertheless
qualified as an act of daring: "And so I dare to hope, / Though
changed, no doubt from what I was when first / I came among
these hills." Having come to this momentary resolution, he

reexamines the change that distinguishes his adulthood from his boyhood, and then he explores the moral this change teaches.

Boyhood is described as a responsive rather than an initiating state in which one is "more like a man / Flying from something that he dreads, than one / Who sought the thing he loved." Daring to hope is grounded in dread. The boy's nature, his "glad animal movements," is not willed and is not tempered by any moral idea; yet dread, haunting passion, and physical pleasure are part of the moral sensibility that necessarily precedes any later moral formulations:

> The sounding cataract
> Haunted me like a passion: the tall rock,
> The mountain, and the deep and gloomy wood,
> Their colours and their forms, were then to me
> An appetite: a feeling and a love,
> That had no need of a remoter charm,
> By thought supplied. . . .

Memory, therefore, not only preserves beauty and records change, but also inspires the thought that interprets that change.

Memory, leading to thought regarded as a new power, enables Wordsworth to accept the loss of youthful spontaneity: "other gifts / Have followed: for such loss, I would believe / Abundant recompense." The power of thought, seen as "Abundant recompense," is also a visionary capability, philosophical in form, but rooted in sensation:

> For I have learned
> To look on nature, not as in the hour
> Of thoughtless youth: but hearing oftentimes
> The still, sad music of humanity.

The stillness of this music is also the stillness in which thought flourishes and comes forth as moral wisdom. Felt, as music is felt, this is silence in which the interpenetration of man and nature finds a voice, as in poetry, and expresses its lesson in morality—a lesson in the possibility of loving rather than dreading the physical world. The music is sad be-

cause it is the music of mortality, containing the burden of
human responsibility. The paradox of music's being "still" is
sustained as Wordsworth speaks of the "presence" this music
represents: "And I have felt / A presence that disturbs me
with the joy / Of elevated thoughts." The ideas seem to be
contradictory, but Wordsworth will have them joined to
stress the inextricability of sorrow and gladness, to show that
adult joy is, indeed, the awareness of disturbance in the form
of "elevated thoughts." The emphasis in the following passage is on the presence as it becomes accessible to thought as
a "sense sublime." The presence exists not only in contemplation but also in "all the mighty world / Of eye and ear,
—both what they half create / And what perceive." Certain
that this presence does live in the world as well as in himself,
Wordsworth is able to extend his earlier conviction that nature contains a health-giving power to the belief that this
very power is also the spirit of his own nature. And so he says
that he is

> well pleased to recognise
> In nature and the language of the sense,
> The anchor of my purest thoughts, the nurse,
> The guide, the guardian of my heart, and soul
> Of all my moral being.

After recognizing that nature is the source of his moral being, Wordsworth fittingly turns to familial and social considerations. Looking at his sister, he sees in her what he once
was; he is concerned because he imagines that she must un-
dergo the same change he has just completed, but he assures
himself that nature guides us all "from joy to joy." The new
joy is a consciousness coming from an awareness of natural
beauty which leads to the strengthening of fraternal love in
the face of "natural sorrow" and social evil. Finally, his new
joy results in self-sufficiency that prevails over loneliness:

> [Nature] can so inform
> The mind that is within us, so impress
> With quietness and beauty, and so feed
> With lofty thoughts, that neither evil tongues,

> Rash judgments, nor the sneers of selfish men,
> Nor greetings where no kindness is, nor all
> The dreary intercourse of daily life,
> Shall e'er prevail against us.

The quiet mind receives and learns and, through memory, retains its treasure, so that no matter what vicissitudes lie ahead, Wordsworth feels that his sister (like himself) will always be protected by the beauty she has already absorbed and by the internalized bond of their love:

> thy mind
> Shall be a mansion for all lovely forms,
> Thy memory be as a dwelling-place
> For all sweet sounds and harmonies: oh! then,
> If solitude, or fear, or pain, or grief,
> Should be thy portion, with what healing thoughts
> Of tender joy wilt thou remember me!

Despite his loss of youthful spontaneity, "An appetite: a feeling and a love, / That had no need of a remoter charm, / By thought supplied," Wordsworth says that the woods, through thoughtful retrospection, shall become "More dear, both for themselves and for thy [his sister's] sake!" and thus protect her from loneliness and grief. The sweet sounds and harmonies will flourish in the silence of her mind as the sublime music of humanity that binds them together even when apart. This is the essence of all familial bonds: the bond from the childhood inheritance of love, which is the covenant that is broken and repaired in the poem "Michael."

When Michael's son, Luke, has to go to the "dissolute city," the covenant is broken because its sustaining influence —the pastoral landscape—is forgotten. And Wordsworth, as Michael's spiritual son, attempts to repair that covenant in his role as poet by leading his reader back into the natural landscape from the "public way." Thus he inherits Michael's roles as both father and guide to future poets:

> I will relate the same
> For the delight of a few natural hearts:
> And, with yet fonder feeling, for the sake

Of youthful Poets, who among these hills
Will be my second self when I am gone.

The covenant is the inheritance father leaves to son, or poet
to reader. The love the child has received is the same love the
grown man in turn will bestow as a gift upon his child. This
is the gift that Wordsworth offers both Dorothy and his readers as moral inheritance. To perceive this pattern (which, as
in "Michael," is always in danger of being violated) as the pattern provided by nature for human growth is also to perceive
nature as a moral order, just as Shakespeare had done in *Macbeth*. Man discerns the presence of such an order in silently
confronting his own consciousness and his own past when
his mind is moved by the imagery of the physical world.

"Tintern Abbey" portrays the power of silence and the kindred power of memory to fortify one in anticipating the process of growing old and the trials of "solitude, or fear, or pain,
or grief." But equally important is what Wordsworth assumes
about the past *that he does not remember*. The "feelings too /
Of unremembered pleasure" are primarily what make possible "that serene and blessed mood / In which the affections
gently lead us on." Unremembered pleasure is emphatical-
ly distinguished from the "beauteous forms" of nature that
he clearly recalls when in "lonely rooms" in the city, yet they
are like the beauteous forms in their effect: both the unremembered pleasures and the remembered "beauteous
forms" make possible "sensations sweet" when Wordsworth
is weary and lonely. Both have a cheering effect as they pass
into the "purer mind" and "influence" his moral instincts,
his "nameless, unremembered acts / Of kindness and of
love."

The "purer mind" is the imagination's medium of silence
in which Wordsworth's mental power is capable of synthesiz-
ing the connections between the present, adult Wordsworth
and the past Wordsworth who in his infancy saw the "visionary gleam." What passes into Wordsworth's "purer mind" are
not thoughts but bodily sensations "felt in the blood, and felt
along the Heart," connecting the unremembered pleasures of
infancy and earliest childhood with the present pleasures of

looking at the "beauteous forms" of nature. In a voice of awe and reverence, he shows how his days are "bound each to each" from the present back to boyhood and back further still to his moral origin—his first home and his infancy. The feelings of unremembered pleasures, then, evoke being fondled and cared for, the total gratification that nursing provides. Nature is connected in Wordsworth's mind with the nurturing mother and home, and the waters of the Wye are suggestive of the sustaining milk at the mother's breast. Wordsworth speaks of nature as "the nurse" and tells us that the beauteous forms "feed with lofty thoughts." The past Wordsworth evokes here is the past of his whole life, and, in "Intimations of Immortality," Wordsworth surmises that memory may go back even beyond birth. The "immortality" following death, then, may be something like the "blessed mood" Wordsworth achieves when these sweet sensations pass into his purer mind.

The "lofty cliffs" are suggestive of a mother's presence from an infant's perspective, because Wordsworth's imagination is working associatively in the realm of the "unremembered." The poem is an act of mind, not merely of consciousness, for it is one's total past that informs the development of one's moral nature. The love Wordsworth received "mutely" as an infant is a love that he still possesses and is capable of giving back to the world as a grown man. In *The Prelude* Wordsworth makes this explicit:

> From early days,
> Beginning not long after that first time
> In which, a Babe, by intercourse of touch
> I held mute dialogues with my Mother's heart,
> I have endeavored to display the means
> Whereby this infant sensibility,
> Great birthright of our being, was in me
> Augmented and sustained.
> (2.265–72)

More particularly, in "Tintern Abbey," the love that he received at home as a child, sustained through his love of nature's beauteous forms, becomes the spiritualized love that he is able to bestow upon his sister. Her appearance toward the end of the poem is the climax that resolves the tensions the poem has set forth. Finally, this is a poem about how human love is connected to the love of nature.

The "best portion of a good man's life" is made up of these unremembered pleasures that become converted in adulthood into instinctual gestures now unconsciously motivated, the "nameless, unremembered acts / Of kindness and of love." Love received becomes love bestowed, and the power to love is now *embodied* in his nature rather than in his consciousness. Kindness and love are the qualities, not the dicta, of the moral person when true to the inheritance that was established in the "unremembered" past. Thus the poem is also about restoration, about renewing what has been lost, as well as about "abundant recompense." What Wordsworth desires to have restored, then, is the "intercourse of touch" as described in the above passage: the soul, "Remembering how she felt, but what she felt / Remembering not, retains an obscure sense / Of possible sublimity." The spiritual bond of love for his sister must replace the "sensations sweet / Felt in the blood." And so "Tintern Abbey" ends with a long "prayer," an invocation of "far deeper zeal / Of holier love" to counteract and lighten "the burthen of the mystery / . . . the heavy and the weary weight / Of all this unintelligible world." The heavy weight of consciousness which, by itself, fails to make the world intelligible or to lighten its burden is relieved by evoking the unremembered pleasures through the agency of the beauteous forms of nature. The blessed mood is achieved again in adulthood as "the affections gently lead us on"—affections like those more explicitly named in "Intimations of Immortality": "those first affections / Those shadowy recollections." The "blessed mood" thus reestablishes the visionary basis for all positive feeling in the poem: "We see into the life of things." This is not vision in the perceptual sense of the word; rather, sensations and affections are felt in bodily repose: "we are laid asleep / In body." The sense of serenity and blessedness emerges when the body is in harmony with itself, so free of conscious thought that body itself takes on the quality of a "living soul." The dichotomy of body and soul here ceases as the mode of consciousness. To become a soul means that the body has achieved harmony with its own desires, and, for a moment deeper than thought, has been cured of "the fever of the world."

Freed from the domination of consciousness, the harmonious body is Wordsworth's characterization of the "living soul" whose emotion is a "blessed mood." But this mood cannot be sustained. Wordsworth falls from its silence back into the noise of the world. What Wordsworth is doubting ("If this be but a vain belief") is the reality of bodily harmony that has been evoked by the beauteous forms whose power finds its source in unremembered pleasures. Those "first affections" suggest the whole constellation of infantile emotions, for nursing (when appetite is assuaged) is exactly such a state of contentment—there is no loneliness, no sense of limitation, no knowledge of mortality. The "soft inland murmur" of the mountain springs that nurtured Wordsworth's conscious memories has brought forth a deep sense of the unremembered past. Secure in the fact that he does, at least, possess this *sense,* Wordsworth's realization of the power of harmony assumes a precious recognition that goes deeper than consciousness, for consciousness inevitably carries with it the awareness of dichotomy and disharmony. The sources of this power precede consciousness *as if* they existed in another life, or, as Wordsworth says in the Immortality Ode: "we come / From God who is our home: / Heaven lies about us in our infancy." But Wordsworth must return to the fact of human limits and loss. We have been barred from the "heavenly home" ("Shades of the prisonhouse begin to close / Upon the growing boy"), and that home can only be replaced in this life by the mind that is able to sense its divine inheritance. So in "Tintern Abbey" Wordsworth prays that his sister shall make her home in her imagination and her "mind / Shall be a mansion for all lovely forms, / Her memory be as a dwelling-place / For all sweet sounds and harmonies."

Wordsworth struggles to accept the mixture of pain and pleasure as it replaces the bliss of infancy and the spontaneity of boyhood, and this acceptance makes possible the affirma-

tion of mature adulthood that requires the paradoxical awareness of a "presence that disturbs me with the joy / Of
elevated thoughts." The "sense sublime," Wordsworth says,
"impells all thinking things," who live in the immediate context of mortality, the fear of loneliness and old age. What this
sense intimates, however, is that man's home is not to be defined only in this immediate context. Man's "dwelling" also
includes what he envisions beyond his perception of nature's
beauteous forms. Since a "sense sublime" is achieved by the
"mind of man" in interaction with natural forms, Wordsworth's love for nature rests not only in his awareness of the
objective beauty of a landscape, but also in his apperception
that intimates the existence of a more harmonious past and
a possibly harmonious future. His love of nature, then, can
provide him with a common language with which to express
the "deeper zeal" of love for his sister:

> Nor wilt thou then forget
> That after many wanderings, many years
> Of absence, these steep woods and lofty cliffs,
> And this green pastoral landscape, were to me
> More dear, both for themselves and for thy sake!

For Wordsworth to describe nature's silence is in part to
create himself out of that silence and to enhance the created
world through his own imagining. Perception thus becomes
inseparable from feeling:

> For feeling has to him imparted power
> That through the growing faculties of sense
> Doth like an agent of the one great Mind
> Create, creator and receiver both,
> Working but in alliance with the works
> Which it beholds. (*Prelude*, 2. 255–60)

Wordsworth believed that man's imaginative response to nature accomplished the dynamic extension of nature. A created world demands a response that continues the work of
that creation. The power to create "in alliance" with the "one
great Mind" was as imperative for Wordsworth as it was for
Coleridge, who argued that man's creativity takes God's cre-

ativity as its model: "The primary IMAGINATION I hold to be
the living Power and prime Agent of all human Perception,
and as a repetition in the finite mind of the eternal act of
creation in the infinite I AM."

I I I

Wordsworth's mind characteristically proceeds from the
noise and clamor of time to the silence of the eternal. He usually begins by contemplating a natural scene and moves to
moral consciousness and the tragic affirmation of "soothing
thoughts that spring / Out of human suffering." Finally, it is
this tragic affirmation that inspires him to compassion and
endurance, and also returns his thoughts to mortal frailty and
worldly limits. When God is glimpsed in nature, however, he
appears in the aspects of both beauty and terror, both blessing
and chastisement. Wordsworth is taught by fear, as well as by
beauty. When as a boy he steals a boat and rides out across
a lake, the opposing cliffs silently rise up as if in somber admonishment. Or, after he steals a bird from someone else's
trap, his guilt takes palpable form:

> I heard among the solitary hills
> Low breathings coming after me, and sounds
> Of undistinguishable motion, steps
> Almost as silent as the turf they trod.
> (*Prelude*, I. 322–25)

The human heart, even through boyhood, is attuned to the
silent, mysterious voices of the world. Silence, as in the admonishing steps coming after him in his boyhood experience,
becomes at this moment the voice of moral and paternal
reprobation. Like Shelley's "white radiance of eternity,"
which is broken down by the dome of life into the "stain" of
many colors, Wordsworthian silence is broken down into
many voices. But the voice of silence remains the source of
Wordsworth's chosen speech for which nature provides the
manifest objectification:

> To every form, rock, fruit, or flower,
> Even the loose stone that covers the highway,

> I gave a moral life: I saw them feel,
> Or linked them to some feeling. (3. 130–33)

Wordsworth describes the natural world as if it might be re-created out of his own feelings and imaginings. The passage, however, continues and complements the idea of Words-worth as the moral animator of nature by reversing that relationship:

> Add that whate'er of Terror or of Love
> Or Beauty, Nature's daily face put on
> From transitory passion, unto this
> I was as sensitive as waters are
> To a sky's influence in a kindred mood
> Of passion was obedient as a lute
> That waits upon the touches of the wind. (3. 136–42)

Here Wordsworth describes himself, instead, as passive, re-flecting nature as water reflects the sky. He is now the instru-ment, not the musician, and he is played upon by fingers of wind. This passage concludes with the bringing together of these apparent opposites, activity and passivity, in a single organization:

> Unknown, unthought of, yet I was most rich—
> I had a world about me— 'twas my own:
> I made it, for it only lived to me,
> And to the God who sees into the heart. (3. 143–46)

The world of nature is both created and perceived by Words-worth, both imagined and actual. What constitutes reality is a dynamically continuous synthesis, and therefore nature is seen as a creation "made" by man as well as by God. Man does not merely praise God's works, he continues God's cre-ation in his imaginative response to it.

The voice of silence speaks to Wordsworth mostly when he is alone; paradoxically, Wordsworth achieves his deepest sense of humanity when he is in isolation. His most sublime figures are men seen in isolation, possessing the "power of solitude," such as the Cumberland beggar, the leech gatherer, the veteran (Prelude, 4. 371–469), the knight (Prelude, 5. 50–

161), or Michael on the "heights." Solitude and silence constitute the atmosphere in which the deepest interpenetration of man and nature may take place. The voices inherent in nature are transformed into Wordsworth's own language of moral sensibility, but *first* the voices enter unawares into his mind. Such influences act upon Wordsworth's mind before he undertakes to affirm them. As with Coleridge's ancient mariner, moral feeling, the blessing received from nature, precedes moral consciousness. The mariner's blessing—to be able to bless and thus to pray—begins as an unconscious response to the beauty of the water snakes:

> O happy living things! no tongue
> Their beauty might declare:
> A spring of love gushed from my heart,
> And I blessed them unaware:
> Sure my kind saint took pity on me,
> And I blessed them unaware.
>
> The self-same moment I could pray . . . (4. 282–88)

To acknowledge the source of this blessing is to bless that source in return in the form of awe, praise, prayer, and imaginative response—in sum, with love.

The boy in Book 5 of *The Prelude* who calls to the owls dies in childhood, and when Wordsworth goes to visit his grave, a bond of silence exists between them: "I believe that there / A long half hour together I have stood / Mute, looking at the grave in which he lies." This silence binds Wordsworth, in a spirit of acceptance, to all human deaths, including his own. He identifies himself equally with the boy and with the ongoing life that survives him, experiencing simultaneously, in a silent moment, both death and immortality. Yet the blessings that come from silence are often threatened by the fear of the possibility of future poverty and the solitude that comes if one loses touch with humanity and with the world:

> I was disturbed at times by prudent thoughts,
> Wishing to hope without a hope, some fears
> About my future worldly maintenance,
> And more than all, a strangeness in the mind,

> A feeling that I was not for that hour,
> Nor for that place. (3. 77–82)

Hoping, where hope is not fully encouraged, changed Wordsworth's early spontaneous power of joy into a more complex power as joy became more difficult to sustain. Wordsworth had to evolve new powers from the old: sensual pleasure and uncontemplative emotion were superseded by the power of philosophy and, above all, by the power of intellectual love. But the powers lost and the powers gained were part of one necessary process through which human beings might achieve the ability to accept and affirm both time and eternity, both death and life.

While journeying through the Alps, Wordsworth experiences his greatest vision of the unity of opposites—death and life, destruction and creation:

> Downwards we hurried fast,
> And with the half-shaped road which we had missed,
> Entered a narrow chasm. The brook and road
> Were fellow-travellers in this gloomy strait,
> And with them did we journey several hours
> At a slow pace. The immeasurable height
> Of woods decaying, never to be decayed,
> The stationary blasts of waterfalls,
> And in the narrow rent at every turn
> Winds thwarting winds, bewildered and forlorn,
> The torrents shooting from the clear blue sky,
> The rocks that muttered close upon our ears,
> Black drizzling crags that spake by the way-side
> As if a voice were in them, the sick sight
> And giddy prospect of the raving stream,
> The unfettered clouds and region of the Heavens,
> Tumult and peace, the darkness and the light—
> Were all like workings of one mind, the features
> Of the same face, blossoms upon one tree:
> Characters of the great Apocalypse,
> The types and symbols of Eternity,
> Of first, and last, and midst, and without end.
> (6. 619–40)

This timeless vision of life both dying and regenerate allows Wordsworth to imagine eternity as the omnipresence of all time, as if all history existed in an instant in God's mind and yet was "without end." Only human beings experience time as sequential. Imitating Milton, Wordsworth suggests the omnipresence of God's eternal time, by placing "midst" *after* "last." He rises out of his "gloom" into ecstatic contemplation of God's created world. The whole passage reveals nature as "the types and symbols of Eternity." Wordsworth's vision brings together both apocalypse and eternal renewal through imagery of a silent and imagined voice ("as if a voice were in them") that speaks through actual phenomena in a sublime moment.

In Book 5 of *The Prelude*, Wordsworth falls asleep after reading Cervantes. In the dream that follows he has an apocalyptic vision of the "knight / Whose tale Cervantes tells: yet not the knight, / But was an Arab of the desert too: / Of these was neither, and was both at once." The knight is riding through the desert to bury a stone and a shell while being pursued by the gathering waters of the deep. Before falling asleep, Wordsworth had been musing about "poetry and geometric truth / And their high privilege of lasting life." In the dream, poetry becomes symbolized as the shell, geometric truth as the stone, and the knight is journeying to bury them (as if burying were impregnation of the earth) that they might survive the coming apocalyptic flood:

> The one that held acquaintance with the stars
> And wedded soul to soul in purest bond
> Of reason, undisturbed by space or time:
> The other that was a god, yea many gods,
> Had voices more than all the winds, with power
> To exhilarate the spirit, and to soothe,
> Through every clime, the heart of human kind.
> (5. 103–9)

This dream image of a dying world reveals as well Wordsworth's individual fear of dying. The wisdom of the stone and the voice of the shell are the means by which he seeks to accept the conditions of life in the context of apocalyptic fears.

Wordsworth's emotional response to the message of the dream, however, is ambivalent. Although he says "I waked in terror," he assumes that his vision of the Arab-knight's quest is not madness: "in the blind and awful lair / Of such a madness, reason did lie couched." Apocalypse is what Wordsworth both dreads and seeks; he identifies himself with the Arab-knight and his quest: "I could share / That maniac's fond anxiety, and go / Upon like errand." The waters that drown the world leave an "illimitable waste," but they are also seen as a "bed of glittering light" which resembles the "celestial light" of the Immortality Ode.

When Wordsworth was a child, this light was directly experienced, but as he grew older, he felt that the vision this light bestowed had to be philosophically, not visually, embodied. The imagination, for him, takes over this embodying function, for it remains in touch with the visionary past. And so the emergence of the imagination as a power capable of restoring and protecting joy marks the development of both the poet and the responsible adult:

> This narrative, my friend, hath chiefly told
> Of intellectual power, fostering love,
> Dispensing truth, and, over men and things,
> Where reason yet might hesitate, diffusing
> Prophetic sympathies of genial faith. (12. 44–48)

Coleridge is the friend whom Wordsworth addresses, and we are reminded that *The Prelude* is written as a letter, with the intention to communicate and with the hope that such communication will nourish friendship and will make "of the whole human race one brotherhood."

Brotherhood includes shared sorrow, and thus Wordsworth propounds the paradox that sorrow, as a source of sympathy, also is a source of joy. As his awareness of the burden of life increases, Wordsworth experiences a heightened sense of compassionate humanity. This compassion, impossible without suffering, supersedes Wordsworth's visionary response to the physical world. The nostalgia for the past never leaves Wordsworth, but that is not, in maturity, where he places his life's emphasis. The visionary past has left him with a "genial faith," but, except as an intimation, it has been lost. What remains is "intellectual power, fostering love," and, in the words of the Immortality Ode, "the human heart by which we live." Wordsworth felt that the proper work of the imagination was to affirm compassion in the context of mortality and to find models for endurance and faith as the visionary past receded. But the "abundant recompense" of the mature man retains some of the sublime power of the mind dwelling in silences. Like the statue of Newton with his "silent face, / The marble index of a mind forever / Voyaging through strange seas of Thoughts, alone," Wordsworth finds his humanity in solitary thoughts of mortal limits and loss that are "too deep for tears" and in the silent voice of God's revelations.

... the primal sympathy
Which having been must ever be.
WORDSWORTH, "Intimations of Immortality"

Softly let all true sympathizers come.
STEVENS, "Esthétique du Mal"

SIX

Wordsworth and Stevens:
Endurance and Sympathy

❦

THROUGHOUT Wordsworth's poetry, thoughts of immortality and thoughts of earthly happiness contend for his deepest allegiance. Stevens's poetry is predicated on the rejection of this Wordsworthian antinomy through Stevens's repeated assertions that heaven and immortality are outworn myths and that one must create happiness in the face of death as an absolute. Stevens demonstrates how the acceptance of death may be transformed from an intellectual necessity to something humanely positive; in this way, death becomes the "mother of beauty." The creation of human values begins anew when reality is faced as "indifferent" and death is seen as a final limit, for in the "predicate that there is nothing else," the mind turns to its own needs and its own resources. Thus Wordsworth presents for Stevens a powerful double model: one to be opposed and another to be embraced. Both of these responses to Wordsworth are fruitful for Stevens in that they release Stevens's poetic energies, his powers of parody and of celebration. Yet it is the earthly Wordsworth that has the most crucial influence on Stevens. When Wordsworth dwells on the immediate sense of mortality, rather than on his visionary glimpses of heaven, the values he evokes are those of endurance and sympathy, and these values become the essence of Stevens's secular humanism.

Wordsworth's visionary moments of "silence visible" invariably express his sense of infinitude and his corresponding desire to reject bodily limits and the fact of mortality. In such moments, he is not at home in the world, but in some realm projected by his imagination into an abstraction of ultimate possibility in which thought, for a moment, becomes its own reality and he is "blest in thoughts / That are their own perfection and reward." Wordsworth describes such a moment:

> . . . when the light of sense
> Goes out, but with a flash that has revealed
> The invisible world . . .
> Our destiny, our being's heart and home,
> Is with infinitude, and only there;
> With hope it is, hope that can never die,
> Effort and expectation, and desire,
> And something evermore about to be.
> (*Prelude*, 6. 600–602, 604–8)

Everything in this passage points to another place, another condition, another realm of time (or timelessness). Desire here does not return Wordsworth to his earthly loves, but leads him in thought to what mortality and finitude do not allow. A direct emotional parallel in Stevens is expressed in the voice of the woman in "Sunday Morning" when she says: " 'But in contentment I still feel / The need of some imperishable bliss.' " The central argument of Stevens's poem is to persuade the woman (an interior voice within the voice of the poem's narrator) that she must relinquish the desire for "imperishable bliss" and accept a love that endures—but only within the mortal limits of "men that perish."

Later in *The Prelude* Wordsworth expresses the exact opposite of this longing for infinitude. Desire does not beckon him beyond time and beyond the world, but back into it, and in this state of mind the earth is experienced as being comparable to heaven, as if Wordsworth lived "among the bowers of Paradise itself." In such a moment, Wordsworth is able to reject transcendent yearnings and find in earthly happiness what Stevens finds in the affirmation of death: "fulfillment to our dreams / And our desires." Paradise is rejected and dismissed when Wordsworth says:

> Not in Utopia, —subterranean fields, —
> Or some secreted island, Heaven knows where,
> But in the very world, which is the world
> Of all of us, —the place where, in the end,
> We find our happiness, or not at all! (11. 140–44)

The consummation of desire is to be found in this world in the form of happiness, not in the revelation of immortality or in God's apocalyptic redemption of history. This passage is unmistakably echoed by Stevens, when, in "Sunday Morning," the poem's narrator replies to the woman who is troubled by nature's ephemerality when she observes: " 'But when the birds are gone, and their warm fields / Return no more, where, then, is paradise?' " Her worldly and sensuous happiness is threatened by natural change, and so the narrator defines what he means by enduring within mortal limits:

> There is not any haunt of prophecy,
> Nor any old chimera of the grave,
> Neither the golden underground, nor isle
> Melodious, where spirits gat them home,
> Nor visionary south, nor cloudy palm
> Remote on heaven's hill, that has endured
> As April's green endures; or will endure
> Like her remembrance of awakened birds,
> Or her desire for June and evening, tipped
> By the consummation of the swallow's wings.

This nostalgic passage is also an act of verbal parody. Stevens is saying that the myth of heaven, with all its delightful imagery, is now remote and obsolete, an ornament of historical memory. Wordsworth's "subterranean fields" has become Stevens's "golden underground"; Wordsworth's "secreted

island" has become Stevens's "isle melodious"; and Wordsworth's rhetorical "Heaven knows where" becomes Stevens's ironic "remote on heaven's hill." Although the tone
differs (Stevens is delighting in his elaborate evocation of the
archaic), Wordsworth and Stevens are both stressing the
mind's need to find consolation, meaning, and happiness in
this world.

There are three aspects of "enduring love" to be found in
the above passage by Stevens, and a fourth aspect, of utmost
importance, is to be found later in "Sunday Morning" in the
lines: "They shall know well the heavenly fellowship / Of
men that perish and of summer morn." All four of these ideas
of endurance have their models in Wordsworth's poetry. Unlike Wordsworth's belief in heaven, which for Stevens no
longer endures as a credible idea, "April's green endures" in
the sense that the natural cycle of the seasons inevitably
brings us back to spring. Change itself is the world's great
freshener. As long as one is alive, the past endures through
memory, "like her remembrance of awakened birds." Memory is a constant within constant change. And there are con-
stants, too, of human need—the need for blossoming and
repose, like the woman's "desire for June and evening." Desire endures as long as human life lasts, and Stevens urges us
to "measure" endurance within mortal limits, what he calls
"the vital boundary." Thus the image of "consummation"
with which Stevens ends canto 4 is one of flight, "the swallow's wings," for consummation is never an ending, but a
fleeting moment in process experienced *as if* it were a finality
only because the moment is "impassioned."

The fourth aspect of Stevens's sense of endurance is the
most deeply paradoxical, and it passes over into the concept
of sympathy. What binds people together is their shared
awareness of their mortality, and this awareness, for Stevens,
can become the enduring basis for values that celebrate life
as precious in the urgency of its vanishing. The communal
worship of the sun, both as symbol and as physical fact, as
the principle of life, acknowledges three things: the world is
indifferent to human need; the awareness of death enters
into every true moment of consciousness; a sense of values,

heightened through celebration, is a human invention. Devotion becomes a communal value that binds people together in mutual sympathy, sharing the energy of life and the poignancy of death. Again in "Sunday Morning," Stevens's image of secular worship thus responds to the inescapable fact that the consciousness of life is equally the consciousness of death:

> Supple and turbulent, a ring of men
> Shall chant in orgy on a summer morn
> Their boisterous devotion to the sun,
> Not as a god, but as a god might be,
> Naked among them, like a savage source.

No system of belief can remain vital unless it acknowledges change and death as absolutes, and human sympathy cannot realize its greatest depth until death has been embraced and celebrated. In this spirit, Stevens cries in "Esthétique du Mal": "Softly let all true sympathizers come. . . . Within what we permit, / Within the actual, the warm, the near, / So great a unity, that it is bliss, / Ties us to those we love."

The paradox of endurance is that one perceives what lasts only in the context of what passes away, and one endures the sorrows of the ephemeral because they intensify and brighten the momentary awareness of *being* when "time flashed again" or when death as the mother of beauty "makes the willow shiver in the sun." The paradox of sympathy, similarly, is that the ties to those one loves would not be choices, and would therefore lack urgency and discrimination, if time were infinite and lovers were immortal. In paradise, girls would remain "maidens," eternally passive, who would "sit and gaze / Upon the grass relinquished to their feet." In answer to the question, "And shall the earth / Seem all of paradise that we shall know?" Stevens's narrator replies with the essential knowledge of death: "They shall know well the heavenly fellowship / Of men that perish." The best and the utmost feelings of which humans are capable, fellowship and devoted love, constitute their divinity ("divinity must live within herself"), and these feelings are contingent upon our inevitable perishing. "Heavenly" feeling is possible only in

this mortal world, for the knowledge of death becomes fruitful knowledge that one tastes from the tree of life, and one
knows, beyond greed and fear, that it is "good death that puts
an end to evil death." Only with the knowledge of "good
death" can the "maidens taste / And stray impassioned in
the littering leaves."

The Stevensian paradox of the "heavenly fellowship of
men that perish" has its direct source in Wordsworth's
"soothing thoughts that spring / Out of human suffering"
and "A deep distress hath humanized my soul." In this respect, Stevens is Wordsworth's heir; he restores the covenant
that is broken by Luke in "Michael." By incorporating
Wordsworth's spirit in benevolent form, Stevens exemplifies
the loyal "son," who cherishes and memorializes the image
of his "father," as Wordsworth had fixed the image of the old
leech gatherer in his thoughts or, as in book 5 of *The Prelude*,
Wordsworth envisions an Arab guide, "who with unerring
skill / Would through the desert lead me." This guide of
fatherly authority enables Wordsworth to confront death and
apocalypse, "the waters of the deep / Gathering upon us,"
and serves as a model of heroic love for Wordsworth who declares his "desire to . . . cleave unto this man." The image of
a guiding father for each son is the heart's deepest blessing of
inheritance.

II

"Resolution and Independence" describes the interrelated
powers of endurance and sympathy which Wordsworth continually sought to strengthen. The dialectical movement
of the poem, gloom and good cheer contending with one
another, is suggested in the first four lines:

> There was a roaring in the wind all night:
> The rain came heavily and fell in floods;
> But now the sun is rising calm and bright;
> The birds are singing in the distant woods.

Wordsworth shows the brightness resulting from the darkness, though they exist necessarily together. After the storm,

facing a sunlit day, Wordsworth feels only a simple delight in
the beauty that surrounds him. Then the thought comes to
him that this present state of boyish ebullience is ephemeral:
"But there may come another day to me— / Solitude, pain of
heart, distress, and poverty." This revelation and its accom-
panying shift in mood have not been unanticipated; the shift
reverses the change from storm to sunlight. Wordsworth
says: "As high as we have mounted in delight / In our dejection do we sink as low," for if joy comes from dejection, then
dejection also must come from joy. Is it a curse or a blessing to
be caught in the cycle of human emotions? And is it even
worse to try to avoid this cycle? These are Wordsworth's innermost questions.

Wordsworth thinks of how little suffering he has undergone: "My whole life I have lived in pleasant thought, / As if
life's business were a summer mood," and considers how
poorly prepared he is to face any hardship that yet may come.
The future has to be met, not only in the future, but now;
what one anticipates as remote may be imminent. Wordsworth says: "I thought of Chatterton, the marvellous Boy, /
The sleepless Soul that perished in his pride," and the suggestion lingers that perhaps Wordsworth's "genial faith" is to
be regarded as a kind of pride. Contemplating this, Wordsworth sinks to the bottom of his depression: "We poets in our
youth begin in gladness, / But thereof come in the end de-
spondency and madness." Nature, however, intervenes, as if
in admonishment, to present Wordsworth with an image of
human endurance from which he can derive strength to overcome his gloom, though Wordsworth leaves open the question as to whether there is a God working intentionally for
his well-being:

> Now, whether it were by peculiar grace,
> A leading from above, a something given,
> Yet it befell, that, in this lonely place,
> When I with these untoward thoughts had striven,
> Beside a pool bare to the eye of heaven
> I saw a man before me unawares:
> The oldest man he seemed that ever wore grey hairs.

Nature seems to include the cures for her own maladies, for the old man—the very opposite of the boy Chatterton—is the living symbol of endurance. Wordsworth describes him as a "huge stone" that resembles a "sea-beast crawled forth." His presence suggests a primeval force; Wordsworth imagines that the burden his life supports is a "more than human weight," and, in wonderment, Wordsworth can again believe in the possibility of triumphing over the seeming impotence of old age. He approaches the old man with awe:

> And now a stranger's privilege I took;
> And, drawing to his side, to him did say,
> "This morning gives us promise of a glorious day."

The "stranger's privilege" rests on the assumption that there is a bond of "one brotherhood" that links all people in their common humanity. But at this point in the poem, it comes as a surprise to Wordsworth that he can make this assumption. It is still surprising to him that other men are not strangers. Only through the realization of this bond with strangers is Wordsworth able to feel that he might emulate the old man's power to endure. The bond in Wordsworth's mind takes on an even more particularized emphasis as he observes that the old leech gatherer is a kind of poet:

> His words came feebly, from a feeble chest,
> But each in solemn order followed each,
> With something of a lofty utterance drest—
> Choice word and measured phrase, above the reach
> Of ordinary men: a stately speech.

The solitary old man possesses a voice of silence within his speaking voice and utters, in effect, the "still, sad music of humanity" which then inspires Wordsworth with new strength:

> The old Man still stood talking by my side;
> But now his voice to me was like a stream
> Scarce heard; nor word from word could I divide;
> And the whole body of the Man did seem
> Like one whom I had met with in a dream;

> Or like a man from some far region sent,
> To give me human strength, by apt admonishment.

The figure of the leech gatherer resembles the Arab-knight in *The Prelude* in that both appear as if in a dream whose source might be found in "some far region." Both dreams and imaginings (the poet's "as if"—"*Like* one whom I had met with in a dream: / Or *like* a man from some far region sent") may express reflections of God's intent, yet Wordsworth turns away from metaphysical speculation and dwells on the human issue of endurance. He chastises himself into self-possession. This strength, however, deserts him when again he thinks of the possible misery to come and of his own death:

> My former thoughts returned; the fear that kills,
> And hope that is unwilling to be fed;
> Cold, pain, and labour, and all fleshly ills;
> And mighty Poets in their misery dead.

But the leech gatherer, his "stately speech" transfigured to a voice "like a stream / Scarce heard," is fixed in Wordsworth's mind. "Motionless and still," his image has become nature's symbol of a spirit that will not suffer the defeat of despair:

> The old Man's shape, and speech—all troubled me,
> In my mind's eye I seemed to see him pace
> About the weary moors continually,
> Wandering about alone and silently.

Wordsworth achieves his own consolation, for his exclamation, "God," though in part an invocation to a transcendent being, is primarily his own self-admonishment to accept the leech gatherer as an example. The bond of sympathy that exists between Wordsworth and the leech gatherer gives Wordsworth a heroic model to imitate. Sympathy and self-sympathy are identified, for Wordsworth must struggle against the perverse temptation to reject himself: "hope that is unwilling to be fed." This image of fortitude in silence and loneliness Wordsworth holds before his eyes and affirms with deliberate intent: "I'll think of the Leech-gatherer on the lonely moor!" This image, this form of thought, has become a choice—an act of will in the "mind's eye."

III

"There came a day, there was a day—one day / A man walked living among the forms of thought," Stevens declaims in "The Owl in the Sarcophagus." The figure at the brink of despair and death, like Wordsworth's leech gatherer, becomes Stevens's primary image of himself in his later poems, and that image often is abstracted into a "form of thought" that, through contemplation, brings consolation and relief. Without such thoughts, one is defeated by the indifferent reality of death, and thus the cure for despair—the disease of the mind —lies only in the mind itself. "The mind . . . is the only force that can defend us against itself," says Stevens in "Adagia," his notebook of thoughts. Even when his figures confronting death have been abstracted into general ideas like "sleep" and "peace," Stevens claims that he can see them as projections of need: "These forms are visible to the eye that needs."

Wordsworth had abstracted his image of the leech gatherer into more than a human individual; he is seen also as a form of thought objectified in nature: "As a huge stone is sometimes seen to lie / Couched on the bald top of an eminence." Wordsworth's image of the leech gatherer as a "huge stone" is transformed through imagination, through *seeming* ("So that it seems a thing endued with sense") into a "sea-beast" that has "crawled forth," as if before his very eyes "sense" is perceived emerging from inorganic matter. He witnesses, in effect, consciousness being born; he witnesses the mind giving birth to its own forms of thought. The huge stone, now a sea beast, reposes on a "shelf / Of rock or sand," seeking warmth and illumination, yet the element of inorganic rock remains for further transformations. The vision of the huge stone as a sea beast, again through seeming, turns into the vision of the leech gatherer as a man both alive and dead: "Such seemed this Man, not all alive nor dead." As a form of thought, he is still being created out of the rock by Wordsworth's imagination. Even after this creation apparently reaches its completion when the leech gatherer speaks with remarkable control and order, with "Choice word and measured phrase," Wordsworth returns to the elemental imagery of stone and water out of which it has emerged: "But now his voice to me was

like a stream / Scarce heard." Once again, what is living is
not seen as divided from what is dead, and the leech gatherer's speech reflects this primal condition: "nor word from
word could I divide." Just as Wordsworth, in his poem, has
created his vision of the leech gatherer out of the rock, so does
Stevens, in his poem "The Rock," declare his own faith in the
power of the imagination when he says: "the poem makes
meanings of the rock."

The rock is Stevens's major symbol for indifferent reality
before that reality has been humanized by the imagination.
Given another emphasis, the rock, and the sun that illuminates it, represent the "first idea"—the idea of a world that
precedes human imagining and exists apart from it as ultimately unknowable. For Wordsworth, physical reality,
nature, can be read as the book of God, and natural objects
can be seen as "the types and symbols of eternity." But for
Stevens—who is consciously rejecting the divine aspect of
Wordsworth's belief in the power of the imagination—physical nature, the rock, has absolutely no meaning other than
what the secular imagination bestows on it. Human beings,
nevertheless, need meaning, for, without purpose, people fall
into the sickness of despair. The poet's function in a secular
age is to provide meaning in the encounter with indifferent
reality and with the inescapable idea of nonbeing. The disease of despair can be cured only by the fabricating imagination, the mind that makes up its mind, that creates itself:

> Of such mixed motion and such imagery
> That its barrenness becomes a thousand things
> And so exists no more. This is the cure
> Of leaves and of the ground and of ourselves.

Just as the image of the leech gatherer has become a healing
thought for Wordsworth, inspiring endurance and sympathy,
so has the rock, for which meanings must be invented, become a healing image for Stevens, since it represents the
place, "the space," where the mind creates itself and makes
itself at home. The world is thus made interior and is loved
as part of the self, and the indifferent rock is regarded as the
goading source and inspiration for human invention and human consolation:

It is the rock where tranquil must adduce
Its tranquil self, the main of things, the mind,
The starting point of the human and the end,
That in which space itself is contained. . . .

The leech gatherer, "not all alive nor dead," has his closest counterpart in the figure of Santayana in "To An Old Philosopher in Rome" who is on "the threshold of heaven," about to die, yet still intensely alive in his mind, as Stevens says: "alive, / Yet living in two worlds." For the mind to be aware of itself on the threshold between life and death is to bring self-apprehension to its most intense pitch. That intensity Stevens often describes as a moment of "effulgence" in which, for example, the candle of the self flares and asserts its own vanishing light: "a light on the candle tearing against the wick." The hero of consciousness exists in an eternity contained within an instant in time, experiencing the fullness of that eternity, yet fully aware that the moment is ephemeral. That experience of mind conscious of itself is the supreme human achievement, and the poem is its memorial: "It is a kind of total grandeur at the end."

Santayana, as a figure of achieved "human dignity," is Stevens's ultimate model; like the leech gatherer, he is both the man himself and a form of thought. Stevens says: "each of us / Beholds himself in you, and hears his voice / In yours, master and commiserable man." As the man who shares "misery," Santayana masters misery, rises above it into sympathy, and, through sympathy, he creates the "grandeur that you need / In so much misery." Death and loss are not transcended through resurrection; they are transcended only in the mind. There are no glimpses of immortality; there is only the "afflatus of ruin," the imagination's held breath, its inspiration of self-realization in the face of extinction. Just as the leech gatherer is seen as a figure in poverty, Stevens, identifying himself with Santayana to the "last drop of the deepest blood," proclaims the source of his poetry: "It is poverty's speech that seeks us out the most." And also as the leech gatherer's words are uttered in "solemn order," Santayana's life becomes the "design of all his words [that] takes form / And frame from thinking and is realized." Through heightened consciousness, "With every visible thing enlarged," thought is "realized" as *the experience of thought* for the man who walks "living" among its forms. The experience of our lives, always at the edge of the knowledge of death, is the "design" we make real in our lives with our words.

I V

The stoical affirmation of "Resolution and Independence" has less personal anguish to overcome than the death of Wordsworth's brother, which is pictured in "Elegiac Stanzas," but the gaining of fortitude and hope through distress anticipates the encompassing affirmation achieved later in the closing stanzas of the Immortality Ode. George Beaumont's painting of Peele Castle portrays a stormy scene, a representation of nature Wordsworth says he would not have chosen before his younger brother, John, drowned in the Indian Sea. Wordsworth pictures the sinking ship from Beaumont's stormy scene as "That Hulk which labours in the deadly swell," in contrast to the tranquil setting that he remembers when "Four summer weeks I dwelt in sight of thee [Peele Castle]." This tranquil memory causes Wordsworth to imagine the painting he *would have done:*

> Ah! Then, if mine had been the Painter's hand,
> To express what then I saw; and add the gleam,
> The light that never was, on sea or land,
> The consecration and the Poet's dream;
>
> I would have planted thee, thou hoary pile
> Amid a world how different from this!
> Beside a sea that could not cease to smile;
> On tranquil land, beneath a sky of bliss.

But Wordsworth breaks free from his nostalgia for a tranquil scene, and his image of the world changes from one of sunshine to one of tempest. The castle, which before was seen as a house of bliss, becomes a fortress, a home of fortitude and endurance. The poet's consecrating touch, the gleam he adds through his own creation, now is regarded by Wordsworth as an illusion. Wordsworth's "light," he now believes, never illuminated anything in nature, and it cannot consecrate nature; it is merely his own dream from which he has awakened:

> Such, in the fond illusion of my heart,
> Such Picture would I at that time have made:
> And seen the soul of truth in every part,
> A steadfast peace that might not be betrayed.

> So once it would have been, — 'tis so no more;
> I have submitted to a new control:
> A power is gone, which nothing can restore;
> A deep distress hath humanized my Soul.

The world of "Elysian quiet" has become for Wordsworth merely "fond" (affection seen as foolish) illusion, and with this new image of the world as a "pageantry of fear," innocent happiness is foregone. Wordsworth has gained a knowledge that is both the burden and the strength of his newly acquired humanity: "A power is gone, which nothing can restore; / A deep distress hath humanized my Soul." Wordsworth is consoled, paradoxically, by his own grief; it is the proof of his human love. Yet for Wordsworth evil is not fully rationalized; God's ways are not "justified." ("We have *more of love* in our nature than He has," wrote Wordsworth in his letter to Sir George Beaumont of March 12, 1805.) Distress, through which sympathy is deepened and the soul humanized, nevertheless remains distress. The knowledge that he will continue to feel distress at his brother's death, also paradoxically, allows Wordsworth the composure to endure his passion, "The feeling of my loss will ne'er be old; / This, which I know, I speak with mind serene," even though this composure is tainted with rationalization.

The crisis of the poem now focuses in this conflict: Wordsworth's "humanized" soul pitted against the amoral nature of the physical world. Although in "Tintern Abbey" Wordsworth could say, "Nature never did betray / The heart that loved her," here he calls the image of nature (as a "peace that might not be betrayed") merely an "illusion." Beaumont's castle, braving the wrath of the natural weather, becomes the symbol of sublime endurance, and, as such, it fills Wordsworth with an excitement that approaches jubilation:

> And this huge Castle, standing here sublime,
> I love to see the look with which it braves,
> Cased in the unfeeling armour of old time,
> The lightning, the fierce wind and trampling waves.

This "huge Castle" is the symbolic home in which man (to be kind, to be mankind) must live, for the poet cannot remain alone. If he stands apart in innocent happiness, he lives in a dream, nurturing himself on illusion, mistaking his blindness for vision. And so Wordsworth must say "Farewell, farewell [to] the heart that lives alone," and to the vision of a benevolent, never-betraying nature.

The happiness that comes from believing that nature is kind and does not betray (Wordsworth's past happiness) is seen now as a dream. Having been "housed in a dream," Wordsworth must reject nostalgia, leave home, and not sink back into that tempting illusion. He must renounce the intimations of immortality and paradise and turn to the sublimity of fortitude and the heroic defiance of whatever misfortune may yet come:

> But welcome fortitude, and patient cheer,
> And frequent sights of what is to be borne!
> Such sights, or worse, as are before me here. . . .

This grim and worldly stance, however, is not the only attitude that resolves the poem. "Not without hope" refers to Wordsworth's personal hope of achieving stoical fortitude, but that hope, so tentatively ("not without") and touchingly put, suggests also the universal hope that somehow, beyond understanding, nature *may be* benevolent—and this benevolence may be the inscrutable grace of God. Wordsworth, however, never fully recovered from his brother's death; it marks the end of his protracted belief in simple happiness: "Such happiness, wherever it be known, / Is to be pitied; for 'tis surely blind." His reading of nature as the "chronicle of Heaven" is replaced by his reading of nature as the chronicle of earth, affording "frequent sights of what is to be borne!" His strength to endure the future became dependent on his power to say "farewell" to past consolations.

V

"Farewell to an idea" is the central refrain of Stevens's great poem, "The Auroras of Autumn," written in his seventieth year. The narrator who meditates this poem is a projection of Stevens, delineated as "The Man who is walking [who] turns blankly on the sand" as he observes the northern lights. No further characterization is appropriate, since Stevens portrays himself only as a figure of old age. Although the idea to which he says "farewell" has many possible referents in Stevens's earlier poetry, such as the "first idea" of an indifferent universe, the main reference within the poem is to the idea of "innocence," which will be developed in the figure of the "innocent mother" and in the concept of an "innocent earth."

Stevens's "innocence" is first related to a past whose remembered forms no longer offer consolation. The past, in effect, seems absolutely gone, its life so completely vanished, that Stevens confronts an image of absence as terrifying whiteness. Everything that Stevens's narrator sees is defined by whiteness that betokens absence: "a cabin stands / Deserted, on a beach. It is white." The past, both historical and personal, has been emptied "as a consequence / Of an infinite course." And yet this whiteness of absence, seen again in the image of "The flowers against the wall / Are white, a little dried," has not entirely ceased to be a token of "a white / That was different," a white that was once a symbol of innocence. The idea of innocence will be revitalized later in the poem, but for now whiteness and absence have become so intensified in the narrator's mind that he himself is defined as being only what he is not. Just as the past for Wordsworth had become an "illusion" and a "Poet's dream," the past for Stevens, as described in "The Auroras of Autumn" and "The Rock," has become an empty illusion: "It is an illusion that we were ever alive."

The refrain of "farewell," however, still must continue, for absence must be confronted by the imagination's power to apprehend loss and the concept of nonbeing, much as Wordsworth chooses to confront the "frequent sights of what is to be borne!" The idea of the consoling mother—"The mother's face"—is brought back only to have her image vanish again. Memory cannot hold before the fact that the past is gone, the mother is dead. What remains of the mother is a memento, not her actual warmth and presence: her "necklace is a carving not a kiss." Her necklace is like her tombstone, and thus the thought of the mother only exacerbates the realization that she is not there, just as Wordsworth had declared in response to the death of his brother, "The feeling of my loss will ne'er be old." For Stevens, memory will not suffice in bringing consolation out of loss until consolation, too, is accepted as ephemeral.

In the third canto beginning "Farewell to an idea," the tone changes radically, for the subject of this and the following canto is the idea of traditional religion and the image of God as a father. The echoes here are not only of Wordsworth, but of Milton as well, and Stevens invariably turns to parody whenever he portrays God or a heavenly paradise. The God whom Wordsworth could imagine as both transcendent and immanent is described ironically by Stevens as "Master O master seated by the fire / And yet in space." Stevens exclaims, "Look at this present throne," pointing to an empty place, for no longer is God to be seen. The consolation of divine authority has been lost, and the image of an ordered and moral world, for Stevens, has given way to an image of chaos: "We stand in the tumult of a festival." Wordsworth's rejection of the image of nature in harmony with itself in "steadfast peace" becomes the spirit of continuous negation that Stevens adopts: "The negations are never final." Wordsworth's sense of betrayal has been transposed into the tones of Stevensian irony.

The "tumult," the chaos, can be regarded as a theater of change and energy, just as Wordsworth's image of a peaceful and gentle nature had been transformed into a "pageantry of fear" represented in images of "The lightning, the fierce wind and trampling waves." Just as God's gleam, reflected in Wordsworth's mind, had been dismissed as "The light

that never was," so, too, for Stevens the primal Wordsworthian elements of cloud, rock, mountain, and water exist only as themselves in a vast and endless spectacle of
transformations:

> It is a theatre floating through the clouds,
> Itself a cloud, although of misted rock
> And mountains running like water, wave on wave,
> Through waves of light. It is of cloud transformed
> To cloud transformed again, idly, the way
> A season changes color to no end,
> Except the lavishing of itself in change.

The spectacle in itself is magnificent, and, apprehended by
the purely aesthetic eye, the elements of earth can be seen reflected in the flaring of the northern lights in all their visual
grandeur. But from another point of view, this is also a spectacle of endless destruction. The human imagination, however, Stevens believes, must contain and express both atti-
tudes toward the spectacle of infinite change, or else that
spectacle will have no human value as a genuine source of
consolation: "This is nothing until in a single man contained, / Nothing until this named thing nameless is / And
is destroyed." Again we see the external world, the cosmos
and its fate of change and annihilation, made interior, and
through this process of interiorization, Stevens finds the
strength to acknowledge his own smallness and his cosmic
fear:

> He opens the door of his house
> On flames. The scholar of one candle sees
> An Arctic effulgence flaring on the frame
> Of everything he is. And he feels afraid.

In this same spirit, Wordsworth had learned to praise Beaumont's painting of a stormy sea as a "passionate work!—yet
wise and well," for in that depiction of "this pageantry of
fear!" his human spirit discovered its own power: "A deep
distress hath humanized my Soul." The symbol of this newly
humanized self is "this huge castle," like the "house" of
Stevens's "scholar of one candle."

The human qualities that the castle represents for Wordsworth are "bravery," "fortitude," and "patient cheer." These qualities are human inventions, and for Wordsworth they replace the power of faith in a benign nature; that "power is gone," Wordsworth declares. Stevens, likewise, depicts the greatest human power as self-humanization. He says in his essay "Two or Three Ideas," "There was always in every man the increasingly human self . . . who had to resolve life and the world in his own terms." The belief that re-solving life is indeed a possibility, that we can create ourselves by means of the ideas of ourselves that we invent, is the essence of Stevens's concept of "innocence" as it emerges in canto 8 in "The Auroras of Autumn." Since innocence "is not a thing of time, nor of place / Existing in the idea of it alone," its manifestation can be found only in the believer's attitude to the idea of innocence as he responds to the thought of death; that response can realize either happiness or unhappiness as Stevens shows in the final canto of his poem. Stevens's resolution of happiness in the face of nature's destructive forces, the "haggling of wind and weather," has its model in Wordsworth's "mind serene" and "patient cheer."

The northern lights exist as physical presence, neither as the book of God nor as symbols of divine immanence; they are not "A saying out of a cloud." Precisely because these lights are nothing but themselves, they can be viewed as an "innocence of the earth"; one can make of them what one wills. These lights, then, become the symbol of what one chooses one's life to be—the psychological fate one creates for oneself. Since they are not symbols of a destiny derived from original sin, "the enigma of the guilty dream," the earth is an "innocent mother" who, through human consciousness, "Created the time and place in which we breathed." And when death arrives as "the mother of beauty" (as she was the "Dark mother" for Whitman), she comes "Almost as part of innocence."

In a late letter (July 1, 1953), Stevens describes the figure of the rabbi as being "exceedingly attractive" because he is a "man devoted in the extreme to scholarship and at the same time to making some use of it for human purposes." Identified with the "scholar of one candle," the rabbi of the final

canto, "fulfilling his meditations," considers how one may
see the possibility of human happiness or unhappiness in response to the conditions of the world. Stevens chooses the
formulation "A happy people in a happy world" because it is
most expressive of human creativity. The image of the serpent, envisioned in the night sky, that opened the poem becomes the "finding fang" of the need for human contrivance,
"This contrivance of the spectre of the spheres." Within the
limits of inevitable change and death, one may contrive "The
full of fortune and the full of fate" in the very attitude the
mind takes toward itself in its interiorization of the physical
world. In the nick of time, in the face of winter death, the
mind is both rescued and consumed by the blazing light of its
own summer imagining: "Like a blaze of summer straw, in
winter's nick." This simultaneous triumph and defeat is the
successor to Wordsworth's castle of fortitude that stands
"sublime" in its ability to brave "old time" and, equally, to
"mourn." The farewell to the dream of the past in both
Wordsworth and Stevens becomes the greeting of a wholly
humanized reality.

VI

The central theme of the Immortality Ode is the transition
from Wordsworth's "farewell" to the "visionary gleam" to its
replacement by the "philosophic mind." Begun after "Resolution and Independence" and "Elegiac Stanzas," and con-
cluded in 1806, the Immortality Ode moves from divine to
human understanding; from the "glory and the freshness of
a dream" through the "earthly freight" of the fear of death, to
the new power of the human heart that comes with its affirmation of both "its joys, and fears." The poem is the history of a growth that involves loss and pain in achieving the
paradoxical triumph of "soothing thoughts that spring / Out
of human suffering." Childhood vision as *sight* is superseded
by adult philosophy as insight; knowledge as sight becomes
knowledge, less immediate, as sound; and hearing and speech
make possible the philosophic mind.

Everything in the first two stanzas is filled with light. The

"freshness of a dream" derives from the clarity of images
known by the eye. The power of sight gives the child his first
knowledge of the world. But immediate vision fails, and
Wordsworth, the adult, cannot experience the dream as reality, nor can he perceive the glory and the celestial light: "The
things which I have *seen* I now can *see* no more." Stanza 2
continues this theme by making an important distinction:
the lights of the world are "beautiful and fair," but they are
not glorious in the specific sense that they are not "celestial
light"; the "heavens" are part of *this* world. In stanza 3 the
world is known by its sound, now that visionary sight (which
sees light as glory) is gone. The world is received joyously, but
as song, not as heavenly glory. Hearing does not have as immediate a focus in the external world as does sight; hearing
moves inward, and as the emphasis in the poem is shifted
from sight to sound, Wordsworth becomes more conscious of
himself; such consciousness is the root of loneliness: "To me
alone there came a thought of grief." Intensely aware of the
falling away of celestial glory, Wordsworth's "thought of
grief" perhaps is his own mortality. But the voice of nature,
"a timely utterance," reminds him of nature's immortality—
"The cataracts blow their trumpets from the steep"—and
Wordsworth recovers himself when he thinks of his voice,
like the echo, partaking of nature's voice, and thus partaking
of nature's immortality: "I hear the echoes through the
mountains throng." Finally, the wind, which symbolized nature's blessing, comes to him as if from childhood, "the fields
of sleep," where previously his vision lay. For the children,
the world is holy; they "keep holiday." They do not yet live in
time.

In stanza 4 the emphasis is still on hearing, but hearing
moves further inward and becomes feeling. What marks the
transition is the paradox, "I see / The heavens laugh," in
which seeing becomes hearing, and hearing then is transformed into empathetic feeling: "The fulness of your bliss,
I feel—I feel it all." This elation is sustained for several lines
while Wordsworth *feels* the sun's warmth but does not *see* its
glory until he cries: "I hear, I hear, with joy I hear!" But hearing is not sight, and Wordsworth's elation drops as he is re-

minded that spontaneous joy is gone. Bliss is experienced only empathetically; the holiday is over:

>—But there's a tree, of many, one,
> A single Field which I have looked upon,
> Both of them speak of something that is gone.

This tree is both an archetype—the tree of life— and a particular tree remembered from childhood; the single field is an actual field, but also the field of sleep that contained the childhood dream. They have lost their glory, but they are left with a voice that can become the "still, sad music of humanity," a voice of distress whose singing has a humanizing effect. Later, this voice will answer the question: "Whither is fled the visionary gleam? / Where is it now the glory and the dream?" by revealing the intellectual growth that results in the philosophic mind. At the end of stanza 4, however, the "visionary gleam," the "glory," and the "dream" are linked and brought into doubt; they are like the "fond illusion" in "Elegiac Stanzas" to which Wordsworth must say "farewell."

Stanza 5, in effect, is a second beginning for the poem. We learn that the child sees the world with the "freshness of a dream" because "Our birth is but a sleep and a forgetting." Waking and sleeping have been reversed. What we ordinarily take to be reality is a dream, and, as the child gets older, he moves further away from God's glory—the source of light— and his dream becomes vague and obscured:

> But trailing clouds of glory do we come
> From God, who is our home:
> Heaven lies about us in our infancy!
> Shades of the prison house begin to close
> Upon the growing boy.

Earth feels progressively less like home and comes to be a prison, until the vision of God and heaven is entirely lost as "Man perceives it die away, / And fade into the light of common day." The youth did not choose his vision, but is attended by it; his spontaneity is passive, for no choice was involved. This passivity is the limitation of the child's "heaven-born freedom." What remains from childhood is not a belief, but an intimation, and from this intimation Wordsworth proceeds to construct a "faith" to supersede the vision that has faded.

The problem Wordsworth now faces is how to make the world a home rather than a prison. He turns to nature for consolation: "Earth fills her lap with pleasures of her own." Although he knows "The homely nurse [nature] does all she can / To make her Foster-child her Inmate Man," the consolation fails. Nature may have "something of a Mother's mind," but the "imperial palace" (the home of infancy) must be left behind. "Inmate Man" becomes a prisoner in an alien world. In stanza 7, the child is portrayed as having a fixed series of roles to play which he must act out to the end:

> The little actor cons another part;
> Filling from time to time his "humorous stage"
> With all the Persons down to palsied Age,
> That life brings with her in her equipage.

An abrupt change of tone takes place in stanza 8 as Wordsworth shifts our perspective on the child from his "exterior semblance" to his interior and invisible soul. He now speaks of the child as the "best Philosopher. . . . On whom these truths do rest, / Which we are toiling all our lives to find, / In darkness lost, the darkness of the grave." The child is a visionary eye, but he cannot communicate for he has no voice; he is "deaf and silent." Also, the child does not possess the truths; they "rest" in his mind like a dream. The child's "heaven-born freedom," like the boy's spontaneous "animal movements," is doomed to the "inevitable yoke" because the child does not possess his freedom. Such freedom does not exist through his own choice nor by virtue of a creative will. The truths are not his at all; they are only a temporary blessing, a gift that is doomed to be lost. The active toiling for truths, though in the darkness of mortality, is the only way in which freedom can be found, for the light of "immortality," which appears to be the alternative, broods over the child as a "Master o'er a Slave."

The young man, however, may choose to affirm the necessity of growing up, to assume the "inevitable yoke," to struggle blindly against his own "blessedness" in order to gain the further freedom of choice. The adult has the possibility of ceasing to be a slave (dependent, passive) as his vision of immortality fades. But the loss of the "heaven-born freedom," the child's visionary power, is still mourned, and the stanza drops off again into gloom:

> Full soon thy Soul shall have her earthly freight,
> And custom lie upon thee with a weight,
> Heavy as frost, and deep almost as life!

One would expect the last word of the stanza, given its downward mood, to be "death," but, surprisingly, it is "life!" A progression has been made from the gloom of lost glory in stanza 4, and this progression prepares for the further surprise of "O joy!" that opens stanza 9. This sudden elation, however, has its basis in reason. Wordsworth is happy because change breeds conscious recognition of what *has been*, and it is just this recognition that brings awareness of the continued possibilities for growth. Not only for childhood "delight and liberty" does Wordsworth raise "The song of thanks and praise," but also for the natural process that leads to adult consciousness: "those obstinate questionings / Of sense and outward things." The new power of "seeing," appropriate to the "light of common day," centers in the mind and not the eye. Consciousness involves remembering that one forgets.

Wordsworth's waking consciousness, knowing that he has forgotten the visionary past, thus opens itself to new contact with that past of "shadowy recollections." Wordsworth can assume that "those first affections" of infancy in the forgotten past constitute the very foundation of his moral life:

> Our Souls have sight of that immortal sea
> > Which brought us hither,
> > Can in a moment travel thither,
> And see the children sport upon the shore,
> And hear the mighty waters rolling evermore.

Paradoxically, what Wordsworth hears is the "eternal Silence"; what he sees is the glory that has been lost. Traveling

back to that "immortal sea" through reconstituted memory
unifies origins and endings by linking the sea in its dawn
moment ("the sunshine is a glorious birth") with the moment of the "setting sun." Darkness and light, like "the
mighty waters" of creation and apocalypse, are celebrated
together as aspects of eternity "rolling evermore."

The jubilation that begins stanza 10 marks Wordsworth's
genuine, though vicarious, participation in nature's celebrating its own spontaneous animal joyousness: "We in *thought*
will join your throng." The paradoxical hearing and seeing of
stanza 9 reconfirms that such thought has its basis in past
experience. Once one actually saw the glory, the immortal
light. This past can be believed because there remain intimations of its having been, but it is now believed in the form of
"faith." Immediate vision, nevertheless, is gone, and Wordsworth reminds himself that this fact must be accepted:
"Nothing can bring back the hour / Of splendour in the grass,
of glory in the flower." Saying farewell to glory, however, has
more than just the virtue of bowing to necessity. Wordsworth's "We will grieve not" goes beyond the consolation
that the loss is at least not total. The loss of "radiance" is the
central, tragic fact of human seeing; accepting this loss has
the further virtue of providing a basis for human sympathy
and compassion "in the soothing thoughts that spring / Out
of human suffering."

Wordsworth's paradoxical view of suffering suggests the
"primal sympathy" of God, and it functions in part as a justi-
fication of his ways. The "faith that looks through death,"
however, does not envision a divine plan that redeems history, but, rather, faith provides a hypothesis for the "philosophic mind" that sees human sympathy coming from suffering and therefore asserts that the vision of lost radiance is as
important as the "shadowy recollections" of past glory. The
mind's awareness of the "human heart by which we live"
leads Wordsworth to assume the view that suffering and
compassion are bound together, and this view of tragic limits
and necessities commands Wordsworth's final attention.

The philosophic mind does not arrive at an *idea* of nature;
it becomes, rather, a vehicle for loving a world that is itself
physical. The movement from infant "glory" to childhood

spontaneity is thus consummated with the achievement of the philosophic mind in the affirming of renewed love: "I love the Brooks which down their channels fret, / *Even more* than when I tripped lightly as they." The transformation realized by the philosophic mind is completed symbolically with the imagery of the "sober colouring" of the "setting sun." In a voice of thanksgiving, Wordsworth can now sing full-throated. This thanksgiving does not encourage the hope for immortality, though it does not reject that hope; it praises the human heart and its treasury of feelings:

> Thanks to the human heart by which we live,
> Thanks to its tenderness, its joys and fears,
> To me the meanest flower that blows can give
> Thoughts that do often lie too deep for tears.

Wordsworth embraces both joy and fear, for together they make possible the tenderness that mitigates human grief for our mortality, attuning us in renewed harmony to nature's profoundest speech—the voice heard in the human heart. Wordsworth's poem affirms a deep sense of necessity: suffering and fear are sources of growth and joy. Since the heart finds its expression in a paradox of united opposites—happiness and sorrow—it sings for Wordsworth a triumphant ("palms are won") but tragic song. The past remains immediate in the "flower that blows" still as nature's original blessing, but the blessing has been transformed into thoughts "too deep for tears." It is, indeed, our fate to weep; yet, the final expression of our sorrow, when humanly understood, need not be sorrowful.

VII

Wordsworth's vision of immortality ("Heaven lies about us in our infancy!") becomes wholly secularized, wholly a vision of earth, in Stevens's "An Ordinary Evening in New Haven," where heaven is seen as a city in Connecticut. With the passing away of Wordsworthian "glory," Stevens can assert that "in an age of disbelief, when the gods have come to an end, . . . men turn to a fundamental glory of their own and

from that create a style of bearing themselves in reality"
("Two or Three Ideas"). "Ordinary Evening" is Stevens's sustained celebration of his "Love of the Real" in the face of the
difficulty of that celebration; in this last long poem he confronts the grimness of reality beyond any effort he has made
earlier. With renewed energy in the search for consolation,
"Our breath is like a desperate element / That we must
calm," Stevens explores the indifference of the world to see if
his imagination can redeem the spectacle of flux. As Wordsworth had made his return to the natural imagery of the
earth, "And O, ye Fountains, Meadows, Hills and Groves, /
Forbode not any severing of our loves!" so, too, Stevens
makes his repeated returns to affirm life in its ordinary forms:
"We keep coming back and coming back / To the real." To
fulfill the inescapable human need for meaning ("The instinct for heaven had its counterpart: / The instinct for
earth"), Stevens again attempts to create his own choir of celebration, his own festival.

The blessing in the "gentle breeze" that opens *The Prelude*, and the visionary winds of the Immortality Ode ("The
winds come to me from the fields of sleep"), become images
of absolute flux in "The Auroras" ("The wind will command
them with invincible sound") and of decay in "Ordinary Evening" ("the wind whimpers oddly of old age / In the western
night"). Stevens's sense of the source of human sympathy—
"This should be tragedy's most moving face"—derives from
his vision of "total leaflessness," reality seen plainly as de-
void of meaning. Yet this bleak vision also contains the potential inspiration for the imagination to create meaning, to
humanize the "bare rock" of the world, and in so doing to
humanize the self. The winter reality of death and barrenness, therefore, also may be seen as a beginning:

>   To re-create, to use
> The cold and earliness and bright origin
> Is to search. Likewise to say of the evening star,
> The most ancient light in the most ancient sky,
> That it is wholly an inner light, that it shines
> From the sleepy bosom of the real, re-creates,
> Searches a possible for its possibleness.

When the imagination responds to reality as the theater of the possible, the human mind reinvigorates itself, knowing that its effort to fill the world with meanings and forms can never come to an end: "Reality is the beginning not the end." If there is no ultimate satisfaction for the mind, no final resting place but only momentary peace, there also is no final emptying of desire, no "cold pastoral" of Keatsian arrest. Within the limits of mortality, one lives in an infinite world of infinite change and possibility, "In a permanence composed of impermanence."

The danger of despair, the mind's disease (what Wordsworth calls "the darkness of the grave"), can be overcome only by a countereffort of the inventing mind. If the ordinary is to be a scene of happiness, "a festival sphere," then one's attitude, one's words, must make it so: "an alteration / Of words that was a change of nature." Only then can the city of New Haven realize its name as "terra paradise." An unsponsored world is a barren world until it is transfigured by human "desire, set deep in the eye / Behind all actual seeing," and, therefore, Stevens argues, it is essential to apprehend that very barrenness as the primary act of imagination:

> The barrenness that appears is an exposing.
> It is not part of what is absent, a halt
> For farewells, a sad hanging on for remembrances.
> It is a coming on and a coming forth.

The farewell to each moment, as it becomes the past, must be understood as a challenge to human energy to begin again, to affirm the "never-ending meditation," which is the mind's life and the poem's form. As long as life lasts, the poet must attempt to "create from nothingness, / The heavens, the hells, the worlds, the longed-for lands."

The tragic sense of limits remains for Stevens what it was for Wordsworth: we lose what we love. As Stevens says of Wordsworth's character Michael, his "simple words become weighted with the tragedy of the old shepherd, and are saturated with poetry." Stevens departs from Wordsworth in his belief that there is no divinity other than what the human mind creates to give meaning and authority to our lives. Stevens's argument with the past—a past that had offered the consolation of religious belief—is absolute; Stevens's poetry begins and ends with the human mind discovering and inventing its own resources "In the predicate that there is nothing else." Yet Stevens's affirmation of the "earth, / Seen as inamorata" and his ceaseless return to both the barrenness of reality and the "reality [that] exists / In the mind" find their model in Wordsworth's poetry. Wordsworth fills the "parental space" of Stevens's imagination, and Wordsworth's thanksgiving to "the human heart by which we live" establishes the mood of holiness and humility that also suffuses Stevens's poetry.

From the point of view of poetic influence, the son's struggle with the "father" and the past can be outgrown. The son can define his differences from his father yet assert himself; he can be true to himself and carry on his father's essential values and concerns. Stevens states in a late letter (July 21, 1953): "My reality-imagination complex is entirely my own even though I see it in others." This is as it should be. Each person, each poet, must claim a single life and assume responsibility for it.

The sense of tradition, which teaches one to endure with compassion and dignity, is as precious as each individual life. In his brief essay "Connecticut," Stevens declares his love for the region because of its "spare colors, the thin light"; he goes on to say, "we live in the tradition which is the true mythology of the region and we breathe in with every breath the joy of having ourselves been created by what has been endured and mastered in the past." The interior Connecticut, a region of the mind, is where "what has been endured and mastered in the past" continues to live. In his mind, Stevens's cultural parents, "the beings of the mind / In the light-bound space of the mind," go on with their lives even in their death. Though Stevens teaches us how to say farewell to our physical lives, he never asks us to relinquish the wish to be remembered. Stevens's muse "cries quickly, in a flash of voice, / Keep you, keep you, I am gone, oh keep you as / My memory." At the threshold of death, Stevens's passion to remember and preserve, like Wordsworth's, finds its most sympathetic voice.

SEVEN

Keats's Letters:
Laughter as Autobiography

❦

I N O U R age of autobiography and confessional poetry
often indistinguishable from narcissism, the relationship between John Keats's life, as revealed in his letters,
and his poetry may have new poignancy and provide
needed instruction for us. Keats's letters engage us with their
good-natured and often humorous concern with worldly and
practical matters; yet what astonishes us is the degree to
which their artlessness approaches art. At their best the letters reverberate with a speculative energy, and beneath that
vitality there sounds a devotion to thought and idea that
gives them their cohesive strength. Certainly, the letters are
not uniformly interesting or significant—what letters are?—
but this operates to their advantage. Incidental news of London, of friends and relatives, mingles with meditations on the
nature of the imagination, beauty, truth, poets, and poetry;
each seems to gain from its proximity to the other. As T. S.
Eliot noted, the letters "are what letters ought to be; the fine
things come in unexpectedly," or to use Keats's own phrase,
they seem to have come "as naturally as the Leaves to a tree."

The letters reflect the organic processes of Keats's mind—a mind precocious in its ability and its willingness to devote itself without embarrassment to speculation about philosophical and aesthetic questions.

Although Keats's letters are frequently profound, they are still more often comic, invested with a humor that ranges from the self-deprecating, playfully ironic to the bawdy. Keats especially delighted in the absurd; he relished the comedy of Smollett and Fielding, and was quick to parody any hint of absurdity in sentiment, style, or situation. Characteristically, he turns his humor upon himself, although never in a maudlin way. In a letter of Thursday, August 6, 1818, to his sister-in-law's mother (Mrs. Wylie), for example, he pokes fun at the picture of himself as a typical nature lover trekking about the Scottish highlands, so that the true focus of his humor is the popular sentimental image of the poet—beside which his own healthy common sense is apparent:

> But I must leave joking, and seriously aver, that I have been *werry* romantic indeed, among these Mountains and Lakes. I have got wet through day after day—eaten oat-cake, and drank Whsky, walked up to my knees in Bog, got a sore throat, gone to see Icolmkill and Staffa, met with wholesome food, just here and there as it happened; went up Ben Nevis, and—N.B., came down again. Sometimes when I am rather tired I lean rather languishingly on a Rock, and long for some famous Beauty to get down from her Palfrey in passing, approach me with—her saddle-bags and give me—a dozen or two capital roast-beef Sandwiches—

This sophisticated sense of humor is present in almost all the letters written before late 1819 when Keats's health began to fail and he took on a darker cast.

Our apprehension of humor as an aspect of Keats's high devotion to poetry and thought leads us inevitably to sympathize with Keats as a man. Combined with our knowledge of the terrible circumstances of his life and his brave response to sickness and poverty, our awareness of Keats's comic sense enlarges our perspective of him as a poet. Unconsummated love and the longing for sexual fulfillment is a major theme in Keats's poetry, as well it might be since sickness, penury, and youth prevented him from marrying Fanny Brawne. Yeats's description of Keats seems apt when he says: "I see a school-boy when I think of him, / With face and nose pressed to a sweet-shop window, / For certainly he sank into his grave / His senses and his heart unsatisfied." In "La Belle Dame Sans Merci," Keats's ironic portrait of the beautiful woman con-sists not in any cruelty perpetrated by her, but in the realiza-tion that the fulfillment she offers is unreal and therefore un-obtainable. Since the questing wight of the poem cannot give up his dream of a fulfilling love, he is doomed to emotional starvation and despair. The poem seems unrelievedly grim in its presentation of the inevitability of human frustration, and it anticipates Freud's pessimism: "Something in the nature of the sexual instinct itself is unfavorable to the achievement of absolute gratification. . . . with the intervention of the in-cest-barrier between the two, the ultimate object selected is never the original one but only a surrogate for it." Neverthe-less, in a letter to George and Georgiana Keats on the stanza that read, "She took me to her elfin grot / And there she wept and sigh'd full sore, / And here I shut her wild wild eyes / With kisses four," Keats reveals his comic awareness of his own sexual obsession:

> Why four Kisses—you will say—why four because I wish to restrain the headlong impetuosity of my Muse—she would have fain said 'score!' without hurting the rhyme —but we must temper the Imagination as the Critics say with judgment. I was obliged to choose an even number that both eyes might have fair play: and to speak truly I think two a piece quite sufficient. Suppose I had said seven; there would have been three and a half a piece—a very awkward affair. (Sunday, February 14–Monday, May 3, 1819)

We might then ask ourselves whether there is some element of humor concealed within the poem. Perhaps humor has been transformed into dramatic objectivity whereby Keats has generalized himself into a collective image of a universal procession of frustrated lovers, "death-pale were they all."

With this possible transformation in mind, a rewarding way to read the letters is to explore what values, such as humor, have taken on related forms in his poetry. Many of the letters function as catalysts for ideas that later are realized in his greatest works. This is most apparent where questions of style and form are concerned. In an early letter (Saturday, November 22, 1817) to John Reynolds, Keats speaks of the concept of "intensity" as it is revealed to him in Shakespeare: "One of the three Books I have with me is Shakespear's Poems: I neer found so many beauties in the Sonnets—they seem to be full of fine things said unintentionally—in the intensity of working out conceits." Through his perception of compression in Shakespeare's verse, Keats was moved to strive for a similar economy in his poetry; that same intensity was to become paramount in his pursuit of a more concentrated style. Combined with that desire for compressed imagery was a propensity, shared with Shakespeare, for empathetic "in-feeling"—the ability to partake of the being of another creature, of the essence of an object; or as Keats expressed it in a famous line from another letter: "If a Sparrow come before my Window I take part in its existence and pick about the Gravel" (To Benjamin Bailey, Saturday, November 22, 1817). Keats believed empathy to be the single most important aspect of a poetic character. Like humor, it enabled him to move outside himself, to free himself from his single and confining life, and thus, as a poet, to project himself into objects and characters other than himself.

In a letter to Richard Woodhouse, Keats outlined the basis for his theory on the impersonality of the true poet:

A Poet is the most unpoetical of any thing in existence; because he has no Identity—he is continually in for— and filling some other Body—The Sun, the Moon, the Sea and Men and Women who are creatures of impulse are poetical and have about them an unchangeable attribute—the poet has none; no identity. . . . When I am in a room with People if ever I am free from speculating on creations of my own brain, then not myself goes home

to myself: but the identity of everyone in the room begins to press upon me that I am in a very little annihilated. . . . (Tuesday, October 27, 1818)

Both of these inclinations—the desire for intensity and the
ideal of the empathetic poet—played a crucial part in the
development of form and style in Keats's poetry, particularly
in the development of the technique of "synaesthesia"—the
fusion of seemingly disparate sensuous impressions in a single concentrated image. Furthermore, the concept of intensity in art led Keats into speculation on the imagination and
its relationship with beauty and truth. Keats had discussed
the imagination (with Milton in mind) in a letter to Benjamin
Bailey on November 22, 1817. What he tried to express
—though Bailey had been somewhat confused as to the import of his remarks—was the validity of the imagination's
creations:

> What the imagination seizes as Beauty must be truth—
> whether it existed before or not—for I have the same Idea
> of all our Passions as of Love they are all in their sublime,
> creative of essential Beauty. . . . The imagination may be
> compared to Adam's dream—he awoke and found it
> truth. I am the more zealous in this affair, because I have
> never yet been able to perceive how any thing can be
> known for truth by consequitive reasoning—and yet it
> must be. Can it be that even the greatest Philosopher
> ever arrived at his goal without putting aside numerous
> objections.

Keats found these ideas difficult to pursue in theory; he con-
fesses, "I must once for all tell you I have not one Idea of the
truth of any of my speculations," but he never ceased to meditate upon their implications.

II

"Ode to a Nightingale" treats the "greeting of the spirit"
through which Keats believed the imagination gives further
life to whatever it perceives, creating a fleeting and question-

able truth from its perception of beauty. And Keats's discussion in the letter of the function of the imagination in relation to those bewildering abstractions—"truth" and "beauty"—is pertinent for consideration of the "Ode on a Grecian Urn," the last lines of which dissolve into the certainty of uncertainty:

> Thou, silent form, dost tease us out of thought
> As doth eternity: Cold Pastoral!
> When old age shall this generation waste,
>   Thou shalt remain, in midst of other woe
> Than ours, a friend to man, to whom thou say'st
> "Beauty is truth, truth beauty, —that is all
>   Ye know on earth, and all ye need to know."

But, for Keats, to be "teased out of thought" is precisely the ultimate function of thought itself. Beauty may be considered as thought dissolving into sensuous form, yet it is form peculiar only to art—an urn, which cannot be ravaged by time. Human knowledge, at best, is feeling what one needs to feel. Perhaps the greatest relevance of the letters here is not that they explain precisely what Keats means in those lines, or where his thoughts were leading—the silence of the urn itself is the best explanation of that—but rather that they illustrate the depth of Keats's commitment to reflection on those concepts and his awareness of the limitation of conceptual thought. Much of our difficulty with Keats's poetry stems from the fact that Keats did not aspire to be a systematic thinker, nor does his poetry work through theory.

Despite his admiration for philosophy, his own nature was, as he well knew, essentially empirical and sensuous. What he accomplished was done through "straining at particles of light in the midst of a great darkness—without knowing the bearing of any one assertion any one opinion." Keats did not feel this to be a disadvantage; rather, it appeared to him that his ability to remain "in the midst of a great darkness" without laboring in search of ultimate explanations was an essential aspect of his character as a poet. To see beauty in honest uncertainty is one way in which Keats's letter on "negative capability" may be scrutinized. There Keats, speculating on "intensity" in art and the importance of beauty and truth for the artist, comes to the conclusion that a great artist is one for whom a sense of the mystery of beauty is paramount:

> at once it struck me what quality went to form a Man of Achievement, especially in Literature, and which Shakespeare possessed so enormously—I mean *Negative Capability*, that is, when a man is capable of being in uncertainties, mysteries, doubts, without any irritable reaching after fact and reason . . . with a great poet the sense of Beauty overcomes every other consideration, or rather obliterates all consideration. (Sunday, December 21, 1817)

Keats's connection between "negative capability" and the "sense of beauty" is paradoxical because it is based on the assumption that the more one passes beyond thought into sensuous apprehension, the more *impersonal* the experience becomes. Keats describes the experience of bodily pleasure as taking one beyond one's individual identity into a collective identity, as if one's body had become the world's body. Therefore, "negative capability," the ability to reach outside oneself, precedes the further capacity to realize the "sense of beauty." Here, too, we encounter another form of laughter if we continue to assume that for Keats the essence of laughter is the freedom that comes with the imaginative power to detach oneself from oneself. At the heart then of Keats's conception of "negative capability" is the ideal of "disinterestedness," which had borne an attraction for Keats since 1817. Great men, Keats believed, possess or attain the ability to empty themselves of their own identities, to immerse themselves through identification in the lives of others—as Socrates and Jesus did, to use Keats's examples.

Contrasted with this ideal is a fault that Keats perceived in Coleridge and to some extent in Wordsworth: the inability to direct the mind to some purpose greater than its own "irritable reaching after fact and reason." Keats felt this inability to be a form of egotism, an assertion of one's own identity that led not to knowledge, but to narrowness of mind. In fear of

such narrowness, Keats eschewed the introspective style of
Wordsworth in favor of the "old Poets"—particularly Milton.
But, in a development that had great implications for his own
poetry, Keats began to reflect on the merits of Wordsworth
and on the importance of inquiry into the nature of man. In
a letter to John Reynolds in May 1818, Keats confessed his
confusion about the validity of what he had formerly believed
to be the highest use of poetry and began to speculate on the
significance of Wordsworth's investigation of "the human
heart":

> I have nothing but surmises, from an uncertainty
> whether Miltons apparently less anxiety for Humanity
> proceeds from his seeing further or no than Wordsworth:
> and whether Wordsworth has in truth epic passion, and
> martyrs himself to the human heart, the main region of
> his song—in regard to his genius alone—we find what he
> says true as far as we have experienced and we can judge
> no further but by larger experience—for axioms in phi-
> losophy are not axioms until they are proved upon our
> pulses: We read fine things but never feel them to the full
> until we have gone the same steps as the Author.

We must read "proved upon our pulses" to imply not only experiences, but also experience extended and re-created as it
finds its way into poetic structure. For Keats, beauty is what
one chooses to feel by virtue of what one chooses to imitate
and to create.

Keats goes on to give his own theory of the development of
human understanding as it leads through thought in order to
move beyond thought:

> I compare human life to a large Mansion of Many Apart-
> ments, two of which I can only describe, the doors of the
> rest being as yet shut upon me. The first we step into we
> call the infant or thoughtless Chamber, in which we re-
> main as long as we do not think—We remain there a long
> while, and notwithstanding the doors of the second
> Chamber remain wide open, showing a bright appear-
> ance, we care not to hasten to it; but are at length imper-
> ceptibly impelled by the awakening of this thinking

principle within us—we no sooner get into the second
Chamber, which I shall call the Chamber of Maiden-
Thought, than we become intoxicated with the light and
the atmosphere, we see nothing but pleasant wonders,
and among the effects this breathing is father of is that
tremendous one of sharpening one's vision into the heart
and nature of Man—of convincing one's nerves that the
world is full of Misery and Heartbreak, Pain, Sickness
and oppression—whereby this Chamber of Maiden
Thought becomes gradually darkened and at the same
time on all sides of it many doors are set open— but all
dark—all leading to dark passages—We see not the bal-
lance of good and evil. We are in a Mist. *We* are now in
that state—we feel the "burden of the Mystery." To this
Point was Wordsworth come, as far as I can conceive
when he wrote "Tintern Abbey" and it seems to me that
his genius is explorative of those dark Passages.

The usual pattern of journeying from darkness to light is here
reversed by Keats so that the very idea of progression is
brought into question and set in a troubling perspective. The
step from infant thoughtlessness into "Maiden-Thought,"
accompanied by an increase in light, seems to suggest that
the next step will involve further thought and more light. But
Keats surprises us, for the "Chamber of Maiden Thought becomes gradually darkened"; we now enter a realm of obscure
mystery, and a sharpening of vision is achieved by an increase
in the ability to "feel," rather than to see or know. Wordsworth's power, as Keats now understands it, is his ability to
explore the wisdom of the body itself. The key word that
Keats uses here is "nerves," and probably Keats is thinking of
Wordsworth's phrase, "Felt in the blood, and felt along the
heart." Likewise, in "Ode to a Nightingale," Keats envisions
in the language of felt uncertainty what literally he cannot
see: "I cannot see what flowers are at my feet, / Nor what soft
incense hangs upon the boughs, / But, in embalmed darkness, guess each sweet. . . ." The entire stanza is filled with
the evocation of the senses, and yet it is darkness itself that
Keats is directly experiencing.

Keats's determination to explore the "dark passages," to

confront what he felt with Wordsworth was the "burden of
the Mystery," may have been his decisive step in achieving
a poetry that would become truly his own. In acknowledging
the importance of his own experience of the darkness within
and beyond thought, Keats confronted the reality of his own
feeling with a courage and a clairvoyance that enabled him to
dedicate himself, never without uncertainty, to his own intellect, his own senses, and the workings of his own intui-
tion. He determined, as he wrote in a letter to Benjamin
Robert Haydon in March 1819, "never to write for the sake of
writing or making a poem, but from running over with any
little knowledge or experience which years of reflection may
give me perhaps." Without this development Keats would
never have been able to write the great odes—all of which
deal with images of things vanishing. Gradually he learned
to trust his own powers, to place his faith and his confidence
in his own ability to confront the complexities of uncertain
knowledge—whether those complexities arose from his own
widening perception of human nature or from the sorrows of
his own life.

III

The circumstances of Keats's life became increasingly complex in the last three years with his brother Tom's death,
financial difficulties, and the onset of illness. With a strength
of character typical of him, he approached these mounting
problems with an eye to converting his difficulties into a for-
tifying poetry of affirmed transience. In a passage from a
lengthy letter to his brother and sister-in-law in America,
Keats expressed his scorn for the Christian paradigm of the
world as a vale of tears from which man is to be redeemed by
God and taken to heaven ("What a little circumscribed
straightened notion!") and presented his own position on the
value of human experience:

> Call the world if you Please "the vale of Soul-making."
> Then you will find out the use of the world (I am speak-
> ing now in the highest terms for human nature admitting

it to be immortal which I will here take for granted for the purpose of showing a thought which has struck me concerning it) I say *"Soul making"* Soul as distinguished from an Intelligence—There may be intelligence or sparks of the divinity in millions—but they are not souls till they acquire identities, till each one is personally itself. Intelligences are atoms of perception—they know and they see and they are pure—in short they are God— How then are souls to be made? How then are these sparks which are God to have identity given them? so as ever to possess a bliss peculiar to each one's individual existence? How, but by the medium of a world like this? . . . Do you not see how necessary a World of Pains and troubles is to school an intelligence and make it a Soul? A Place where the heart must feel and suffer in a thousand diverse ways! Not merely is the Heart a Hornbook, It is the Minds Bible, it is the Minds experience, it is the teat from which the Mind or intelligence sucks its identity. (Thursday, April 15, 1819)

This brave response to his own experience takes another, more mature, form in the affirmation of process and the acceptance of melancholy in several of the odes where the narrative emphasis falls on the transformation of thought and intelligence into emotion so that the "heart must feel and suffer in a thousand diverse ways." The mind, in Keats's image from the letter above, becomes the body of an infant; identity is nourished by pure sensation; and thus the body becomes a Bible, a sacred text of mysterious knowledge, just as it had for Wordsworth's nursing infant in *The Prelude:* "Along his infant veins are interfused / The gravitation and the filial bond / Of nature that connect him with the world."

In "Ode on a Grecian Urn," Keats also focuses on the idea of immortal fulfillment and the desire to escape the reality of life's processes through art; but he recognizes that the only escape from life, from the "hungry generations," is into a realm of silence where thought is impossible. The cry "Cold Pastoral!" has the ring of a forlorn bell that returns Keats to the realm of time from the unthinkable conception of eter-

nity. It is Keats's reminder to himself that art cannot create
a new nature that can free man from process, from generation
unto death. Nevertheless, Keats can live in the sensuous
moment of art and think in the logic of its own metaphorical
structure, for it is a moment in which what one thinks *is*
what one feels—and that unity may glimpse the very quality
of eternity. Nor should the reader overlook, as critics usually
do, the comic aspect of Keats's poem, since a talking urn,
which is also an "unravish'd bride," can only be taken seri-
ously on a high level of philosophical farce. In the face of the
most powerful emotions, thought necessarily collapses upon
itself, or it dissolves in laughter. The body's own inherent
power to laugh and to enjoy is achieved by Keats's "strenuous
tongue":

> O for a life of sensations rather than thoughts! It is "a
> vision in the form of Youth" a shadow of reality to
> come—and this consideration has further convinced me
> for it has come as auxiliary to another favorite specula-
> tion of mine, that we shall enjoy ourselves here after by
> having what we call happiness on Earth repeated in a
> finer tone. (Saturday, November 22, 1817)

For Keats, bodily pleasure, free of the duality and uncertainty of thought, becomes a model of what heaven might be
like if one could imagine happiness purified, refined, and sustained through eternal youth. Our perceptions of earth, however, are shadowy and to be compared to dreaming, and yet
death may become an awakening into a clearer reality, as
Keats says, "The imagination may be compared to Adam's
dream—he awoke and found it truth." The final question of
"Ode to a Nightingale"—"Do I wake or sleep?"—has, therefore, the primary meaning: Is pleasure on earth indeed a fore-
shadowing of paradisiacal pleasure yet to come?

   Keats's immediate models for such speculation again are
Milton and Wordsworth. Raphael tells Adam in book 5 of
Paradise Lost:

>   . . . Yet, for thy good
> This is dispensed; and what surmounts the reach
> Of human sense I shall delineate so,

By likening spiritual to corporal forms,
As may express them best—though what if Earth
Be but the shadow of Heaven, and things therein
Each to other like, more than on Earth is thought?

Exactly as in Keats's letter, Milton depicts earth as a shadow of heaven, and there is a direct correspondence between worldly pleasure and spiritual bliss. Later, in book 8, Adam questions Raphael again about the resemblance between earth and heaven; particularly, he wants to know if love in heaven resembles love on earth. Adam asks, "Love, thou sayest, / Leads up to Heaven, is both the way and guide; / Bear with me, then, if lawful what I ask. / Love not the heavenly Spirits, and how their love / Express they—by looks only, or do they mix / Irradiance?" In a rare moment of humor, more typical of Keats than of Milton, Raphael blushes "with a smile that glowed / Celestial rosy-red, Love's proper hue," and he replied to Adam: "Let it suffice thee that thou know'st / Us happy, and without Love no happiness . . . if Spirits embrace, / Total they mix, union of pure with pure. . . ." The comedy here is to be compared with the passage in Keats's letter to Dilke where his description is an apotheosis of pleasure:

Talking of Pleasure, this moment I was writing with one hand, and with the other holding to my Mouth a Nectarine—good god how fine. It went down soft pulpy, slushy, oozy—all its delicious embonpoint melted down my throat like a large, beatified strawberry. I shall certainly breed. (Wednesday, September 22, 1819)

Perhaps such speculation anticipates Yeats's description of heavenly fornication:

There is no touching here, nor touching there,
Nor straining joy, but whole is joined to whole;
For the intercourse of angels is a light
Where for its moment both seem lost, consumed.

Yet in "To Autumn," Keats rejects the notion of escape or transcendence by fully affirming process itself; the central impact of the poem is the assertion that man must intensely experience the world around him in all its change, all its transient fullness and beauty. In this respect, Keats is the literary father of Wallace Stevens. Here, most convincingly in Keats's poetry, thought and the rejection of thought become a single act: "Where are the songs of Spring? Ay, where are they? / Think not of them. . . ." This self-contradictory gesture (since Keats is thinking about spring in exhorting himself not to do so) contains all that Keats hopes for and fears. It is an act of will to hold himself in an instant of perception and speculation as if he were in eternity. The reader's sense at the poem's end of the "gathering swallows" is at once that they are gathering to leave and to remain. Keats offers us this equivocal image to be held and to hold to as the limit of truthful consolation, and he foreshadows Stevens's difficult meditation in "Credences of Summer" when Stevens says: "This is the barrenness / Of the fertile thing that can attain no more," and "This is the refuge that the end creates." So, too, in "Bright Star," by what appears to be sheer force of will in defiance of logical thought, Keats asserts the unity of natural process, watching "his fair love's ripening breast," with eternal stasis—as if the process of *ripening* could be possessed in a still, unchanging moment of ecstasy. In response to such a passionate Keatsian wish, Stevens cries out: "Does ripe fruit never fall?" and Yeats exclaims: "Things that are thought too long can be no longer thought."

The torments of sexual deprivation could draw humorous responses from Keats, but most often his typical reaction to hardship reflected his strong sense of responsibility and a desire not to escape, but to deal with problems honestly and honorably. In money matters, for example, Keats was strict in his sense of duty to those from whom he had to borrow, and prided himself justifiably on his "sense of squareness." Where poetry was concerned, his difficulties elicited a similarly earnest response. "I must choose," he wrote in a letter to one of the Jeffrey sisters in May 1819, "between despair and Energy—I choose the latter." The principle of energy was essential in Keats's character; his favorite metaphors—in speaking, for instance, of setting himself to work on a poem—were military: "I have done little to Endymion—I hope to finish it in one more attack." He, like Blake ("Energy is eternal delight"), admired energy in almost all its manifestations: "Though a quarrel in the streets is a thing to be hated, the energies displayed in it are fine," Keats proclaims.

In opposition to energy, as he noted in the letter to Miss Jeffrey, was despair, a state of mind that implied not simply the lack of energy (Keats, as can be inferred from "Ode on Indolence," could also take great satisfaction from a pleasurable passivity), but an inability to face what had to be faced, to take action when action was required. A corollary of despair, for Keats, was melancholy, that state in which the thought of pleasure led inevitably to the thought of its loss, as he pictured it in "Ode on Melancholy":

> She dwells with Beauty—Beauty that must die;
> And Joy, whose hand is ever at his lips
> Bidding adieu; and aching Pleasure nigh
> Turning to Poison while the bee-mouth sips:
> Ay, in the very temple of Delight
> Veiled Melancholy has her sovran shrine. . . .

Melancholy, as well as Delight, is a deity to be worshipped. If we can speak of Keats's vision as a tragic one, it is precisely because celebration and lamentation are inseparable; they are part of the dialectic of experience as they are of poetry. Thus the typical Keatsian oxymoron ("aching Pleasure") is the signature of his character as well as of his style.

I V

The cause of much of Keats's melancholy and despair in the last year of his life was, of course, his illness and the knowledge that even as he felt himself to be approaching a truly fine poetry, the possibility of ever achieving a great poem would be denied him. But a great deal of the pain in this last year, as his letters reveal, stemmed from his unfulfilled and unfulfilling relationship with Fanny Brawne. Women had always perplexed Keats; he shared in the prevailing scorn for bluestockings, and in his more uneasy moments thought women of little use—except perhaps as objets d'art, as he writes in

a letter to his brother and sister-in-law, "I never intend hereafter to spend time with Ladies unless they are handsome—
you lose time to no purpose." Much of his prejudice against
women, as he well knew, was a result of his inability to understand them through his accustomed mode of empathy. In
a letter to Benjamin Bailey, he describes his frustration with
women and vows earnestly to make an effort to overcome his
dislike:

> I am certain I have not a right feeling towards Women—
> at this moment I am striving to be just to them but I can-
> not—Is it because they fall so far beneath my Boyish
> imagination? When I was a Schoolboy I thought of fair
> Woman a pure Goddess, my mind was a soft nest in
> which some one of them slept, though she knew it not
> —I have no right to expect more than their reality. I
> thought them etherial above Men—I find them perhaps
> equal—great by comparison is very small. . . . When I am
> among Women I have evil thoughts, malice spleen—I
> cannot speak or be silent—I am full of Suspicions and
> therefore listen to nothing—I am in a hurry to be gone—
> You must be charitable and put all this perversity to my
> being disappointed since Boyhood. (Saturday–Wednes-
> day, July 18–22, 1818)

Keats took an ironic view of lovers even after he was caught
up in his passion for Fanny, and he could see the amusing side
of love. Of his own passion, he writes to Fanny:

> at night, when the lonely day has closed, and the lonely,
> silent, unmusical Chamber is waiting to receive me as
> into a Sepulchre, then believe me my passion gets entire-
> ly the sway, then I would not have you see those Rhapso-
> dies which I once thought it impossible I should ever give
> way to, and which I have often laughed at in another, for
> fear you should think me unhappy or perhaps a little
> mad. (Thursday, July 1, 1819)

The fact that his ballad "La Belle Dame Sans Merci" and
the sonnet "To Fanny" are so similar in language and in tone
indicates that Fanny must have been in Keats's mind as he

wrote "La Belle Dame." In both poems Keats speaks of a woman's "thrall" under which the lover has fallen; both poems conjure up the specter of a living death, where the lover searches for, yet never finds, the fulfillment of love. Whether or not the woman of "La Belle Dame" is a nonexistent creature who represents the ideal that the lover seeks, for Keats the specter of a living death was all too real. The cruelty of La Belle Dame, one must remember, is not that she chooses to injure or enslave, but rather that she is an unrealizable dream, and thus cannot offer the paradisiacal meal, the fulfillment, that the dream enacts.

Keats considered it a living death to awake from such a dream, know that it is a dream, and also know that the dream can never be forgotten. This knowledge is the "cold hill side" of the mind, forever corrupted by desire. The wish for romantic fulfillment remains a fatal wish. Keats was not able to heal himself according to Wallace Stevens's injunction to "exile desire for what is not." And yet the poem's narrative structure—in which the wretched lover lost in the desolate landscape is the speaker's alter self—objectifies the romantic despair the poem describes. The cyclical patterns of dream within dream, of return and recurrence, are broken only by imaginative awareness in the form of the poem itself as a mirror of its own confining structure—as in Blake's vision of the limbo of nature's cycles in "The Mental Traveller." In other words, Keats demonstrates a liberating separation between his own obsessed psychology and his visionary understanding of the sickness of unlimited desire.

The letters of late 1819 and 1820 reflect the terrible pain and frustration Keats felt as it became evident to him that he, like his brother Tom, was going to die. In this respect the most striking theme that may be followed in the letters from the time of Tom's illness through the last months of Keats's own life—a theme paralleled in the poems—concerns the question of immortality. Alluding to his brother's death in a letter to his brother and sister-in-law early in 1819, Keats says that he had "scarce a doubt of immortality of some nature or other." But that assertion may have sprung more from his love for Tom than from any deep conviction on the existence of an afterlife because Keats had never been religious. What thoughts he had on immortality were a matter of speculation rather than faith, and his less deliberate references to immortality were generally associated with fame and his desire to be numbered among the English poets after his death. Early in 1820, this concern still received his greatest emphasis. In February of that year he considered the possibility of his death in a letter to Fanny Brawne: " 'If I should die,' I said to myself, 'I have left no immortal work behind me—nothing to make my friends proud of my memory—but I have loved the principle of beauty in all things, and if I had had time I would have made myself remembered.' " As the fact of his impending death became evident, he felt an anguish before his uncertainty about an afterlife, an anguish that was exacerbated by the pain of losing the possibility of Fanny's love. Tormented by a desire indistinguishable from despair, he vacillated, in his letters, between the hope for life after death and the desire to escape life completely. He wrote to Fanny in July 1820, "I long to believe in immortality. I shall never be able to bid you an entire farewell." And again to Fanny, a month later: "the world is too brutal for me—I am glad there is such a thing as the grave—I am sure I shall never have any rest till I get there."

Perhaps the keenest expression of the agony he had to endure lies in a letter written to Charles Brown on Saturday, September 30, 1820. Stirred into acute awareness by the thought of Fanny Brawne, Keats gave voice to what seems a cry of bewilderment that bespeaks both the hell of his existence and the excruciating longing to believe in immortality:

> The thought of leaving Miss Brawne is beyond every thing horrible—the sense of darkness coming over me— I eternally see her figure eternally vanishing. Some of the phrases she was in the habit of using during my last nursing at Wentworth place ring in my ears. Is there another Life? Shall I awake and find all this a dream? There must be we cannot be created for this sort of suffering.

As in "Ode to a Nightingale," the possibility that life is a dream and death an awakening is held to, though tentatively.

The refinement of sensation in poetry is perhaps a prophecy of a further refinement to come through death as Wordsworth had conjectured: "Our birth is but a sleep and a forgetting." The "tender-taken breath" of Keats's late sonnet "Bright Star," by which Keats imagines himself to "so live ever," may exist on either side of the grave. But in Keats's extremity, these are all speculations nursed at the breast of despair. Transience is not one with the principle of earthly loveliness as in Stevens's "Death is the mother of beauty"; rather it defines the condition of Keats's emotional damnation in which "I eternally see her figure eternally vanishing." It is the moment of loss now, not the moment of sensuous beauty, that is fixed, as if permanently, in Keats's mind.

Despite the anguish, the terrible pain, and the fear Keats felt in his last months, his letters nevertheless end on a note that we might regard as a kind of triumph. Ever committed to that Shakespearean ideal of the man who is able to exist in uncertainties, mysteries, and doubts, Keats had undergone the utmost trial of his conviction and had succeeded in finding an attitude of grace and humor where others would have found no consolation at all. His last letter, to Charles Brown, reflects the calm and fortitude of a man resigned to death, yet still concerned with the living, a man whose spirit has indeed moved outside of himself—like Hamlet addressing Horatio as if Horatio were Hamlet who himself, at his death, might be described "as one, in suffering all, that suffers nothing." It is as if the tragedy of Keats's early death were given a comic gesture, "an awkward bow," to bring his life and art together in some inexplicable consummation beyond thought:

> Remember me to all my friends, and tell Haslam that I should not have left London without taking leave of him, but from being so low in body and mind. Write to George as soon as you receive this, and tell him how I am, as far as you can guess; and also a note to my sister--who walks about my imagination like a ghost—she is so like Tom. I can scarcely bid you goodbye, even in a letter. I always made an awkward bow. (Thursday, November 30, 1820)

The ultimate act of "negative capability" for the lyric poet is to fill his own life, tell his own story, as if it were another's. Much of the self-indulgence and narcissism of contemporary American poetry might well be alleviated if the poet tried to imagine how he would represent his own sorrows in verse if Keats had invented him. The paradox of Keats's realization of himself through poetic negation is that the essence of his style is one of passionate detachment. We do not find in Keats's poetry the personal details of his private life that are abundant in his letters. There is a willed projection of the self into the world of objects, representative characters and types, and the energy behind Keats's power to free himself from the constraints of his own life, it seems to me, is the inebriated energy of universal laughter that, even in the face of sober "Melancholy," still "Can burst Joy's grape against his palate fine." The "finer tone," the phrase Keats used to describe heavenly pleasure, after all, is to be found with certainty only in the living body; joy was not merely his to lose in its possessing, but everyone's.

EIGHT

Yeats as Spectator to Death

❦

Y EATS'S obsession with death takes many forms, ranging from stoical defiance to longing for an escape from the painful duality of consciousness. When his spirits are exhilarated, Yeats sets himself the task of writing poems "for such men as come / Proud, open-eyed and laughing to the tomb," but when his mood darkens into quiet meditation, he flatly asserts that "what disturbs our blood / Is but its longing for the tomb." As in Keats's swooning cry to join his immortal nightingale, "I have been half in love with easeful Death," Yeats imagines death as a sexual consummation in which man's "soul's a bride," or as a visionary moment of ecstasy in which he realizes that "Eternity is passion." Sexual desire and artistic vision are dual aspects of Yeats's ambivalent attitude toward death, wishing on the one hand to defy death and turn to worldly passion even if it be "life to pitch / Into the frog-spawn of a blind man's ditch," or, on the other, to consider art a kind of spiritual substitute for bodily desire in being "constructed there in nature's spite."

From his earliest poems, Yeats describes the self as bifurcated and in conflict, simultaneously seeking to face the

tragic truths of reality and to escape them. Yeats views consciousness itself as an aspect of man's mortality and his suffering. And yet consciousness of consciousness may achieve
a cure or, at least, offer a respite from the groping desire to be
released from the torment of duality. The possibility of the
mind's alleviating its own disease of despair is the paradox of
art itself which, in thinking, seeks to soothe the wound of
thought. For Yeats, art is a "vision of reality" in which the
artist confronts his deepest temptation to remain blind to his
own condition.

II

In "A Dialogue of Self and Soul" the poem's structure as a dialogue portrays the duality of Yeats's mind, the breach in the
house of thought.

I

> *My Soul.* I summon to the winding ancient stair;
>   Set all your mind upon the steep ascent,
>   Upon the broken, crumbling battlement,
>   Upon the breathless starlit air,
>   Upon the star that marks the hidden pole;
>   Fix every wandering thought upon
>   That quarter where all thought is done:
>   Who can distinguish darkness from the soul?
>
> *My Self.* The consecrated blade upon my knees
>   Is Sato's ancient blade, still as it was,
>   Still razor-keen, still like a looking-glass
>   Unspotted by the centuries;
>   That flowering, silken, old embroidery, torn
>   From some court-lady's dress and round
>   The wooden scabbard bound and wound,
>   Can, tattered, still protect, faded adorn.
>
> *My Soul.* Why should the imagination of a man
>   Long past his prime remember things that are
>   Emblematical of love and war?
>   Think of ancestral night that can,
>   If but imagination scorn the earth

And intellect its wandering
To this and that and t'other thing,
Deliver from the crime of death and birth.

My Self. Montashigi, third of his family, fashioned it
Five hundred years ago, about it lie
Flowers from I know not what embroidery—
Heart's purple—and all these I set
For emblems of the day against the tower
Emblematical of the night,
And claim as by a soldier's right
A charter to commit the crime once more.

My Soul. Such fullness in that quarter overflows
And falls into the basin of the mind
That man is stricken deaf and dumb and blind,
For intellect no longer knows
Is from the *Ought*, or *Knower* from the *Known*—
That is to say, ascends to Heaven;
Only the dead can be forgiven;
But when I think of that my tongue's a stone.

II

My Self. A living man is blind and drinks his drop.
What matter if the ditches are impure?
What matter if I live it all once more?
Endure that toil of growing up;
The ignominy of boyhood; the distress
Of boyhood changing into man;
The unfinished man and his pain
Brought face to face with his own clumsiness;

The finished man among his enemies?—
How in the name of Heaven can he escape
That defiling and disfigured shape
The mirror of malicious eyes
Casts upon his eyes until at last
He thinks that shape must be his shape?
And what's the good of an escape
If honour find him in the wintry blast?

I am content to live it all again
And yet again, if it be life to pitch
Into the frog-spawn of a blind man's ditch,
A blind man battering blind men;
Or into that most fecund ditch of all,
The folly that man does
Or must suffer, if he woos
A proud woman not kindred of his soul.

I am content to follow to its source
Every event in action or in thought;
Measure the lot; forgive myself the lot!
When such as I cast out remorse
So great a sweetness flows into the breast
We must laugh and we must sing,
We are blest by everything,
Everything we look upon is blest.

Yeats's conception of consciousness as the mind divided against itself is more complex than Marvell's "Dialogue between the Soul and Body" in that Yeats's "Self" in the poem represents more than the claims of the body. As it becomes apparent later in the poem, the Self has a soul of his own—a soul that chooses bodily life over death—in contrast to the Soul who speaks in section 1, effusively expressing the temptation to die.

The Soul's opening address to the Self has an incantatory effect as it tries to cast a spell that would enable the Self in his "wandering thought" to focus on the single task of climbing the "winding ancient stair" to the "crumbling battlement" from which to view the timeless heavens. According to Yeats's arcane symbolism of historical cycles as represented by the cycles of the moon, the Soul tries to tempt the Self into relinquishing himself to the darkness beyond life by employing thought to reject thought, as if peace, darkness, and freedom from consciousness were synonymous. In effect, the Soul is tempting the Self to die and escape the humiliation of both mind and body—as Marvell described our mortal predicament as being trapped "in Chains / of Nerves, and Arteries, and Veins. / Tortur'd, besides each other part, / In a vain Head, and double Heart."

The Self refuses to be distracted by the Soul from his own chosen distraction, "Sato's ancient blade," the heirloom given to his family. Meditating on the male and female aspects of the sword and its embroidered scabbard—the "razor-keen" sword can still protect and the scabbard made "From some court-lady's dress" can still adorn—the Self chants his own counterincantation in his resistance to the Soul's temptation. Just as the Soul had constructed its speech on the rhetorical repetition of the word "upon," so, too, the Self responds rhetorically in his orchestration of the word "still." What the reader hears, of course, is Yeats's voice divided into two voices as if they were truly separate, each trying to seduce the other into a single and unambivalent emotion.

Responding to the Self's refusal to be attentive, the Soul then tries to humiliate the Self by reminding him that he is "Long past his prime," and that it is demeaning for an old man to be thinking about the sword and the scabbard, "Emblematical of love and war." Since the Self can only think about love and war, he can also, by thinking (so the Soul argues), reject the attractions of love and war. Again the Soul urges the Self to "scorn the earth" and turn only to the thought of "ancestral night," of timeless and soothing oblivion—like Keats's wishing to "cease upon the midnight with no pain." With a sophistical twist, the Soul defines the rejection of earth as a kind of antibirth out of the medium of nature and time. Thought negating itself can "Deliver"—like a spiritualized birth—the Self from nature's cycles of "death and birth." The natural cycle of renewal returning to death is judged to be a "crime" by the Soul, since it allows no peace from the torments of desire—the corrupt intermixture of sexuality and aggression, love and war.

But the Self continues to fix his thoughts upon the sword and its long history, not on "ancestral night." He sees in the embroidery an emblem of love's passion, "Heart's purple," which he adopts as a symbol of his choice to remain in time, in opposition to the symbol of the tower, which would lead him out of the day into the night of eternal death. The Self asserts a lover's passion and a "soldier's right" to return in thought to the world of the living and thus to commit the "crime once more" of loving and hating, creating and destroying, in their impure and tormenting mixture. Only the Soul, however, is convinced by its argument, and so the Soul turns its attention from the Self to its own dissolving thought of the purity of oblivion in that quarter of the moon "where all thought is done." When the duality of imperfect thought —the division between subject and object—is healed and thus "intellect no longer knows / *Is* from *Ought*, or *Knower* from the *Known*," the Soul in effect passes beyond this world and "ascends to Heaven." With the final awareness that nature and its reflection in consciousness are themselves a crime, and that therefore "Only the dead can be forgiven," the Soul has no more to think or say and becomes the stone monument to the ultimate choice of silence, leaving the Self behind in the world of time to contend with ambivalence and corruption.

Left alone and now in soliloquy, as if without a Soul, the Self confronts his own blindness, the uncertainty of his own thought, the incompleteness of his identity from boyhood on. The source of the Self's redemption from the "crime of death and birth" is to be found in the paradox that the Self can see his own blindness. The power of humility released by that paradoxical seeing enables the Self to look back into his past, and this recapitulation of his personal history releases the further power of visionary seeing at the poem's end when the earth, the "blind man's ditch," is envisioned as blest.

But the condition of blessedness on earth, in body and in thought—in opposition to the Soul's purity of silent and oblivious darkness—only can be achieved through a cathartic recounting of one's humiliations from childhood on: the "ignominy of boyhood"; the degrading image of oneself as seen through the "malicious eyes" of others; the rejection by women which leads only to the "folly" of seeking love where it will not be returned. And yet, as the paradox deepens, the Self's perception of his own clumsiness, his own "disfigured shape," and his own folly, leads him to assert a countersense of honor in that he will not allow his humiliation to provoke him to escape from his condition into death. Rather, with defiant energy, he turns back to confront the "wintry blast." The real option of the Self is not what life he will choose to live, but his deliberate return in thought to the life already fated for him. In that choice, his mood of despair begins to change, and he is able to say: "I am content to live it all again / And yet again." Memory becomes an eternity that can be repeated by a willed act of thought.

In reliving—through the choice of memory—his suffering for having wooed "A proud woman not kindred of his soul," the Self, with casual inadvertence, seems to ignore the dramatic fact that the Soul has disappeared from the scene back into "ancestral night." But the Soul who has vanished into silence was only that part of the Self that had truly desired death. The "soul" that remains as a living part of the living Self must now be regarded as the Self's capacity to choose the very life that he has lived. In making this choice, in affirming the necessity of his own history, the Self's contentment is repeated in the phrase "I am content," and thus the action of retrospection follows "to its source / Every event in action or in thought." Having chosen to confront and accept his own history, the Self (no longer passive) does not need forgiveness as the Soul had claimed was the blessing of the dead, for the active Self now is able to "forgive myself the lot!" This act of self-forgiveness completes the series of mental choices made by the Self in generating his own freedom, so that his culminating choice to "cast out remorse" manifests a magical freedom. As Adam was cast out of the garden of Eden, the Self, in casting out remorse, chooses to live in the inherited fallen condition of the ditch of life.

This worldly ditch, suitable it seemed only for the spawning of frogs, stagnant, and with only a drop for the blind man to drink, now begins to gather fresh energy, so that "a sweetness flows into the breast." The ditch of bitter and frustrated desire is redeemed in the heart of the Self as desire for what has been; hence, a final paradoxical transformation of the Self occurs. Having affirmed his own individual history, the Self —through the power of human freedom to choose the necessity of its mortal nature—becomes a collective Self. The speaking voice of the Self shifts from an "I" to a "We," from "I am content" to "We must laugh." Argument and complaint pass over into the voice of art, whose essence is laughter and song. Having recounted his fallen corruption, the collective voice of the Self takes on a Blakean innocence, which Yeats had defined earlier in "A Prayer for My Daughter" as the transfiguration achieved when "all hatred driven hence, / The soul recovers radical innocence." Like Blake's concept of "organized innocence," Yeats's willed return to the ditch is literally "radical," for it is a return to the ambivalence of the human heart and thus to our emotional human roots. In this return, the eyes of the blind are opened, and the Self sees, both in himself and in the world, a vision of blessedness. This is not blessedness of death beyond thought, but the blessedness of art that is capable of accepting ambivalence and thereby capable of rejecting the escapist wish to die. In this representative victory over his own Soul, the Self shares the ecstasy of collective laughter.

I I I

In his late poem "The Man and the Echo," just as in "A Dialogue of Self and Soul," Yeats dramatizes the division of the Self through the structure of alternating speakers, Man and Echo.

Man

In a cleft that's christened Alt
Under broken stone I halt
At the bottom of a pit
That broad noon has never lit,
And shout a secret to the stone.
All that I have said and done,
Now that I am old and ill,
Turns into a question till
I lie awake night after night
And never get the answers right.
Did that play of mine send out
Certain men the English shot?
Did words of mine put too great strain
On that woman's reeling brain?
Could my spoken words have checked

That whereby a house lay wrecked?
And all seems evil until I
Sleepless would lie down and die.

Echo

Lie down and die.

Man

         That were to shirk
The spiritual intellect's great work,
And shirk it in vain. There is no release
In a bodkin or disease,
Nor can there be work so great
As that which cleans man's dirty slate
While man can still his body keep
Wine or love drug him to sleep,
Waking he thanks the Lord that he
Has body and its stupidity,
But body gone he sleeps no more,
And till his intellect grows sure
That all's arranged in one clear view,
Pursues the thoughts that I pursue,
Then stands in judgment on his soul.
And, all work done, dismisses all
Out of intellect and sight
And sinks at last into the night.

Echo

Into the night.

Man

         O Rocky Voice,
Shall we in that great night rejoice?
What do we know but that we face
One another in this place?
But hush, for I have lost the theme,
Its joy or night seem but a dream;
Up there some hawk or owl has struck,
Dropping out of sky or rock,

> A stricken rabbit is crying out,
> And its cry distracts my thought.

The Man, "old and ill," is alone in a cavern, described as a "cleft," as he cries out his "secret to the stone." His need for secrecy comes from the shame he feels in believing that thought has failed him since he "never [gets] the answers right"; all life "seems evil" to him, and therefore he wishes to "lie down and die." Like the Self in "A Dialogue of Self and Soul," his distress drives him to recount his own personal history:

> Did that play of mine send out
> Certain men the English shot?
> Did words of mine put too great strain
> On that woman's reeling brain?
> Could my spoken words have checked
> That whereby a house lay wrecked?

But this time Yeats's rehearsal of his past does not have a cathartic effect, leading to acceptance. His questions remain unresolved, contributing to his sleeplessness and the agitation of his thoughts from which the peace of death seems to offer the only relief. The answering voice of the Echo, ironically repeating the Man's last words, "lie down and die," expresses the momentary dominance of the Man's wish to escape the burden of his consciousness which sees all as evil.

The Man recoils, however, against the very attractiveness of escape through death, trying to persuade himself that artistic thought, "The spiritual intellect's great work," must be attempted and sustained to the very end. Echoing the melancholy Hamlet's suicidal conjecture that "he might his quietus make / With a bare bodkin," the Man rejects his wish to escape from the remainder of his life by arguing that there is "no release / In a bodkin or disease" as long as there is still work for his intellect. The Man believes that his soul will not be prepared to stand judgment unless "all work" is done. This is his equivalent of Hamlet's belief that God has "fix'd / His canon 'gainst self-slaughter." The goal of life is death (as Freud also argued), but only after life has run its full course.

The Man's defense of work as the artist's attempt to clean "man's dirty slate" is the moral imperative that continues to hold him in his life.

For the aging Man whose body has ceased to provide respite from thought now that "wine or love" no longer drugs "him to sleep," the intellect is driven to put its house in order "in one clear view." There is not even a temporary escape for the restless mind of the Man who gives ironic thanks for the body's stupidity, its capacity for the oblivion of sleep—a blessing old age has taken away. The burden of intellect unflinchingly confronting the evil of life cannot be lifted until the intellect completes its work; only further thought (so it seems to the old Man) can free him from thought so that, at last, he can then dismiss all "Out of intellect and sight." When thought is complete, then the old Man can submit to his wish for peaceful death and sink "at last into the night." The Echo again repeats his final phrase, "Into the night," suggesting that the relief of death might occur that very instant and that the old Man will be gathered into the unity of "ancestral night" as if returning to his mother's arms. Then, to lie down where he is, at "the bottom of a pit," would return him to the womb of the earth.

In his final speech, the Man addresses the Echo, "O Rocky Voice," as if he were speaking to someone who had already died and knew what death was like. The Man asks the ultimate question about whether death brings happiness: "Shall we in that great night rejoice?" Instantly, he realizes that "Rocky Voice" is only an external projection of his inner self, and that it is his own self he is confronting—"we face / One another"—in his own mind, the pit that has become for him both grave and womb. In seeing death as part of his living self, he commands the Echo—that part of himself that seeks death beyond life—to be quiet. "Hush," he says, and, indeed, the Echo is not heard again. The poem's pattern, whereby the Echo repeats the last phrase spoken by the Man, is broken. The theme that the Man has lost is the speculation of what death might be like, and so the question of whether or not the night of death brings joy appears now to the Man merely as a vain thought, "a dream."

There will be no revelation from the sky, from the "star that marks the hidden pole," where the Soul, in "Dialogue of Self and Soul," had asked the Self to "fix" (in both senses of the word) his thoughts. What appears "Up there," instead, is an actual bird, "some hawk or owl," which drops from the sky and seizes "A stricken rabbit." This is not a moment of divine incarnation, as when Zeus mysteriously becomes "the brute blood of the air" and rapes Leda in the guise of a swan; rather, this is worldly violence, the cruelty and evil of nature itself. Nothing is "engendered" by this descent as a new historical era is engendered by Zeus's seed in Leda, except further distraction in the mind of the Man. Yeats evokes the pain of the Man's response to the rabbit's "crying out"—as if in the repetition of the word "cry" the rabbit's agony were an extension of his own—in the harsh rush of consonants that dominate the conclusion of the poem: "ha_wk_," "stru_ck_," "s_k_y," "ro_ck_," "stri_ck_en," "_cry_ing," "_cry_," "distra_cts_." The Man's final distraction, unlike the Self's sense of blessedness, turns him away from the contemplation of the possible joy of death and gives his emotions a focus of their own. That focus is the moral claim all suffering life has on the sympathetic self. The paradox at the heart of the poem is that suffering holds the Man in his life even against the temptation of imagining that death may bring happiness. In this astonishing reversal, the final effect of this poem is the same as that of "A Dialogue of Self and Soul," for in both poems the temptation to escape life into death, though for opposite reasons, is overcome.

I V

In *A Vision* Yeats writes, "Man seeks his opposite or the opposite of his condition," and that statement surely applies to Yeats's own poetry. In seeking to create a poetry that is as "cold and passionate as the dawn," Yeats resembles the Shakespeare that Yeats portrayed as a "man whose actual personality seemed faint and passionless," but who nevertheless created "through Mask and Image . . . the most passionate art that exists." The most passionate realizations of

Yeats's own alterself in his poetry, nevertheless, are to be found in the figures of Maud Gonne, the woman he loved for most of his life, and the fictive Crazy Jane. Both of these women are depicted as passionate in the extreme: Maud is compared to Helen of Troy—"What could have made her peaceful with a mind / That nobleness made simple as a fire. . . . Was there another Troy for her to burn?"—and Crazy Jane is epitomized in the line, "Love is like the lion's tooth." In portraying these women, Yeats extends his own identity, through his opposite into a larger androgynous Self that can be realized through his art. Yeats's art embodies a bisexuality that releases a passion beyond his own limited character. Only his poetry can accomplish a fusion of bodily passion with willful control, and this is what Yeats means when he speaks of "passion and precision" being one.

In "Lapis Lazuli" precision is lacking in the "hysterical women," who do not understand that control is the essential gift of art and who, therefore, "are sick of the palette and fiddle-bow."

> I have heard that hysterical women say
> They are sick of the palette and fiddle-bow,
> Of poets that are always gay,
> For everybody knows or else should know
> That if nothing drastic is done
> Aeroplane and Zeppelin will come out,
> Pitch like King Billy bomb-balls in
> Until the town lie beaten flat.
>
> All perform their tragic play,
> There struts Hamlet, there is Lear,
> That's Ophelia, that Cordelia;
> Yet they, should the last scene be there,
> The great stage curtain about to drop,
> If worthy their prominent part in the play,
> Do not break up their lines to weep.
> They know that Hamlet and Lear are gay;
> Gaiety transfiguring all that dread.
> All men have aimed at, found and lost;
> Black out; Heaven blazing into the head:

Tragedy wrought to its uttermost.
Though Hamlet rambles and Lear rages,
And all the drop-scenes drop at once
Upon a hundred thousand stages,
It cannot grow by an inch or an ounce.

On their own feet they came, or on shipboard,
Camel-back, horse-back, ass-back, mule-back,
Old civilisations put to the sword.
Then they and their wisdom went to rack:
No handiwork of Callimachus,
Who handled marble as if it were bronze,
Made draperies that seemed to rise
When sea-wind swept the corner, stands;
His long lamp-chimney shaped like the stem
Of a slender palm, stood but a day;
All things fall and are built again,
And those that build them again are gay.

Two Chinamen, behind them a third,
Are carved in lapis lazuli,
Over them flies a long-legged bird,
A symbol of longevity;
The third, doubtless a serving-man,
Carries a musical instrument.

Every discoloration of the stone,
Every accidental crack or dent,
Seems a water-course or an avalanche,
Or lofty slope where it still snows
Though doubtless plum or cherry-branch
Sweetens the little half-way house
Those Chinamen climb towards, and I
Delight to imagine them seated there;
There, on the mountain and the sky,
On all the tragic scene they stare.
One asks for mournful melodies;
Accomplished fingers begin to play.
Their eyes mid many wrinkles, their eyes,
Their ancient, glittering eyes, are gay.

Lacking control, the passion of these hysterical women is without a proper goal, their emotion is self-defeating, they are indeed sick, as they themselves unintentionally acknowledge. The alternative to these women will be seen later in the poem in the image of the actresses who play Ophelia and Cordelia and who "Do not break up their lines to weep." Control is to be found in the representation of Ophelia and Cordelia through the art of the actresses who play them. No true actress may impose her own personal sorrow on the lines given her to speak by the playwright. Furthermore, the actresses who play Ophelia and Cordelia know that the actors who play Hamlet and Lear "are gay," because, as professional actors who have mastered their personal emotions, they, too, will not break up their lines to weep.

Unlike the hysterical women who do not regard themselves as players in a vast historical drama of many scenes in the rise and fall of civilizations but rather as the victims of their own historical moment, actress and actor may possess a double perspective. They may see themselves through the eyes of the characters they play as if they were those characters, and they may see themselves as if they were the spectators of that play. The "dread" of violence that men and women feel when facing the destruction of their own civilization and immediate bodily harm may be transfigured into gaiety, Yeats's speaker asserts, if one can see one's life as if separated from it. Then it is possible to feel the thrill of aesthetic exaltation, just as one does when watching Shakespeare's *Hamlet* or *Lear*, even though what is being seen is the tragedy of one's own life. As Yeats made explicit in his essay "The Cutting of an Agate": "Later on, [a man] can see himself as but a part of the spectacle of the world and mix into all he sees that flavor of extravagance, or of humour, or of philosophy, that makes one understand that he contemplates even his own death as if it were another's."

The transfiguration of personal "dread" into impersonal "gaiety" is what, according to Yeats's speaker, "All men have aimed at," and this radical shift of perspective occurs in a moment in which everything is "found and lost." This moment in which the personal self is annihilated so that the mind "Black[s] out" is also the moment of ultimate revelation in which "Heaven blaze[s] into the head." In all stages (in both senses of the word) of human history, whenever a life or an era is coming to an end, "And all the drop-scenes drop at once / Upon a hundred thousand stages," the tragedy of human life reaches its "uttermost intensity" and "cannot grow by an inch or an ounce." For Yeats, then, a shift takes place from the contemplation of death as afterlife to the moment of death. This moment of intensity at the threshold of death becomes a model for Yeats against which to measure all life so that passion itself becomes the goal of experience. As Yeats had said in "A General Introduction for My Work," quoting Lady Gregory's ideal for theatrical art, "Tragedy must be a joy to the man who dies." All civilizations are "put to the sword," and time destroys everything human beings build as when "sea-wind swept the corner"; yet for the spectators who do not mourn their own deaths because they see creation and destruction as inseparable, "All things fall and are built again, / And those that build them are gay."

The "I" that speaks at the opening of "Lapis Lazuli" is Yeats's personal self, located in Ireland, surrounded by "hysterical women," himself in danger of being drawn into a fashionable despair that sees all issues in political terms. The "I" does not appear again until halfway through the last stanza of the poem, and then the reassertion of the self takes place as a projective act of the imagination when the speaker depicts the Chinamen *beyond* the point where they are carved on the lapis lazuli. From the text of the poem, all the reader sees is "Two Chinamen," a third Chinaman behind them who "Carries a musical instrument," a "half-way house" on the side of a mountain toward which the Chinamen are climbing, and the cracks and dents on the stone that are the accidents of eroding time, not part of the design of the original artist. The culmination of Yeats's poem derives from what the poem's transfigured speaker envisions on the stone as his imagination superimposes further details on what is literally there.

"Discoloration," "crack," and "dent"—markings on the stone without artistic intent—are converted by the speaker's speculating imagination into images that might belong to the depicted mountain scene. Still tentative for a moment in the act of seeing an image where one seems to be, the speaker hypothesizes the mind's visual options: "a water-course or an avalanche, / Or lofty slope where it still snows," but immediately the *seeming* of imaginative sight passes over into certainty as the scene is fleshed out and composed in the speaker's mind: "though doubtless plum or cherry-branch / Sweetens the little half-way house / Those Chinamen climb towards." Now, beyond doubting the veracity of his vision, the speaker returns in the poem from the passive "I have heard" at the opening, reappearing as an emphatic "I." The pronoun declaring his own self is stressed as it appears at the end of the line immediately after a caesura, and is given additional stress by the enjambment that breaks the phrase connecting pronoun and verb: "I / Delight."

No longer merely a listener, the speaker performs a further act of imagination in the full delight of exercising the emergence of his visionary power: "and I / Delight to imagine them seated there; / There, on the mountain and the sky." Again the speaker extends the scene he observes on the stone by picturing the Chinamen as having moved past the half-way house to the top of the mountain where it meets the sky —where life and death meet. The reimagined scene has become so certain to him that he virtually can point to it, "*There*, on the mountain and the sky," and we, as readers, now realize that the mood of hysteria has been transfigured into gaiety in the speaker himself as he becomes spectator to the scene that he has in part created.

The speaker has both gained his identity as spectator and lost himself in the imaginative projection of himself into two Chinamen who themselves remain significantly undifferentiated. So, too, are sexual differences obliterated in the androgynous condition of old age and the collective wisdom of the Chinamen. Having reached the top, the limit of imaginative thought, the Chinamen do not claim that they have earned the right to die as the Man in "The Man and the Echo" had anticipated: with "all work done, [he] dismisses all / Out of intellect and sight / And sinks at last into the night."

Rather, they turn back to survey the "tragic scene" (like the "frog-spawn of a blind man's ditch") out of which they have climbed. The speaker participates fully in the gesture of the Chinamen's mental return, just as the Self in "Dialogue of Self and Soul" had fixed upon "Sato's ancient blade" as his oriental emblem representing his choice to turn back to life despite its tragedy. In this image of the Chinamen's visionary return to the scene of dying civilizations, Yeats finally comes as close as he ever will to resolving the essential split within him—the split between his wish for immortality and peace and the wish to accept the life of the limited body. What the Chinamen stare upon and see, in effect, is the fall of Ireland along with the rest of Western civilization which, of course, includes Yeats's historical "I" as well. But in bearing witness to this "last scene" as the "great stage curtain" comes down, Yeats, in the projected figure of himself as the collective "Chinamen," survives as spectator to his own death in the heightened moment of visionary intensity.

Such a moment of imagination, for Yeats, is the proper ambition for art itself, and thus it is appropriate that the Chinamen's culminating moment of vision be accompanied by music. The artist, as "serving-man" (in the enlarged sense of that phrase), begins to play the requested "mournful melodies," so that the speaker's healed split between weeping and gaiety is reflected in the unity between the artistic expression of mournful sorrow and artistic beauty itself in the form of melody. Yeats once commented: "In Greece the tragic chorus danced." The passion of the resolved antinomy between tragedy and comedy, or, more generally, between sorrow and joy, only can be achieved through artistic impersonality and control, and so Yeats emphasizes the "accomplished fingers" of the musician whose playing attends the scene. Again, Yeats shows us that passion and precision must be one. In the "glittering eyes" of the Chinamen, through which the speaker now sees, all history becomes story—a divine play created by God as if for his own entertainment. It is a play that Man must teach himself to enjoy. Seen as a spectacle, both nature and history may be experienced as redeemed by art, just as spectators in the audience enjoy the suffering they see on the stage if it is well performed. The essence of such watching, for the spectator, is laughter, even when bearing witness to his or her own life and death.

For Yeats, there is a time to help relieve suffering and a time to watch in awed detachment. The historical part given one to play invites action on the moral assumption that one is free to change the course of events. But the self as spectator sees the unfolding of time as a necessity—the play of history already has been composed by God and must be acted out— and thus he watches it in the mood of aesthetic contemplation. The passion of action in love or war is wrought to its ecstatic uttermost in the passion of the observing artist who, though lover and soldier at heart, watches all from his mountain peak as if he himself were the God of creation, saying to himself that his creation is good.

V

The motif of artistic laughter, and the linking of such laughter to ecstatic detachment, runs throughout Yeats's poetry, though it becomes most prominent in his later work. In "Upon A House Shaken By the Land Agitation," for example, Yeats compares the values of social reform for the general welfare with the value of protecting aristocratic privilege, because such privilege, as Yeats sees it, provides the leisure that enables art to flourish. Yeats makes the plea that from the house of art come the "gifts that govern men," since the house—Yeats's symbol for tradition—sustains through memory what is most noble in the human spirit, "the sweet laughing eagle thoughts that grow / Where wings have memory of wings." The gift of art—which Yeats believes enriches all society and creates the myths that give a culture its identity—is evoked at the poem's conclusion as "gradual time's last gift, a written speech / Wrought of high laughter, loveliness and ease." Just as sublime laughter is the final gift of art in this early poem, so, too, does the Self's triumph over despair and the temptation to die in "A Dialogue of Self and Soul" result in ecstatic laughter: "We must laugh and we must sing." Such laughter, however, must not be understood

merely as humor (it is not dismissive), but also as the manifestation of a spiritual strength capable of overcoming the
dread of death. Yeats said in his essay "Poetry and Tradition":

> the free mind permits itself aught but brief sorrow. That
> we may be free from all the rest, sullen anger, solemn vir-
> tue, calculating anxiety, gloomy suspicion, prevaricat-
> ing hope, we should be reborn in gaiety. . . . for pure joy
> masters and impregnates; and so to world end, strength
> shall laugh and wisdom mourn.

The many allusions to and invocations of laughter in
Yeats's last poems make essentially the same point and have
the same effect: like George Bernard Shaw's metaphysical
stage direction, "Universal laughter," which concludes his
play *Man and Superman*, Yeats's laughter carries with it the
sense of a final judgment. In "News for the Delphic Oracle,"
for example, "The ecstatic waters laugh" as they watch the
"ancestral patterns" of sexual desire being enacted again and
again throughout time. The waters bear witness to the spectacle of human beings who, like animals or gods, "Copulate
in the foam," as if the waters were the voice of a chorus in
a tragic drama. In a similar image in "High Talk," Yeats
depicts the sea again in the metaphor of "great sea-horses,"
and he concludes his poem with the rousing assertion that
"Those great sea-horses bare their teeth and laugh at the
dawn." Finally, in "Under Ben Bulben," the poem Yeats
wrote to conclude his life's work and compose his own epitaph—"Cast a cold eye / On life, on death. / Horseman, pass
by!"—Yeats describes the ecstatic moment, as spectator, to
which his work ultimately has led him:

> Something drops from eyes long blind,
> He completes his partial mind,
> For an instant stands at ease,
> Laughs aloud, his heart at peace.

The most sublime moment that typifies Yeats's transcendence of his personal self into that of an impersonal spectator is not that extreme instant when things "thought too
long can be no longer thought," but the moment of laughter
that turns him back to his involvement with life and the

living. Such a moment can be found in Yeats's ballad, "John Kinsella's Lament for Mrs. Mary Moore":

> A bloody and a sudden end,
>   Gunshot or a noose,
> For Death who takes what man would keep,
>   Leaves what man would lose.
> He might have had my sister,
>   My cousins by the score,
> But nothing satisfied the fool
>   But my dear Mary Moore,
> None other knows what pleasures man
>   At table or in bed.
> *What shall I do for pretty girls*
>   *Now my old bawd is dead?*
>
> Though stiff to strike a bargain,
>   Like an old Jew man,
> Her bargain struck we laughed and talked
>   And emptied many a can;
> And O! but she had stories,
>   Though not for the priest's ear,
> To keep the soul of man alive,
>   Banish age and care,
> And being old she put a skin
>   On everything she said.
> *What shall I do for pretty girls*
>   *Now my old bawd is dead?*
>
> The priests have got a book that says
>   But for Adam's sin
> Eden's Garden would be there
>   And I there within.
> No expectation fails there,
>   No pleasing habit ends,
> No man grows old, no girl grows cold,
>   But friends walk by friends.
> Who quarrels over halfpennies
>   That plucks the trees for bread?
> *What shall I do for pretty girls*
>   *Now my old bawd is dead?*

Speaking in the persona of John Kinsella, Yeats invents Kinsella's memory of his "old bawd," Mary Moore, who had provided him with what "pleasures man / At table or in bed,'' and, shockingly, he depicts Mary Moore as if she were Jehovah, the God of creation. Like the Chinamen, Mary's identity encompasses the duality of the sexes, and, like the Old Testament God, she is willing to make bargains—a comic version of God's willingness to enter into a covenant with man: "Though stiff to strike a bargain, / Like an old Jew man, / Her bargain struck we laughed and talked / And emptied many a can." This bargain-covenant is contracted in the spirit of laughter, and it releases the artist's power to see and represent the world as a story to be told, so that John Kinsella exclaims in a moment of revelation:

> And O! but she had stories,
>   Though not for the priest's ear,
> To keep the soul of man alive,
>   Banish age and care,
> And being old she put a skin
>   On everything she said.

Like Adam and Eve, John Kinsella and Mary Moore have been banished from "Eden's Garden," but in their laughter and storytelling they are able, in spirit, to reverse the consequences of their banishment; they are able to "Banish age and care." The soul need not depart from the body to achieve its own life and freedom, since Mary Moore's profane stories have the power "to keep the soul of man alive," and in doing so, her gift of narration reincarnates her life out of her dying: "And being old she put a skin / On everything she said." Her speech functions to restore spirit in the form of bodily "skin." Turning back to life at the threshold where life and death meet—as on the Chinamen's mountain top or on the "crumbling battlement" where Soul and Self have their dialogue— John Kinsella and Mary Moore become laughing spectators to the story of life as if (to use King Lear's phrase) they were "God's spies." Free for a visionary moment from their own individual fates, they look upon "all the tragic scene" in the spirit of Blake's "eternity is in love with the productions of

time" or of Yeats's similar words as spoken by his visionary
fool, Tom, who declares: "The stallion Eternity / Mounted
the mare of Time, / 'Gat the foal of the world."

The laughter of the spectator in passionate detachment—
"We that look on but laugh in tragic joy"—enters back into
the world as man's narration of his limited self. By means of
such narration the artist acknowledges the debt of mortality
he owes to nature and to God; yet he also survives himself as
if he has entered the mind of God who watches the story of
his creation unfold in the medium of historical time. "The
world only exists to be a tale in the ears of coming generations," Yeats said, and, in the context of historical time,
Yeats's own death and the agony of modern Ireland—as Yeats
came to perceive in gaiety—are but a blink of the eye or
another drop of the "great stage curtain" to mark the end of
a scene.

NINE

Frost's Enigmatical Reserve: The Poet

as Teacher and Preacher

❦

IN DESCRIBING one of his own poems, Robert Frost
says that it has the "proper enigmatical reserve." Frost
believed that the surface of a poem, like speech, should
be simple and immediate, yet that, upon further scrutiny, the poem should reveal itself as elusive. After all, life
does not readily yield up its meaning and purpose—indeed, if
it has any. The poet must be accurate in describing his limited sense of the mysteries of nature and of God, and he must
be true to his own "confusion"—to use one of Frost's favorite words. What the poem contains is not merely private
knowledge but the poet's own uncertainty, and the order the
poem imposes on this uncertainty functions to dramatize,
not simplify or dismiss, what it is that puzzles him. Frost
said, "I don't like obscurity or obfuscation, but I do like dark
sayings I must leave the clearing of to time." If Frost as poet is
also to be thought of as teacher and preacher, then we, as
readers, must regard his poems as if they are parables. His
poems speak most profoundly when they speak by indirec-
tion; they are indeed "dark sayings," engagingly "enigmati-

174

cal," and the best of them maintain Frost's characteristic "reserve."

The dark qualities of a Frost poem, however, do not neces- sarily determine that the poem will be without humor. There is often an element of playfulness even in Frost's most se- rious poems. The play of the poem—the poet's power to create a design—is what Frost summons to contend with darkness and confusion. He takes delight in the resistance to uncertainty and disorder that humor can provide. About "The Road Not Taken," Frost said, "it's a tricky poem, very tricky." Frost had his own games to play with the game life demanded that he play:

> Forgive, O Lord, my little jokes on Thee
> And I'll forgive Thy great big one on me.

Frost's poems, then, are "tricky" out of a mischievous sense of delight in the intricacies of tone and image that a poem can organize, and "tricky," too, in that they themselves resemble the dangerous paths toward possible forgiveness and salva- tion that people must choose to follow in the course of their days. The image of the road appears in many poems, but it is always uncertain as to what revelation the road leads to, even when the destination or place is as specific as the "frozen wood" in "The Wood Pile" or the old couple's new home in "In the Home Stretch."

Frost begins "The Oven Bird" with a playful and strategic lie: "There is a singer everyone has heard," he says. A reader, unaccustomed to Frostian trickery, will simply accept this line for what it states, but Frost knows perfectly well that not every reader has heard the call of an oven bird. And certainly no one has heard an oven bird that says "leaves are old" or "the early petal-fall is past" as he does in this poem:

> There is a singer everyone has heard,
> Loud, a mid-summer and a mid-wood bird,
> Who makes the solid tree trunks sound again.
> He says that leaves are old and that for flowers
> Mid-summer is to spring as one to ten.
> He says the early petal-fall is past

When pear and cherry bloom went down in showers
On sunny days a moment overcast;
And comes that other fall we name the fall.
He says the highway dust is over all.
The bird would cease and be as other birds
But that he knows in singing not to sing.
The question that he frames in all but words
Is what to make of a diminished thing.

Frost is playing a game with the reader's credulity, for the
question of what we can believe on the basis of the little that
we know is precisely the problem Frost is exploring here.
What Frost is leading the reader toward is the contemplation
of the design of the poem itself. Although the literal sound
the bird makes is described merely as "loud" and is, in this
sense, distracting, Frost invites the reader with him to
"make" of this sound some speech that is humanly useful.
Nature only speaks when man makes it speak. What man believes, beyond what he hears and sees, is necessarily of his
own invention.

The oven bird's milieu is "mid-summer" and "mid-
wood," yet the bird speaks of the "highway dust." Both man
and bird, as it were, are midway in the journey of their lives,
and though this road inevitably leads to dust and death, what
matters most is the kind of song that man freely chooses to
sing along the way. As Emerson says, "In popular experience
everything good is on the highway." (Frost commented about
Emerson, "I owe more to Emerson than anyone else for troubled thoughts about freedom.") The poet, lying his way hope-
fully toward the truth, tells us the bird "makes the solid tree
trunks sound again." This new sound becomes the sound of
the poet's voice incorporating and extending the literal call of
the oven bird, just as Frost describes Eve in the garden of Eden
listening to birds: she "added to their own an oversound."
This addition is the result of human making, the invention of
metaphor. Metaphor is fabrication, a lie the poet builds in the
name of the truth, and thus it contains the reality of what the
poet adds to what is there. Yet this making, enigmatic and
uncertain, remains the only source of human belief. Such

making is what Frost calls "real art . . . believing the thing into existence, saying as you go more than you even hoped you were going to be able to say."

The season of fall is linked in "The Oven Bird" with the fall from the garden of Eden by the poetic act of naming: "And comes that other fall we name the fall." The poet has merged his voice with the oven bird, as Adam, in the book of Genesis, names the animals. So, too, the linking of literal meanings, speech, with poetic meanings, song, accomplishes the design by which the total poem exists in its own form and its own right. It is both sung prose and spoken song that enables Frost—as an oven bird—to know "in singing not to sing," for as speech can become song, and song can incorporate speech (as it does in this poem), so, too, can fact become metaphor, and metaphor, fact. These are the linkings that constitute poetic truth.

Belief for Frost is always grounded in the questions out of which belief emerges. As the maker of belief, this is what Frost teaches and what the poet proclaims is the virtual effect of the bird's song, which in reality is Frost's poem: "The question that he [both Frost and the oven bird] frames in all but words." The question is framed, just as the form of the sonnet constitutes a structural frame, and thus the question *implies* more than the words themselves can literally ask. The question embodies the *feeling* of the enigma of what man can make of himself and of his world: "Remember that the sentence sound often says more than the words," Frost once asserted. It is only because (like the bird's song) the poem is framed, because it is a made thing, that the question it asks, and the answer of belief that it implies, can remain dynamically in tension. The poem remains open to the reader's own scrutiny. Such is the style of Frostian teaching.

The question asked by the oven bird is "what to make of a diminished thing." It comes at the end of the poem and thus it throws us back to the beginning, so that the poem makes a kind of circle. But the question, though specific enough, is also enigmatic: What "diminished thing"? Summer is a diminishing from spring, as the oven bird says, "as one to ten." Fall is a diminishing from summer. The fall from the garden of Eden is a mythical diminishing. Death, the highway "dust," is the diminishment of life. (What can one make of death?) The poem is a diminishing of the oven bird's loud call and its *possible* meanings. (All poetic form is made by choice and selection and is thus a diminishing of nature's plenitude.) Aging on the highway, Frost, too, is a diminishing thing. The poem itself, however, is the poet's only answer to these questions, for it is, indeed, what the poet has made. It is an order, a design, to set against uncertainty, to set against "the fall" and against death. As Frost consoled, "When in doubt there is always form for us to go on with." And thus the reader is left with the enigma of what to make of the poem, a thing "diminished" into shape from the chaos of life. Frost offers us a man-made form, and it is for us to be strengthened by it as such, to find in its own framed coherence what Frost himself believed to be there, "a momentary stay against confusion." And those readers who actually have heard the call of an oven bird (or have looked it up in Roger Tory Peterson's *A Field Guide to the Birds*) will know that what the oven bird says is: "Teacher! Teacher!"

I I

If the role of the poet-teacher is to make nature speak with a human voice, the role of the poet-preacher is to dramatize for the reader the mystery of divinity in the face of which belief must be given shape. In this role, too, one finds the characteristic Frostian reserve:

> There may be little or much beyond the grave,
> But the strong are saying nothing until they see.

Or, in a lighter mood:

> And I may return
> If dissatisfied
> With what I learn
> From having died.

But Frost must speak—he must bear witness to the enigma

of God in nature and offer his reader the story of that confrontation.

Frost describes a solitary man in his poem, "The Most of
It," who walks out to a "boulder-broken beach," repeatedly it
seems, to wake a voice that would answer his cry.

> He thought he kept the universe alone;
> For all the voice in answer he could wake
> Was but the mocking echo of his own
> From some tree-hidden cliff across the lake.
> Some morning from the boulder-broken beach
> He would cry out on life, that what it wants
> Is not its own love back in copy speech,
> But counter-love, original response.
> And nothing ever came of what he cried
> Unless it was the embodiment that crashed
> In the cliff's talus on the other side,
> And then in the far distant water splashed,
> But after a time allowed for it to swim,
> Instead of proving human when it neared
> And someone else additional to him,
> As a great buck it powerfully appeared,
> Pushing the crumpled water up ahead,
> And landed pouring like a waterfall,
> And stumbled through the rocks with horny tread,
> And forced the underbrush—and that was all.

The solitary man in the poem cries out as if to a god, unheed-
ing or asleep, who might respond to his call if properly sum-
moned. In his naïve wish, he is like the boy of Winander in
Wordsworth's *Prelude*, who "both hands / Pressed closely
palm to palm," as if in unconscious prayer, "Blew mimic
hootings to the silent owls, / That they might answer him."
But, unlike Frost's man, Wordsworth's boy does receive a certain answer, and he does hear a voice speaking in the silence.
The owls "shout again / Responsive to his call." What Frost's
man receives is merely the "mocking echo of his own" voice,
and so the narrator tells us "He thought he kept the universe
alone." The man is literally alone, and alone in the deeper
sense that he is without a god who is the keeper, the protec-

tor, of the universe. A man may keep promises, but the universe is more than a man alone can keep or protect, more than he can keep watch over.

What the man cries out for, like Adam before the creation of Eve, is "counter-love, original response." He wishes for God's love, counter to man's need, and God's original creative presence. Without God, man's world is only a "boulder-broken beach," and man's voice calling out "on life" is a mockery of man's deepest desires. The narrator tells us that

> . . . nothing ever came of what he cried
> Unless it was the embodiment that crashed
> In the cliff's talus. . . .

The whole mystery of this poem hangs on the open word "unless," on what the man (and the reader) makes of that crashing embodiment. The poem's enigma is whether to regard that embodiment as a kind of incarnation or revelation, or merely as a physical phenomenon that has occurred "some morning" by chance. If it is seen as an incarnation of God's design, then it is, indeed, the "most of it," the most the man can wish for: it is revelation. If it is merely a physical event and not God's "voice in answer," it must be seen as the limiting "most" man can receive from nature. The design of nature, then, would be no more than the design of nature alien to man.

The narrator describes the effect of the crashing embodiment literally, yet the impression the reader receives is uncertain and mysterious. There is a series of echoes. First, we hear the crash of loosening and tumbling stone. Then we hear the boulders splashing in the water. But what follows is a strange gap after which the boulders in the water *seem* to turn into a "great buck." The narrator says that this happens "after a time," as if it might be evolutionary time, as if the man has witnessed divine causality unfolding in a visionary instant. The narrator's difficult syntax suggests that it was the embodiment that allowed this transformation to take place. But even as the buck appears, it does not fulfill the man's expectation or hope. The buck is not seen as "original response," as "someone else additional to him." Like Adam

naming the animals before the creation of Eve, the man
senses that something is still missing in his world that has
not yet been revealed. Described by the increasingly elusive
word "it," the buck is not regarded as the "most of it," although its natural power, like that of a waterfall, is awesome.
The question still remains: Has the man witnessed more
than a display of natural power?

What are the man, the narrator, the reader, to believe? The
buck, with bountiful energy, "Pushing the crumpled water
up ahead," seems to know what it is doing there, to have direction. But is this nature's random energy and force that
"stumbled through the rocks," or is there the suggestion of
a design that is to be read symbolically, as if life is to be seen
here emerging from chaos and inorganic matter, pushing,
landing, stumbling, forcing? The way the buck "forced the
underbrush" resembles the way the image of the buck enters
the mind of the man who is watching. That a powerful image
is perceived is certain, but what can the mind make of that
image, uniting rational thought with subconscious implications? It is as if the buck gets born in the mind of its perceiver.
The narrator draws no conclusions, makes no assertions, and
says flatly "that was all." Just as the title of the poem is firmly
ambiguous in that "most" might mean everything the man
hopes for, revelation, or merely the limit of what nature offers, so, too, is the last word, "all," ambiguous in the same
way. Another voice echo occurs, "all" becomes an echo of
"most." The phrase "that was all," therefore, with Frostian
tonal irony, may imply disappointment, in that the man,
hoping for a "voice in answer," sees only a buck, or "that was
all" may suggest the man's jubilation in witnessing a gesture
of divine revelation—all, everything. The buck, though not
what the man expected, may be regarded as an embodiment
of God's presence in nature—an embodiment that at least for
Adam led to the creation of Eve. The poem keeps these alternative possibilities clearly and absolutely in balance. The
readers, like the man in the poem, are left to believe, if they
will, one or the other, or perhaps, more accurately, they are
left, knowing the extremes of possibility—belief or disbelief—unable to choose, confirmed only in their uncertainty.

III

Can one become "whole again beyond confusion"? We see
Frost again and again in his poems walking out into the darkness or venturing into an equivalent interior darkness, "To
scare myself with my own desert places." Frost's intellectual
heroism is his refusal to avoid such confrontation or to escape
into comforting dogma. In his sonnet "Acquainted with the
Night," written in Dantean terza rima, Frost is in his own circle of hell, locked into an obsessive "I" of self-consciousness:

> I have been one acquainted with the night.
> I have walked out in rain—and back in rain.
> I have outwalked the furthest city light.
>
> I have looked down the saddest city lane.
> I have passed by the watchman on his beat
> And dropped my eyes, unwilling to explain.
>
> I have stood still and stopped the sound of feet
> When far away an interrupted cry
> Came over houses from another street,
>
> But not to call me back or say good-by;
> And further still at an unearthly height
> One luminary clock against the sky
>
> Proclaimed the time was neither wrong nor right.
> I have been one acquainted with the night.

The poem returns at the end to the line with which it begins,
for there seems to be no way out of this circle. The speaker's
movements outward in body and inward in thought both lead
to the same darkness, the same "night." The "city light," and
later the moon, the "luminary clock," paradoxically illumi-
nate only this essential darkness, this absence of meaningful
self-identity. We see the isolated speaker as if he were trying
to walk beyond life itself to confront death, the ultimate isolation. In doing so, he detaches himself from the sorrow of
human affairs as he looks back at the "saddest city lane," and
feels a pang of guilt as he passes "the watchman on his beat"
for the extreme alienation he has perversely chosen. And so
he drops his eyes, "unwilling to explain," even if he could, for

he knows that the watchman is there to guard human lives and protect against the darkness, while he has elected to submerge himself in it.

How much death, how much isolation, can one experience and still return to tell of it? When the speaker says, "I have stood still and stopped the sound of feet," the reader may feel that the speaker's heart has virtually stopped, or worse, that his spirit has died within his stilled body. That this is indeed spiritual death is suggested by the speaker's reaction to the anonymous "cry" that comes from the city of human suffering: the cry, he feels, has nothing to do with him, it does "not call me back or say good-by." Having "outwalked the furthest city light," the speaker, in his imagination, journeys "further still," even beyond the world, to an "unearthly height," and envisions the moon as a clock. But time, the cosmos itself, is regarded as being without moral content and thus without meaning: it is "neither wrong nor right." To feel this way, in effect, is to be in hell. Such is the dark night that Frost confronts and finds within himself.

But the speaker does return, just as the poem returns to its first line. Close to death as he has come, he has not died and experienced the ultimate isolation, nor has he wrung from death its mystery. He says, having said it before, "I have been one acquainted with the night," and the reader knows that he has been, is, and will continue to be so acquainted. He will go on. He will, for a time, outwalk the death within him. He is "one"—he feels himself to be alone—but such confining isolation is not equal to death itself. He still does not *know* death, for he is merely *"acquainted* with the night." This is what he comes back to tell us. As far as we may journey into darkness, we can never know the final darkness or discover what ultimately it may reveal. All we can know is that we are lost. With this paradoxical knowledge, we may begin our journey again, and if we are "lost enough to find [ourselves]," we will go on trying to assert form—such as the circle this poem strategically makes—where there is darkness.

What every Frostian confrontation with nature teaches is that God's ways and his purpose for men are obscure, and the poet, the preacher, must lead the reader to prayer without denying or sentimentalizing the divine mystery. Frost's courage is to live within the circle of doubt and yet still to try to approach God through prayer. But as he says, "People should be careful how they pray. I've seen about as much harm as good come from prayer. It is highly doubtful if man is equipped for judicious prayer" (Lawrence Thompson, *Robert Frost: The Early Years, 1894–1915* [New York: Holt, Rinehart and Winston, 1966], pp. 673–74). The paradox of "judicious prayer" is that it is not the result of reason, but of belief, and belief, for Frost, is always an invention. Frost, in the voice of God speaking to Job, says in "A Masque of Reason," "There's no connection man can reason out / Between his just deserts and what he gets." Frost must be the inventor of prayer, guiding his reader, in the hope that the human drive toward making form and order corresponds to something like a divine command to do so. And yet human order, the poem, must always acknowledge that in nature itself God's meaning is not to be discerned. The poet-preacher must teach his readers to pray that they be able to pray; he must teach them the absolute humility—that man is not capable of judging his own works or his own worth. If there is a divine mercy, perhaps it is God's response to such humility, or as Frost says in "A Masque of Mercy":

> Our lives laid down in war and peace, may not
> Be found acceptable in Heaven's sight.
> And that they may be is the only prayer
> Worth praying.

I V

In "The Draft Horse," an anonymous couple, like Adam and Eve late in the world's history, are seen on a typically unspecified journey:

> With a lantern that wouldn't burn
> In too frail a buggy we drove
> Behind too heavy a horse
> Through a pitch-dark limitless grove.

And a man came out of the trees
And took our horse by the head
And reaching back to his ribs
Deliberately stabbed him dead.

The ponderous beast went down
With a crack of a broken shaft.
And the night drew through the trees
In one long invidious draft.

The most unquestioning pair
That ever accepted fate
And the least disposed to ascribe
Any more than we had to to hate,

We assumed that the man himself
Or someone he had to obey
Wanted us to get down
And walk the rest of the way.

We do not know whether this couple are leaving home or returning home. They are in "too frail a buggy," suggesting the
frailty of their bodies, and their lantern, suggesting their
reason, sheds no light. It is "pitch dark," nothing can be seen.
The narrative of the poem is enacted in this total darkness, so
that, in effect, everything that takes place is imagined as in
a nightmare vision. The grove through which the couple
move is "limitless." It would seem that there can be no end to
their journey, no destination that might reveal the purpose
and meaning of their travel's effort. The thought of infinitude
is itself a tormenting part of their dilemma. Suddenly, a figure, described blankly as "a man," comes out of the woods
and stabs their horse dead. His action is assumed to be deliberate, but for what intent and purpose, we do not know. Since
the act occurs in absolute darkness, the reader can only assume that the speaker of the poem *assumes* that it is a man. It
might as well be an angel or a devil or the speaker's own
guilty fantasy. And the assumption that this is a deliberate
act is also enigmatic: Has the man done this out of evil, merely to harm, or is there some purpose in the act, since it forces
the couple to dismount and make their way through the dark
entirely by the strength of their own spirits?

Having first been described as "too heavy a horse," the
"beast" goes down "ponderous" with the weight of its own
mortality. Everything weighs finally what death weighs.
Death determines the measure of all things, and the "shaft,"
which seemingly gave the horse direction and purpose, is
broken. If the "little horse" in "Stopping by Woods on a
Snowy Evening" shows an instinct to return home, not to remain in the dangerously enticing woods, the heavy horse in
this poem reveals only that this basic wish may be defeated.
And just as the mysterious man has come "out of the trees,"
so, too, does the night move "through the trees" as if the man
and the night were the same or were directed by the same
force. The night moves in an "invidious draft," enwrapping
and destroying the "draft horse"; their names merge, agent
and victim become one, and all is reduced to a wind. The
work of the draft horse has been completed, but nothing that
the poem's speaker can understand through reason has been
accomplished.

Can anything be made of this apparently meaningless and
random event? The speaker describes himself and his companion as an "unquestioning pair." They are not, however,
unthinking; they seem to know that knowledge has its limits
in this "limitless grove," and, quite simply, they must accept
this. They accept "fate" as a necessity, knowing that their
freedom, if it exists at all, exists only in the attitude they take
toward their fate, and thus the speaker says that they are "the
least disposed to ascribe / Any more than we had to to hate."
In their reluctance to respond to this event as the design of
a malevolent force (a "design of darkness to appall"), they
begin to define their own humanity. They will have to make
something positive from this seemingly rebuking event—
something that derives from their own humanity, though
they will never be certain that they are right to attribute this
generosity to anything other than themselves. They will
have only the fragile certainty of what belief provides. And
yet the believer may speculate that this is precisely what God
wants, precisely what his design demands: that we must
respond to nature, and thus to God, out of our own believing,
not God's revelation. Therein lies our freedom. In this sense,

it is the meaning that we make out of unmeaning that reveals
us in our greatest humanity. God says to Job in "A Masque of
Reason":

> Too long I've owed you this apology
> For the apparently unmeaning sorrow
> You were afflicted with in those old days.
> But it was of the essence of the trial
> You shouldn't understand it at the time.
> It had to seem unmeaning to have meaning.

The ability to make meaning of "apparently unmeaning sorrow" is synonymous with our ability to pray. We must not
pray *for* something; rather, we must *make* something and
hope the trial of that uncertain making will lead to our salva-
tion, if not beyond the grave, at least within the measure of
time.

And so, in "The Draft Horse," the couple make what may
be called a creative *assumption*. They choose to accept the
apparently causeless punishment of fate as having a positive
aspect. They assume that nature and human events must
"obey" the laws of fate and that there is intent behind this
design that must remain obscure to them. The man—that
mysterious agent—no less than themselves, obeys the author
of this design. The grove, the night, the wind, the man, the
journeying couple—all are part of the design. And the only
free act that the couple can perform is to "assume" that there
is meaning in this enigmatical design. The closest Frost
comes to naming God in this poem is when he refers to
"someone [the man] had to obey," yet an unknowable God is
there by implication. What this obscure, controlling force
demands, or so the couple choose to assume, is only that they
"get down / And walk the rest of the way." Why this "someone" wants this, they are not told, and they do not know. Just
as the grove is limitless, so, too, are the possible explanations
for what the couple have experienced and what the reader has
been given to witness. Although reason cannot unravel the
mystery of what is limitless, Frost's parable is rich with implications that he, as poet-preacher, has locked into the poem
with firm intent. The poem itself resists the darkness that it

confronts, both as a man-made order and as an assumption
that the outer darkness, the cosmos, is also an order, and, as
such, may be believed to contain a benevolent intent. This is
the inherent prayer the poem makes and invites the reader to
participate in. And so to this darkness the poet-teacher must
unceasingly turn, for it is the source of all that he is and all
that he may become, as Frost said in his letter to "The
Amherst Student":

> The background [is] hugeness and confusion shading
> away from where we stand into black and utter chaos;
> and against the background any small man-made figure
> of order and concentration. What pleasanter than that it
> should be so? . . . This confusion . . . we like it, we were
> born to it, used to it and have practical reasons for want-
> ing it there. To me any little form I assert upon it is
> velvet, as the saying is, and to be considered for how
> much more it is than nothing. (*Selected Prose of Robert
> Frost* [New York: Collier Books, 1968])

Perhaps, then, the readers themselves may assume that
there is indeed good in the couple's having to "walk the rest
of the way," entirely on their own. They are compelled to
make of "the way" what they can and what they will, just as
the poet has made the finite form of his poem out of unlimited darkness. Where the "way" will lead, the poem does
not tell us, but as Frost says, "The one inalienable right is to
go to destruction in your own way. What's worth living for is
worth dying for." What lies beyond the grave the strong do
not venture to guess at. There may be nothing, and that
enigma remains part of the darkness in which we live. But if
Frost as teacher, preacher, and poet, "acquainted with the
night," is to keep going along the way, and if he is to be true to
the God he believes in but does not know, he must imitate his
enigmatical creator and maintain his own "proper enigmatical reserve" in the making of his poems.

TEN

Stevens's Sufficient Muse

❧

P oetry / Exceeding music must take the place / Of empty heaven and its hymns," says Wallace Stevens in "The Man with the Blue Guitar." Stevens's poetry proceeds from the assumption that there is no God, no paradise beyond death, and that people must relinquish their traditional religious beliefs if they are to find their own mortal humanity sufficient. He hopes, in "Esthétique du Mal," that "the health of the world might be enough." Yet the rejection of religious belief and the subsequent focusing on what one can make of this world within its mortal limits does not remove the problem of belief: What kind of credence can one give, inspired by his or her muse, to one's own created structures—one's ideas, one's poems? If the poet is the maker of "fictions," as both Stevens and Frost contend, what is the nature of the truths that these fictions may contain and celebrate? Stevens formulates this problem paradoxically in his collection of aphorisms, "Adagia," in *Opus Posthumous*: "The final belief is to believe in a fiction, which you know to be a fiction, there being nothing else. The exquisite truth is to know that it is a fiction and that you believe in it willingly." The ability to believe in a created fiction as an "exquisite

truth" is to achieve a renewed innocence, and, in this state of
innocence, ideas—including the idea of innocence itself—
are considered to be as real as anything in the material world.
If trees grow in nature, ideas grow in the human imagination,
and their existence is sufficiently manifest in their verbal expression. What exists fictively in language thus also exists in
nature. The "innocent" poet sees no unbridgeable dichotomy
here, and so Stevens can say in "The Auroras of Autumn":

> There may be always a time of innocence.
> There is never a place. Or if there is no time,
> If it is not a thing of time, nor of place,
>
> Existing in the idea of it alone,
> In the sense against calamity, it is not
> Less real.

Although the made things of the mind—its fictions—are not
rooted in time and place, as material things are, they have
their own certain forms that spring from human need, and if
this need is not met, the result will be psychic "calamity."
Human need is surely real, and the fictions that derive from
that need may be given fulfilling credence as long as they do
not violate what Stevens, in "Credences of Summer," calls
"the limits of reality." Mortality and endless change, seen as
absolutes, are such "limits," and the belief in "Terra Paradise," of which Stevens dreams, must find its credibility
within these limits.

Stevens's muse, whose benevolent power enables Stevens
to give credence to his own created beliefs, to search "a possible for its possibleness," is also a muse who defines and accepts limits, who is true to "things exactly as they are."
Infinite possibility, in this sense, exists within finite possibility. Stevens's muse is the power within him to achieve
tranquillity through giving credence to his own fiction that
life is good because he chooses to see it as good, and, though
death is something he has no choice about, it too may be seen
as good because it is the conclusion of *life*. He can choose his
attitude toward death, as he can toward life, and thus death
can be fictionalized also. The fictionalization of death en-

ables Stevens to see death as good: "Be tranquil in your wounds," Stevens says. Though death is an absolute limit, it still may be regarded as either good or evil. In the absence of God, people may remake themselves out of their need to do so, in the way they fictionalize their world.

In *The Prelude*, Wordsworth speaks of having "a saving intercourse with my true self," and Stevens's poem "Final Soliloquy of the Interior Paramour" may be thought of as such a "saving intercourse":

> Light the first light of evening, as in a room
> In which we rest and, for small reason, think
> The world imagined is the ultimate good.
>
> This is, therefore, the intensest rendezvous.
> It is in that thought that we collect ourselves,
> Out of all the indifferences, into one thing:
>
> Within a single thing, a single shawl
> Wrapped tightly round us, since we are poor, a warmth,
> A light, a power, the miraculous influence.
>
> Here, now, we forget each other and ourselves.
> We feel the obscurity of an order, a whole,
> A knowledge, that which arranged the rendezvous.
>
> Within its vital boundary, in the mind.
> We say God and the imagination are one . . .
> How high that highest candle lights the dark.
>
> Out of this same light, out of the central mind,
> We make a dwelling in the evening air,
> In which being there together is enough.

The Interior Paramour is his muse, speaking within his mind, soothing him as a mother consoles, wrapping the two of them together, as if one, in a "single shawl." Her soliloquy begins as a kind of ceremony in which she instructs the poet to light the candles of his room—which is also his mind—as if he were lighting the "first light," Venus, the evening star. The paramour-muse, in effect, is trying to make him feel restful and at home in his own mind, and out of the reason of need, she fictionalizes that mind-room so that it becomes the "world imagined." She urges him to believe, beyond the proof of reason, that such a world may be *felt* to be the "ultimate good." Stevens expresses this urge to believe as follows: "In an age of disbelief, when the gods have come to an end, when we think of them as the aesthetic projections of a time that has passed, men turn to a fundamental glory of their own and from that create a style of bearing themselves in reality." This inner "fundamental glory" of the Interior Paramour is invoked to light the room as if it also were the outer light from Venus.

The rendezvous in this literal room and in the poet's mind is the rendezvous of the poet's thoughts with his mothering female self, and also the rendezvous of the poet's imaginings with the fact and "boundary" of the room—the real world. The intensity of the rendezvous results from the realization that thought can contain itself as thought, and thus both images of the world and ideas can be brought together. In this spirit of unity, the muse says: "we collect ourselves." This gesture of synthesis and invention is accomplished in the face of the indifference of unhumanized reality, the world merely as it is, and in the face of human indifference as well.

Although poet and muse are "poor" in that reality itself offers them only indifference, they are able to find in their unity of the fictive and the real "a warmth, / A light, a power, the miraculous influence." The influence is miraculous because the poet's imagination has been able to transform the outer world he lives in by investing it with warmth and light and by giving it value. The laws of causality have not been suspended, but the poet, through his muse, has performed a *natural* miracle in creating his own mood of contentment.

In the intense immediacy of this present moment, "here, now," poet and muse "forget each other" as separate entities and forget their collective selves ("ourselves") as well in the sense that knowledge becomes feeling. They become aware of "the obscurity of an order," *as if* nature, by intent, had arranged their rendezvous. Their fictive belief has transformed the quality of the room in the way they have "create[d] a style of bearing themselves in reality." The boundary of the room has become the boundary of their collective mind, yet it is

felt to be a *"vital* boundary," a limit that brings forth ex-
panded life rather than a limit that diminishes their sense of
possibility. At this point, a fictive assertion of belief may
fully be made: "We say God and the imagination are one. . . ."
The traditional belief in a healing and consoling God has been
replaced by a belief, with equal credence, in God as metaphor
for the imagination's miraculous power. Stevens says in his
essay "The Irrational Element in Poetry" that "the poet who
wishes to contemplate the good in the midst of confusion is
like the mystic who wishes to contemplate God in the midst
of evil."

The candle that the muse has instructed her poet-son
to light at the poem's ceremonial opening has become the
candle of his imagination, and now it lights not only the room
and his mind, but the whole night sky: "How high that highest candle lights the dark." This light, which has flared up in
the dark "out of the central mind," the mind that acknowledges its need for solace, is able then to provide that solace. In
meeting this need, the fictive light is thus affirmed as real,
and in this light the poet can make himself at home in the
"dwelling" of his mind, just as Wordsworth, in "Tintern
Abbey," had wished for his sister:

> . . . thy mind
> Shall be a mansion for all lovely forms,
> Thy memory be as a dwelling-place
> For all sweet sounds and harmonies.

The memory of Stevens's mother dwells in his mind in the
form of the muse. His mother, however, has been generalized
and transformed to become his "Interior Paramour," a collective figure for all the women who have loved him, and thus an
image of his own sense of worthiness. If the world, through
fictive belief, can be made interior, then Stevens can indeed
feel his love for the earth as the earth's love for him—all
within his memory and imagination. Although the poet is
literally alone in his room, he has the feeling of "being there
together," and that feeling is so powerful that the sense of
limits and boundaries vanishes. Nothing further is desired
beyond such harmony—it "is enough." Stevens's poem

dramatizes the feeling of being at one with the loved persons
and objects that literally are always outside oneself, yet here
they are made interior, as if speech can become touch. Such
consolation, as many of Stevens's poems show, is not final,
though it evokes the *feeling* of finality. What Stevens has
described in this poem is the momentary *feeling* of consummation which achieves an abatement of desire—desire that
must return.

The muse as earth mother, regarded only as the bringer of
death through inevitable change, is portrayed by Stevens in
"Madame La Fleurie" as a "bearded queen, wicked in her
dead light." This image evokes the desolation Stevens feels
when he acknowledges the collapse of his fictive credences.
The limit of reality, seen as desolation, is "evil death," the
opposite of the imagined "ultimate good." The imagination's
effort is spent, and Stevens must cry out: "And yet what good
were yesterday's devotions? / I affirm and then at midnight
the great cat / Leaps quickly from the fireside and is gone."
The "great cat," Stevens's symbol for the imagination's fictive effulgence—"the auroral creature musing in the mind"
—must necessarily vanish just as Stevens's solacing affirmation must collapse, leaving him to confront again the
midnight darkness. The warmth of the fireside does not suffice when Stevens feels abandoned and alone in his own
mind. Confronting this desolation, the poet must begin again
to make a new affirmation "in the imagination's new beginning, / In the yes of the realist spoken because he must / Say
yes, spoken because under every no / Lay a passion for yes
that had never been broken." The realist, then, is one who
knows that all consolation and affirmation must fail. Yet the
realist knows equally well that the need to create affirmation
out of a "passion for yes" is also a human absolute, and that
the imagination will again flourish its warming fictions.

II

Stevens's poem "Autumn Refrain" begins with a sense of
diminishment and loss. The poet, as literal realist, must describe the desolate scene as it is, mirroring his own mind:

The skreak and skritter of evening gone
And grackles gone and sorrows of the sun,
The sorrows of sun, too, gone . . . the moon and moon,
The yellow moon of words about the nightingale
In measureless measures, not a bird for me
But the name of a bird and the name of a nameless air
I have never—shall never hear. And yet beneath
The stillness of everything gone, and being still,
Being and sitting still, something resides,
Some skreaking and skrittering residuum,
And grates these evasions of the nightingale
Though I have never—shall never hear that bird.
And the stillness is in the key, all of it is,
The stillness is all in the key of that desolate sound.

The poem is set, not in autumn, but at the end of autumn and at the end of evening. The sounds of summer have diminished to a "skreak and skritter," and now even these reduced sounds are gone except that they reside in the poet's memory as a residuum. In fact, he is hearing what is there only as an aftermath, a refrain in his mind. The late grackles are also gone, and so, too, are the sorrows of the season's ending, which reminds him of the continuity of sorrow. The poet cannot refrain from thinking of sorrow; just as the sun must go down, the moon must rise, and the hard *sk* and *g* sounds are counterpointed with soothing *oo* and *ow* sounds. These are sounds of loss and bereavement, and they evoke not only the past season and the completed day, but also the poetic past—Keats's immortal nightingale, and the past of religious belief that held to the idea of an immortal God. The appropriate song of immortality is one of "measureless measures," like that of Keats's nightingale, but the poet is compelled to declare that it is "not a bird for me." His own "measures," his poem, must sing of limits and of annihilation as Stevens made explicit in his essay "Two or Three Ideas":

To see the gods dispelled in mid-air and dissolve like clouds is one of the great human experiences. It is not as if they had gone over the horizon to disappear for a time; nor as if they had been overcome by other gods of greater power and profounder knowledge. It is simply that they came to nothing. . . . It was their annihilation, not ours, and yet it left us feeling in a measure, we, too, had been annihilated. It left us feeling dispossessed and alone in a solitude, like children without parents, in a home that seemed deserted, in which the amical rooms and halls had taken on a look of hardness and emptiness.

The poet cannot deny his nostalgia for the lost belief in "measureless measures," but he must assert that such belief no longer is credible. The "nameless air" of the nightingale is an air he cannot breathe and a musical "air" he cannot sing. There is pain in the acknowledgment that he "shall never hear" immortal song, but that is the ineluctable fact. The "moon of words," his imagination, leads him necessarily back to this fact so that he names the nightingale for the illusion it symbolizes. His imagination's first allegiance must be to the measuring of limits: the poet's primary muse is thus reality itself, and the mortal grackle, not the nightingale, must be his chosen bird. If, by the moon's light, solace is to be found, it must derive from the grackles' ugly sounds.

With the statement of bereavement, "I have never—shall never hear," the poem comes to a heavy pause. Out of this pause, this silence, the poet (and reader) must draw a new breath and begin again to re-create himself as if from nothing, from the "stillness of everything gone." His voice pours forth a powerful "and yet"—a sharp phrase that is counter in its energy to the exhaustion that the poem's long first sentence has exacted. Stevens then shows the progression that "stillness" makes from the essence of absence to an encompassing presence: first, "stillness of everything gone"; second, "being still"; third, "being and sitting still"; fourth, "the stillness is"; finally, "the stillness is all." As these phrases unfold, they take on personification and being, and finally become embodied fully in a musical key.

The silence out of which the second half of the poem emerges is also the silence of memory, the residuum of sounds from the past autumn's "skreaking and skrittering." These sounds reside in his mind where he must again try to make himself at home. From these mere sounds, heard by the mind in silence, he must again compose "an alphabet / By which to spell out holy doom." What saves him from despair is the power of his memory to confront the collapse of the past and, from the ruins, to create a musical form, a refrain, that can console and affirm. Thus the muse of memory and the muse of reality become a single mothering force in the poet's mind, personified by Stevens as "she that in the syllable between life / And death cries quickly, in a flash of voice . . . is the mother of us all."

The voice of memory "beneath / The stillness" speaks in the *gr* sound of the grackles, the bird of reality that has become the poet's source of inspiration, which "grates" in a rough music against the nightingale's "evasions," its failure to accept the ultimate reality of loss and death. Although the note of nostalgia returns as another refrain in the poem, "I have never—shall never hear that bird [the nightingale]," this phrase takes on a musical presence more powerful than what the words literally say. Again the poem comes to a pause and, with another energetic breath, the poet speaks from the stillness—taking stillness as his theme, creating himself anew in the very act of completing his poem. He has found "the key"; it is a musical key, and both he and the stillness come fully alive in the key word of being, the word "is"—"the stillness *is* in the key, all of it *is* / The stillness *is* all." The musical refrains of the poem indeed have emerged from "desolate sound." Paradoxically, the poet has not had to refrain himself; his muse has flourished. Confronting the "negations" of time and death, he has made music out of skreaks and skritters, out of the gutterals of grackles, and though this music, too, at the end of its season, will return to desolate sound and to silence, the poet has won a moment of "ecstatic freedom":

> For the sensitive poet, conscious of negations, nothing is more difficult than the affirmations of nobility and yet there is nothing that he requires of himself more persistently, since in them and in their kind, alone, are to be found those sanctions that are the reasons for his being and for that occasional ecstasy, or ecstatic freedom of the mind, which is his special privilege. (Wallace Stevens, "The Noble Rider and the Sound of Words")

III

If, like "the earliest single light in the evening sky," the poet
"creates a fresh universe out of nothingness by adding [him-
self]," then reality, regarded first as "silence" or "nothingness," must be the source of his need to create. "Nothingness" is the starting point of a "necessary" process, which
can lead to a vision of nature that includes what is humanly
imagined "Within what we permit, / Within the actual."
This awareness of a necessity to be "Born / Again in the sav-
agest severity, / Desiring fiercely," is inherent in Stevens's
poem, "The Plain Sense of Things," where reality is stripped
down to its perceived minimum:

> After the leaves have fallen, we return
> To a plain sense of things. It is as if
> We had come to an end of the imagination,
> Inanimate in an inert savoir.
>
> It is difficult even to choose the adjective
> For this blank cold, this sadness without cause.
> The great structure has become a minor house.
> No turban walks across the lessened floors.
>
> The greenhouse never so badly needed paint.
> The chimney is fifty years old and slants to one side.
> A fantastic effort has failed, a repetition
> In a repetitiousness of men and flies.
>
> Yet the absence of the imagination had
> Itself to be imagined. The great pond,
> The plain sense of it, without reflections, leaves,
> Mud, water like dirty glass, expressing silence
>
> Of a sort, silence of a rat come out to see,
> The great pond and its waste of the lilies, all this
> Had to be imagined as an inevitable knowledge,
> Required, as a necessity requires.

After the mind has negated its own structures of thought,
it confronts a void both in itself and in nature, so Stevens begins his poem, "After the leaves have fallen, we return / To a
plain sense of things." The falling of the leaves, like the nega-

tions of thought, has left the landscape and his mind virtually empty, and the poem's speaker must regard this emptiness to see what he can make of it. Although he seems to have "come to an end of the imagination," this very proposition has the effect of a beginning, a renewal. The speaker cannot regard the plain sense of things plainly; rather, he makes an imaginative hypothesis from the crucial phrase "as if"—a phrase that recurs throughout Stevens's poetry. The speaker feels "Inanimate in an inert savoir," since he has not yet found a use for the knowledge of things as fallen, and yet, his imagination has indeed begun to define this fallen condition.

He says "It is difficult even to choose the adjective / For this blank cold," but the phrase belies its statement: he has, in fact, chosen the adjective "blank." The choice, in a time of diminished energy, which has been described as "difficult," is seen by the reader as having been made, although the still inert speaker has not yet added his own cause—his need for a new structure in the mind—to nature's cyclic pattern of change. Not only has summer come to an end, but also the imagination's fictive creations have become a "minor house" in which the speaker now dwells. It is a house without the exotic flourishing of images or thought: "No turban walks across the lessened floors." The speaker must continue to examine his own desolate mind even as his mind is preparing to gather up new energy to reassert the belief that "poetry is part of the structure of reality."

The "greenhouse" is an effective image to convey the unity of natural growth with human design; it, too, is a structure that requires human care. The greenhouse's need for paint corresponds to man's need to create structures, which is rooted in man's nature. In the image of the slanting chimney we see a structure both enduring and needing to be repaired. The past summer's blossoming and the past structures of the imagination have failed. What was once a "fantastic effort," in the sense that it was a great effort, is now seen as "fantastic" in the sense of fantasy—no longer can it be given credence. The cycle of flourishing and collapse is seen as a mere "repetitiousness of men and flies," as if men have no more cause in the world than flies do. The speaker has not yet been able to make his "savoir" (his knowledge) animate; he has not yet been able to transform repetition into a musical structure that will express his own humanity and thus enhance and redeem the plain sense of things. At this point in the poem, the speaker cannot "think of resemblances and the repetitions of resemblances as a source of the ideal."

As in "Autumn Refrain," the word "Yet" marks a sudden release of energy and a leap of the imagination that had been prepared for earlier by the speaker's tentative "as if." The speaker now realizes that his imagination, seemingly inert, has begun its own recovery by confronting its own failure and its own blankness. The experience of inanimateness and nothingness, nevertheless, is both a necessary and a real experience. One must measure what one is against the void, against "absence," and so the speaker can propose succinctly that "the absence of imagination had / Itself to be imagined." Affirming this necessity, the speaker is then able to look at the "great pond," reality itself, and see it as both "great" and "plain" at the same time. It is great in that it can contain and reflect many things, yet the speaker imagines its plainness, "without reflections," as if it can be seen apart from his own reflecting thoughts. Paradoxically, his mind has added itself to the scene by imagining the scene as existing independently from his mind. In this sense, the scene is not merely silence itself, since, through the mediation of the poet, the scene is capable of "expressing silence." The poet has created a fictive voice so that the silence may speak and articulate man's need for connection with his world.

Seeing begins as plain, ignorant, animal seeing, "of a rat come out to see," yet there is a potent energy in this animal instinct. The wish to confront literal reality is the basis of the need for humanized seeing that results from having looked "with the sight / Of simple seeing, without reflection." Through the eye of a rat, the great pond of reality first is seen as containing only "its waste of the lilies," yet what the poet also sees is the necessity of viewing this waste and transforming it into a structure of acceptance. This is the necessity of the imagination as it confronts the "mud" of the pond, the fallen world. The varied repetition of the phrase "Had to be

imagined" is then no longer experienced as a "repetitiousness of man and flies," but as a musical form that celebrates
a required "inevitable knowledge." Necessity ceases to be a
painful limit, for the knowledge of necessity is not wasted,
and the poet, summoning his muse—the "angel of reality"—
may again seek out the possibilities of the actual, searching a
"possible for its possibleness." As Stevens's "Professor Euca-
lyptus" puts it: "The search / For reality is as momentous
as / The search for God."

The "possibleness" of the actual is inherent in what the
mind can make of what it sees, so Stevens says, "The mind
turns to its own creations and examines them, not alone from
the aesthetic point of view, but for what they reveal, for what
they validate and invalidate, for the support that they give."
In the face of a world that is always vanishing, Stevens's mind
has the power to create its own solace through his musical
fictions. Stevens resembles Wordsworth speaking to Coleridge at the end of *The Prelude* when Wordsworth says, "we
shall still / Find solace—knowing . . . how the mind of man
becomes / A thousand times more beautiful than the earth /
On which he dwells." In this sense the poet as maker must
also be regarded as the poet as guide whose role is to help people live their lives.

I V

Stevens begins his poem "The Woman in Sunshine" with a
tentative simile comparing the "warmth and movement" of
the sun, which his senses perceive, with those same qualities
in an imagined woman:

> It is only that this warmth and movement are like
> The warmth and movement of a woman.
>
> It is not that there is any image in the air
> Nor the beginning nor end of a form:
>
> It is empty. But a woman in threadless gold
> Burns us with brushings of her dress

And a dissociated abundance of being,
More definite for what she is—

Because she is disembodied,
Bearing the odors of the summer fields,

Confessing the taciturn and yet indifferent,
Invisibly clear, the only love.

Stevens's potentially solacing muse, the woman of the mind, is first considered to be "only that," as if she may be easily dismissed as a fantasy. The speaker must acknowledge the fact that there is no "image in the air" and that his sense of a woman's presence has emerged *out* of the air, out of nothing. In the literal sky there is neither "the beginning nor end of a form." There is nothing in nature itself that necessarily leads to the production of a woman's image. The air "is empty." The embodied image emerges only because there is something in the speaker, responding to the sunshine, that requires it, and the woman's form is thus "visible to the eye that needs." The mind's leap from simile to vision is made in the stressed word "but," in which the human need to imprint human desire on the world is enacted: *"But* a woman in threadless gold / Burns us." Her image is not a "sleek ensolacing" because the undeceived speaker knows that she does not exist in nature; rather, she is a necessary creation.

Beholding what is not there, the speaker apprehends the form of the woman delicately between "It is" and "It is not," and yet the form "burns" and illuminates like the sun. As his mind continues to assert itself, the speaker both sees a visible image, the "brushings of her dress," and apprehends the woman as an abstraction—a "dissociated abundance of being." The form of the woman does not exist as a necessary association with the image of the sun, but as an overflow from the speaker's need for abundance, the largesse of his own being. Although the woman does not exist as a physical body, she can be seen through the poet's fiction, both as image and as idea, and thus "More definite for what she is." As a figure created out of the innocence of the poet's need, she is a "pure principle [whose] nature is its end." To apprehend the woman as disembodied is to apprehend the mind's power of embodiment—the power to create a solacing fiction from a sense of absence.

The mind, however, does not create wholly out of nothingness. Though it begins each new cycle of invention by confronting its own blankness and therefore discovers its own need to fill that emptiness, the mind also, through the senses, confronts a physical world. Stevens says, "The greatest poverty is not to live / In a physical world." There is no limit to the possibilities of poetic invention, yet the poet's fictions always must adhere to physical reality. In the poet's "desire for resemblance [the poem] touches the sense of reality, it enhances the sense of reality, heightens it, intensifies it." There *is* a resemblance between the woman and the sun—they both give warmth—which is rooted in physical actuality and which the speaker may extend. So, the woman, though disembodied (since she is a fiction), may be embodied fictively in the poem as the essence of summer fruition, "Bearing the odors of the summer fields."

"Bearing" implies both *making apparent* and *giving birth.* The image of the woman evokes and reveals the memory of summer fragrance in the reader's mind (who may be perusing this poem in winter), and in this sense the odors of summer emerge from the poem itself. Guiding the reader, the poet has turned to his own creation for the "support it gives." Though summer is evoked through sight and smell, the speaker must confess—through his image of the woman—that the sunshine is "taciturn," for it resembles a woman only by virtue of the poet's act of imagination. Still, physical reality remains "indifferent" to the poet's creation. The woman is both there and not there; she is to be seen and not to be seen; she is "Invisibly clear." As the "fiction that results from feeling," she exists as "the only love," the imagination's love for the real which must include the imagination as well. Thus the woman in sunshine becomes an interior paramour, and the tentative "only" of the poem's opening becomes an affirmative "only" at the poem's conclusion.

If it is true, as Stevens says, that "A poet looks at the world as a man looks at a woman," then what he adds to what he sees is *value,* his own feeling of love. That love (in the strictest, physical sense) is not out there in nature, yet it does exist by virtue of the fictions, "the unreal," that the poet propounds from his need for purpose and values: "If the imagination is the faculty by which we import the unreal into what is real, its value is the value of the way of thinking by which we project the idea of God into the idea of man." For Stevens, the "idea of man" must be sufficient to provide meaning and solace through man's own inventions.

In his poem "Note on Moonlight," Stevens again confronts the "mere objectiveness of things." He sees the "various universe" *as if* it had been created so that the poet might humanize it by adding his or her fictions to it. This "as if" assumption, the poet knows, is itself a fiction—yet the power of sight passes over so naturally into the power of fictive envisioning that the poet cannot separate knowledge of the universe's indifference from the imagination's sense of purpose: "the various universe, intended / So much just to be seen—a purpose, empty / Perhaps, absurd perhaps, but at least a purpose." And so the poet composes another musical "note" of certitude that he "know[s] to be a fiction," an absurdity, and he is renewed and given solace by its being "Certain and ever more fresh. Ah! Certain, for sure . . ."

Sure as this note may be, nevertheless it dissolves in the air. The poem, ending with three dots, provides an image of the note's vanishing as the last word, "sure," dwindles away in the reader's ear. The muse of reality both gives and takes away. So, too, the poet, knowing the limits of what is real, must unname the very creations he has given fictive form "until this named thing nameless is / And is destroyed." For the affirming poet, it must be sufficient to know that solace cannot be permanently solacing; he must be able to feel that the desire for the solacing muse—like desire for an actual woman—is not "too difficult to tell from despair." The need to create anew, as a principle of energy and a source of human striving, necessarily leads to defeat, yet defeat quickens the "passion for yes" in the poet's wintry mind. This "inevitable knowledge," this equivocal blessing, Stevens chooses to see as sufficient, and thus he can "forego / Lament." The modern poet, he says, "has to find what will suffice." Stevens's muse teaches him that there is no conclusion to this search, but she knows, too, that the search itself is an ultimate good. Stevens's fictive music is founded on the "rock" of the world whose "barrenness becomes a thousand things," and thus it takes the place of belief in "empty heaven" and enables him to bear himself within the limits of reality as an "adventurer / In humanity."

PART THREE

ELEVEN

Separation and Fatal Desire

❦

I N   H I S   poem "The Aërolite," Thomas Hardy invents ("Or so I dreamed") a little cosmic parable about how consciousness began on earth, and he also surmises how it might end. The uniqueness of human suffering, "the mortal moan / Begot of sentience," is identified with intelligence, specifically the capacity to conceptualize death, and this capacity itself, Hardy asserts, is a form of sickness, which he describes as "this disease / Called sense." In the evolutionary scheme, consciousness seems to be nature's tragic mistake, and with ironically bitter hopefulness, Hardy concludes his poem with the speculation that maybe "Normal unawareness waits rebirth":

> I thought a germ of Consciousness
> Escaped on an aërolite
>   Aions ago
> From some far globe, where no distress
> Had means to mar supreme delight;
>
> But only things abode that made
> The power to feel a gift uncloyed
>   Of gladsome glow,

And life unendingly displayed
Emotions loved, desired, enjoyed

And that this stray, exotic germ
Fell wanderingly upon our sphere,
          After its wingings,
Quickened, and showed to us the worm
That gnaws vitalities native here,

And operated to unblind
Earth's old-established innocence
          Of stains and stingings,
Which grin no griefs while not opined
But cruelly tax intelligence.

"How shall we," then the seers said,
"Oust this awareness, this disease
          Called sense, here sown,
Though good, no doubt, where it was bred,
And wherein all things work to please?"

Others cried: "Nay, we rather would,
Since this untoward gift is sent
          For ends unknown,
Limit its registerings to good,
And hide from it all anguishment."

I left them pondering. This was how
(Or so I dreamed) was waked on earth
          The mortal moan
Begot of sentience. Maybe now
Normal unawareness waits rebirth.

The power of this poem lies in its emotional assertion
through self-tormenting irony that the awareness of death
forever poisons the possibility of human happiness.

Hardy's attempted rejection of thought fails, of course, because even the denial of thought is an act of thought. The profound distress of consciousness is inescapable, as Keats says
in "Ode to a Nightingale," "where but to think is to be full of
sorrow / And leaden-eyed despairs," except through suicide
or illusion. And so Hardy is torn between his need to believe

in the illusion of immortality, which in denying death cures thought of its despair, and his commitment to the Promethean dignity of thought, whose criterion is truthfulness, but which, in acknowledging the finality of death, causes human misery. Thought, therefore, is an inescapable form of duality, separating one both from oneself and from nature. If one thinks and is truthful, one must be unhappy; if one would be happy, one must necessarily lie. Since human beings are trapped, as Hopkins says of himself, "in this tormented mind / With this tormented mind tormenting yet," only that snickering physician, Death, seems to offer a cure for a mind infected with the idea of death.

I I

The paradigmatic model for separation both from the self and from nature is to be found in the poet's idealized image of woman which includes in repressed form the abandoning or forbidden mother. The "wretched wight," for example, in Keats's "La Belle Dame Sans Merci" is described as drained of blood and deathly pale, "With anguish moist and fever dew," from prolonged and frustrated desire, just as in Shakespeare's underlying Sonnet 147 where the speaker declares love to be a disease, "My love is as a fever," and asserts "Desire is death":

> Ah, what can ail thee, wretched wight,
>   Alone and palely loitering;
> The sedge is wither'd from the lake,
>   And no birds sing.
>
> Ah, what can ail thee, wretched wight,
>   So haggard and so woe-begone?
> The squirrel's granary is full,
>   And the harvest's done.
>
> I see a lily on thy brow,
>   With anguish moist and fever dew;
> And on thy cheek a fading rose
>   Fast withereth too.

I met a lady in the meads
　Full beautiful, a fairy's child;
Her hair was long, her foot was light,
　And her eyes were wild.

I set her on my pacing steed,
　And nothing else saw all day long;
For sideways would she lean, and sing
　A fairy's song.

I made a garland for her head,
　And bracelets too, and fragrant zone:
She look'd at me as she did love,
　And made sweet moan.

She found me roots of relish sweet,
　And honey wild, and manna dew;
And sure in language strange she said,
　"I love thee true."

She took me to her elfin grot,
　And there she gaz'd and sighed deep,
And there I shut her wild sad eyes—
　So kiss'd to sleep.

And there we slumber'd on the moss,
　And there I dream'd, ah woe betide,
The latest dream I ever dream'd
　On the cold hill side.

I saw pale kings, and princes too,
　Pale warriors, death-pale were they all;
Who cry'd—"La belle Dame sans mercy
　Hath thee in thrall!"

I saw their starv'd lips in the gloom
　With horrid warning gaped wide,
And I awoke, and found me here
　On the cold hill side.

And this is why I sojourn here
　Alone and palely loitering,
Though the sedge is wither'd from the lake,
　And no birds sing.

The story that Keats's speaker tells the "wretched wight," his doppelgänger, describes his apparent seduction of a "lady in the meads." The lady appears innocently at first as a "fairy's child," though the emphasis on her bodily parts, her hair, her foot, and her eyes, already is charged with implications of sexual invitation. The account of this meeting with the lady and their journey on horseback to her "elfin grot" is presented structurally as a dream within a dream, and the imagery is replete with sexual symbolism: riding together on his "pacing steed" suggests intercourse, and dressing her ("I made a garland for her head, / And bracelets too"), through dream reversal, implies its opposite, as in "The Eve of St. Agnes" where the lady is spied upon undressing: "Of all its wreathed pearls her hair she frees; / Unclasps her warmed jewels one by one; / Loosens her fragrant bodice by degrees / Her rich attire creeps rustling to her knees." Like La Belle Dame, the lady in "St. Agnes" also utters an enticing moan.

The love banquet that La Belle Dame serves the speaker is the food of paradise, "honey wild, and manna dew," and thus eating and sexual intercourse become inseparable images. Here the "language strange" of love is that of the body seemingly uncorrupted by thought. As the love journey progresses, the speaker becomes less in control; La Belle Dame seizes the initiative—"She took me to her elfin grot"—as she leads him into the genital landscape, from which her body is indistinguishable, where the speaker will regress even further into sleep. Her "wild" eyes, an image of sexual energy earlier in the poem, now reveal their prophecy of sorrow to come, so that when the speaker shuts her "wild sad eyes," he himself is drawn back into sleep and dreaming. But this dream is now recognized as one in an endless sequence of dreams in which the distinction between actuality and fantasy is lost. The apparent reality of the "cold hill side" is now revealed as the phantasmagorical projection of the speaker's self into his doppelgänger image of the "wretched wight" as a result of the speaker's waking from the dream of paradisiacal fulfillment. Since reality cannot fulfill his infinite desire for absolute bodily gratification, reality in the form of a desolate nature where "no birds sing" becomes a visionary nightmare in which all men, "pale kings, and princes too, / Pale warriors, death-pale were they all," suffer from the same disease of un-fulfilled desire. This procession of starved and yearning lov-ers, fixed in their obsession for an unobtainable object that they cannot reject, becomes the central focus of the speaker's consciousness. Yet their warning cry to the speaker, "La belle Dame sans mercy / Hath thee in thrall," is ineffective be-cause La Belle Dame, in her guise as lover, represents the un-diminished infantile wish for the nursing mother—a wish for the impossible.

The procession of lovers is the equivalent, but reverse, image of Freud's "endless series" of love objects that charac-terizes the instability of neurotic love and the failure to make a permanent choice. In "A Special Type of Object Choice," Freud says: "The pressing desire in the unconscious for some irreplaceable thing often resolves itself into an endless series in actuality—endless for the very reason that the satisfaction longed for is in spite of all never found in any surrogate [for the mother]." All lovers are "starved," including the poem's speaker, because mortal food and actual sexuality cannot pro-vide the satisfaction that the unconscious mind, in retrospec-tion, fantasizes was once offered by the mother. In this sense, La Belle Dame is without mercy because she is unreal, a dream, a fantasy of the past—therefore unobtainable, and thus her very attraction is the fatal aspect of her cruelty. The emotional reality of unfulfilled desire obliterates all other considerations and traps the speaker, as if damned, in his mind which projects itself upon the landscape so that he can see only his own barren self wherever he goes. The hellish circle of the torment of thought seems inescapable; no re-deeming or consoling song seems possible; and the waters of the lake do not bring forth new life—rather, these waters, as if poisoned, contribute to the withering of the surrounding sedge. Freud writes: "Something in the nature of the sexual instinct itself is unfavorable to the achievement of absolute gratification."

In Thomas Hardy's ballad "The Well-Beloved," which is a rewriting of Keats's ballad (Hardy himself continuing the procession of starved lovers), the landscape again represents inner psychic forces. The speaker's journey to his "dear one's home" is given a cosmic and fatalistic setting as he is guided "by star" along an immemorial path:

> I went by star and planet shine
>   Towards the dear one's home
> At Kingsbere, there to make her mine
>   When the next sun upclomb.
>
> I edged the ancient hill and wood
>   Beside the Ikling Way,
> Nigh where the Pagan temple stood
>   In the world's earlier day.
>
> And as I quick and quicker walked
>   On gravel and on green,
> I sang to sky, and tree, or talked
>   Of her I called my queen.
>
> —"O faultless is her dainty form,
>   And luminous her mind;
> She is the God-created norm
>   Of perfect womankind!"
>
> A shape whereon one star-blink gleamed
>   Slid softly by my side,
> A woman's; and her motion seemed
>   The motion of my bride.
>
> And yet methought she'd drawn erstwhile
>   Out from the ancient leaze,
> Where once were pile and peristyle
>   For men's idolatries.
>
> —"O maiden lithe and lone, what may
>   Thy name and lineage be
> Who so resemblest by this ray
>   My darling?—Art thou she?"
>
> The Shape: "Thy bride remains within
>   Her father's grange and grove."
> —"Thou speakest rightly," I broke in,
>   "Thou are not she I love."

—"Nay: though thy bride remains inside
    Her father's walls," said she,
"The one most dear is with thee here,
    For thou dost love but me."

Then I: "But she, my only choice,
    Is now at Kingsbere Grove?"
Again her soft mysterious voice
    "I am thy only love."

Thus still she vouched, and still I said,
    "O sprite, that cannot be!" . . .
It was as if my bosom bled,
    So much she troubled me.

The sprite resumed: "Thou has transferred
    To her dull form awhile
My beauty, fame, and deed, and word,
    My gestures and my smile.

"O fatuous man, this truth infer,
    Brides are not what they seem;
Thou lovest what thou dreamest her;
    I am thy very dream!"

—"O then," I answered miserably,
    speaking as scarce I knew,
"My loved one, I must wed with thee
    If what thou sayest be true!"

She, proudly, thinning in the gloom:
    "Though, since troth-plight began,
I have ever stood as bride to groom,
    I wed no mortal man!"

Thereat she vanished by the lane
    Adjoining Kingsbere town,
Near where, men say, once stood the Fane
    To Venus, on the Down.

—When I arrived and met my bride
    Her look was pinched and thin,
As if her soul had shrunk and died,
    And left a waste within.

As in Keats's poem, the romantic drama of disillusionment
can take place at any moment in history; indeed, as the poem
suggests, love worship is a universal religion. From the beginning, Hardy's speaker's beloved is exalted: she is called "my
queen," and the fact that she lives at "Kingsbere" already
sounds an ominous note that she belongs to someone else
more powerful than he, the king, and is therefore unobtainable. Yet the speaker's idealization continues in his image of
her as representative of "perfect womankind," until an apparition appears as the double of his bride.

At first, Hardy's speaker cannot distinguish between his
bride and the visionary shape, and he asks her name as if her
origin, her lineage, contains the mystery of her elusive identity. The shape declares that, despite the resemblance, she is
not his bride who remains within the confinement of her
"father's walls," but then, to the speaker's shock, the shape
asserts that she, not the bride, is the object of the speaker's
love. Still holding to the illusion that he has a "choice" as to
whom he loves, the speaker protests, but to no avail, for a
fatal passion, "as if my bosom bled," has been activated.
Her accusation, "Thou hast transferred / To her dull form
awhile / My beauty," reveals a truth that hitherto had been
hidden, and that now cannot be resisted. The sprite, like
Keats's "fairy child," despite her apparent innocence, is
the true queen and mother, the first love, and the bride
is merely a surrogate for her. "Brides are not what they
seem," as the sprite says, precisely because they are images
invented through projection by the lover's wishful fantasy.
The sprite's further assertion, "Thou lovest what thou
dreamest her; / I am thy very dream," makes verbally overt
the psychic fact that the speaker's fidelity is to a dream of
love, to an unobtainable image of La Belle Dame Sans Merci,
not to an actual woman of mortal and imperfect reality. Nevertheless, the speaker, trapped in his passion, cannot free
himself from the grip of his dream, and it is to the dream that
he pledges himself, as if this were a conscious choice. The
sprite's chilling reply, "I wed no mortal man," has a double
meaning: it acknowledges her unreality, but also it is an invitation to the speaker to die. If he were *immortal*, her tempt-

ing words imply, then she might marry him. Again we see, as in Shakespeare's phrase, that "Desire is death."

The sprite vanishes as if the speaker had wakened from his dream of her, just as Keats wakes on the hillside to find La Belle Dame is gone, and what Hardy's speaker sees in her place is the temple of Venus, reminding him that he is merely the latest in an endless procession of love worshipers. When he arrives at the house of his actual bride, she appears "pinched and thin," diminished in comparison to the beauty of the shape within his dream. His own hunger—an image of sexual dissatisfaction like the "starv'd lips" of the kings and princes in Keats's poem—is projected upon the woman. Because the speaker has emotionally wedded himself to the dream woman, and thus can no longer live in the world of waking reality, he sees his own spiritual death in the image of his bride, "As if her soul had shrunk and died, / And left a waste within." Like the desolate landscape at the end of Keats's poem where the "sedge is wither'd from the lake," Hardy's image of the "waste within" describes the punishment for uncontained desire as if desire, like hell, were a place of torment for a forbidden and impossible attachment to a queen-mother-goddess whose power over the lover remains unbroken. The speaker's psychic death, as if it were a marital consummation, thus both fulfills a wish and constitutes a punishment for the guilt contained within the wish.

One of the traditional attributes of ballad form is that character or incident are brought to the fore to give emphasis to psychological patterns that do not belong to any particular historical moment. The indefinite past in the ballad becomes an eternal present because the aspect of human nature being portrayed has not and will not change. The ballad, one might argue, is the mythic epic contracted within the space of the lyric. Yeats's ballad "The Cap and Bells" resembles Keats's and Hardy's ballads in this respect, but, like theirs, Yeats's poem also is conceived as a dream of love, and, indeed, it is based on a dream Yeats claimed he actually had: "I dreamed this story exactly as I have written it." The central themes of the poem are desire, separation, and duality, prefiguring Yeats's masterful late ballad, "The Three Bushes":

The jester walked in the garden:
The garden had fallen still;
He bade his soul rise upward
And stand on her window-sill.

It rose in a straight blue garment,
When owls began to call:
It had grown wise-tongued by thinking
Of a quiet and light footfall;

But the young queen would not listen;
She rose in her pale night-gown;
She drew in the heavy casement
And pushed the latches down.

He bade his heart go to her,
When the owls called out no more;
In a red and quivering garment
It sang to her through the door.

It had grown sweet-tongued by dreaming
Of a flutter of flower-like hair;
But she took up her fan from the table
And waved it off on the air.

'I have cap and bells,' he pondered,
'I will send them to her and die';
And when the morning whitened
He left them where she went by.

She laid them upon her bosom,
Under a cloud of her hair,
And her red lips sang them a love-song
Till stars grew out of the air.

She opened her door and her window,
And the heart and the soul came through,
To her right hand came the red one,
To her left hand came the blue.

They set up a noise like crickets,
A chattering wise and sweet,
And her hair was a folded flower
And the quiet of love in her feet.

The jester in Yeats's poem is a comic and debased version of the royal lovers in Keats's ballad, and his desperate love for the "young queen" adds him to the procession of men who long for an unobtainable object. If a woman cannot be possessed, for whatever reason, she becomes invested with the lover's wishes and fantasies, and in this crucial respect, she becomes a dream, an illusion of his own projection. The jester's desire is spiritualized as "He bade his soul rise upward / And stand on her window-sill," but his carnal motive is unmistakable in his fascination with the lady's "light footfall," just as Keats's attention is given to La Belle Dame's body, "her foot was light." The lady's window and door, through dream displacement, represent the lady's genital mystery, but her deadly effect, dressed in her "pale night-gown," is made manifest in her decisive rejection of the jester's advances: "She drew in the heavy casement / And pushed the latches down."

Since the lady has rejected the jester's soul (or spiritualized body), he now offers her his body—"He bade his heart go to her"—but still she will not have him. The jester's third attempt or strategy, like the mythic third wish, is that of a sacrificial offering. Again he offers her his body, but this time in castrated form: "I have cap and bells, he pondered, / I will send them to her and die." His comic identity as jester-child, as well as his sexual body, is represented by his "cap and bells," and in sending them to the lady a paradoxical wish is enacted: by giving up this part of his body he is rewarded by the lady's bodily acceptance of him. Only his death can win the love of this queen, this fatal La Belle Dame: "She opened her door and her window, / And the heart and soul came through." The fallen garden at the beginning of the poem—an externalized image of the body's dissatisfaction, like Keats's cold hillside—becomes at the end the garden of sexual activity identified with the woman's body whose "hair is a folded flower." But this final image of completed satisfaction, "the quiet of love in her feet," is in actuality the quiet of death. Death has been sexualized, and the fatal lady has exacted her price for the jester's desire for impossible passionate fulfillment. So, too, in "The Three Bushes" lady and chambermaid, dual aspects of a single self, both love the same minstrel, one with her soul and the other with her body. Yet, unity can be achieved only after all three die and are buried together with a rose tree planted upon their common grave: "And now none living can, / When they have plucked a rose there, / Know where its roots began." The separation between lover and loved one, between reality and the dream of fulfillment, becomes the conditions of the mind divided within itself, the torment of thought, to be healed, it seems, only by death.

III

A poem, like playing or like dreaming, may give symbolic expression to desire; it may enact a wish, but, also like playing or dreaming, the poem often will represent such a wish in divided form. In most play there is a formalization of obstacles and both a loser and a winner; similarly, most dreams have a troubling element, an aspect of nightmare. Both play and dream, then, give expression to the wished fulfillment of a desire *and* to the counterwish that the desire not be fulfilled and make manifest the anxiety attending the hidden awareness of the consequences of the desire should it indeed be realized. This hidden sense of threat (losing) or consequence relates to an inner awareness of reality that the act of dreaming, even in its solipsism, does not entirely lose. Thus the ballads by Keats, Hardy, and Yeats discussed above are both expressions of sexual desire and, equally, the dramatizations of punishment for the fantasies that these poems enact. The poems are emblems of a torturous split in the mind, and they serve to portray the truth of an essential psychic reality. Painful as is the thwarted desire these poems reveal, yet they possess the stoical dignity of simply facing the truth of the human condition. Perhaps we can say that there is another kind of pleasure that belongs to poet and scientist alike which is to be found in the courage of truthfulness. Yeats himself asserted: "Art is but a vision of reality."

Still, the poet must search for consolations in life itself, not merely in the visionary dignity and control of his art. Wallace Stevens, in his great poem of old age, "The Auroras

of Autumn," expresses a separation from his own aging
body, which he envisions as vanishing, "being visible is being white." Separated from the landscape as well, "A cold
wind chills the beach. / The long lines of it grow longer,
emptier," Stevens seeks consolation in his attempt to recall
his "mother's face," and he defines this attempt as the "purpose of the poem." For a moment he succeeds as the memory
of his mother becomes so vivid that her imagined presence
"fills the room. / They are together, here, and it is warm."
But the moment cannot be sustained. The vision of the comforting mother vanishes, "And yet she too is dissolved, she is
destroyed," and Stevens is confronted with the reality of
desolate separation and with obliterating change symbolized
by the "invincible sound" of the "cold wind," much as Keats
had awakened from his dream on the "cold hill side."

It is precisely because Stevens can acknowledge that his
mother is lost, however, that he is able to bring her back in
a remembered form that is free of fantasy. His own "innocence" is projected upon the mother in his rejection of the
wish that she take the form of a lover or that the reality of her
death be denied, so that, for Stevens, there is no separation
between waking and sleeping thought. His reward, then, is
that his imagination is liberated to enjoy the recollection of
his mother within the limits of the fact that it is only a recollection, and that the poem is only a created structure of words
whose reality is a conscious "as if" fiction:

> As if, awake, we lay in the quiet of sleep,
> As if the innocent mother sang in the dark
> Of the room and on an accordion, half-heard,
> Created the time and place in which we breathed . . .

Innocence, for Stevens, lies in the discipline to wish only for
the possible, for what reality permits; thus, finally, innocent
thought requires both the acceptance of death and the con-
comitant acceptance of the fact that the love of one's mother
never can be replaced. The failure to achieve this acceptance,
Stevens fully realized, would transform the image of the
mother into a destructive force like La Belle Dame who
starves rather than nurtures her lover. The limitations, then,

of mortal love could not be a source of pleasure, but only the cause of frustration and grief as Stevens shows in his poem "Madame La Fleurie," where he portrays the "heartbreak" of the lover yearning for infinite satisfaction: "His grief is that his mother should feed on him, himself and what he saw, / In that distant chamber, a bearded queen, wicked in her dead light."

The discipline of accepting reality must begin with the recognition, grounded in emotional conviction, that the model for connection and bodily fulfillment is to be found through contemplating the reconstructed image of the nursing child. This recognition was Wordsworth's pre-Freudian discovery, and Wordsworth's emphasis that this scene of connection was not a memory as such, but the reconstruction of an event based only on the evidence of feeling, was of equal significance in defining the powers and limitations of his imagination.

> . . . blest the Babe,
> Nursed in his Mother's arms, who sinks to sleep
> Rocked on his Mother's breast; who with his soul
> Drinks in the feelings of his Mother's eye!
> For him, in one dear Presence, there exists
> A virtue which irradiates and exalts
> Objects through widest intercourse of sense.
> No outcast he, bewildered and depressed:
> Along his infant veins are interfused
> The gravitation and the filial bond
> Of nature that connect him with the world.
> (*Prelude*, 2. 234–44)

The experience of nursing establishes the paradigm for connection, and the feeling of being connected becomes the emotion evermore to be desired. To be separated from the mother, the inevitable fate of growing up, turns each of us into an "outcast." And yet this feeling of fulfilled unity, consubstantial with the milk he has imbibed at his mother's breast, is not entirely lost. Rather, it becomes a part of the sleeping or unconscious mind and thus remains in the body "Along his infant veins."

Not only does the body retain the feeling of connection for possible later restoration, but also the little noises of nursing which accompany touch become the foundation for language itself, as Wordsworth surmises of his infant self: "by intercourse of touch / I held mute dialogues with my Mother's heart." The motive for learning language, then, takes root in the body as the need to reestablish touch when physical connection with the mother has been severed. And it is no accident that Wordsworth's favorite, even obsessive, pattern of alliteration throughout his poetry is based on the letter *M*— as in the key words "milk," "murmur," and "mother." Wordsworth goes on to tell us that later, as a young man, he "would walk alone / Under the quiet stars . . . listening to notes that are / The ghostly language of the ancient earth," as if he could hear in the "distant winds" the origin of the language of connection when his mother was for him all of the "earth" he knew.

Wordsworth describes listening to the wind through the metaphor of drinking, "Thence did I drink the visionary power," as if on a subliminal level he is nursing again, just as Keats describes the reverse correlative of frustrated desire through the metaphor of starvation. In this moment of visionary listening the infant soul is reactivated and brought into adult consciousness even though the content of consciousness is only the awareness that something has been forgotten: "the soul, / Remembering how she felt, but what she felt / Remembering not, retains an obscure sense / Of possible sublimity." The very knowledge that something precious has been lost or forgotten becomes the effective motive to reconstruct the "unremembered" past on the basis of one's obscure feelings and from the evidence of dreams. Paradoxically, Wordsworth is most in touch with the origins of his deepest feelings of connection when he is alone and in an inward mood, so that a "holy calm / Would overspread my soul, that bodily eyes / Were utterly forgotten, and what I saw / Appeared like something in myself, a dream."

Wordsworth was orphaned when he was still a child, and although he was left "destitute," he writes: "Early died / My honored Mother, she who was the heart of all our learnings and our loves." His mother remains a source of enduring strength to Wordsworth because his love for her passes over into his love for nature, providing that his excessive expectations of nature also are contained: "Nor with impatience from the season asked / More than its timely produce; rather loved / The hours for what they are." Wordsworth's image of his mother is not repressed only to return in the form of desire for a woman who can provide complete and unambivalent fulfillment. Just as his mother "Was not puffed up by false, unnatural hopes," so, too, Wordsworth disciplines himself to accept the grief of her loss while retaining the consolation of her memory. Like Stevens, Wordsworth describes the rejection of false hope as innocence, and he attributes this potentiality for renewed innocence to the gift of God who provides each man with the ability to accept the limitations of his own nature: "He / Who fills the mother's breast with innocent milk, / Doth also for our nobler part provide, / Under His great correction and control, / As innocent instincts and as innocent food." Without man's acceptance of death and the control of desire, nature herself is violated, human aspiration becomes unnatural, love becomes a torment to the lover, and thought, impossibly, seeks to avoid itself.

I V

Pope's "Rape of the Lock" is no less profound than Wordsworth's *Prelude* in its dramatization of the dangers inherent in the repression of the natural fact of death, even though Pope's style is one of "good Humour" and his cure for psychic denial is "to laugh" at folly. Although Pope invokes a comic muse, his exploration of the motive in his heroine, Belinda, to reject sexuality—"what stranger Cause, yet unexplored, / Cou'd make a gentle Belle reject a Lord?"—in favor of chastity is deeply serious in his insistent correlation of the fear of sexuality with the fear of death. The poem begins at dawn with the sun rising, "Sol thro' white Curtains shot a tim'rous Ray," and Pope never allows us to forget that time is passing as the poem moves through its course, "Mean while declining from the Noon of Day, / The Sun obliquely shoots his burning Ray," and ends at night with the anticipation of Belinda's death as the closing of her eyes is identified with the setting of the sun: "When those fair Suns shall sett, as sett they must, / And all those tresses shall be laid in Dust." If Belinda is to think without self-deception, if she is to laugh and to love, she must confront the reality of her eventual death. Not to do so would doom her to remain in a state of "infant Thought," narcissistically worshiping herself as if she were a goddess, "A heav'nly Image in the Glass appears, / To that she bends," her passions merely vanities, no more than a "moving Toyshop."

Belinda's protecting sprite, Ariel, represents her narcissistic wish to remain chaste, which Pope reveals to be at heart her fearful defense against loving someone other than herself, and thus Ariel sets himself against time itself, the "Birth of Fate," as if Belinda need never mature into adult sexuality: "Whoever fair and chaste / Rejects Mankind, is by some Sylph embraced." The fantasy of Belinda that Pope exposes is her dream of immortality in the form of eternal childishness. Yet her willed chastity turns the belle, Belinda, into another version of La Belle Dame Sans Merci; her rejection of sexuality and love have the perverse effect of making her attractive precisely because she is unobtainable. And so Pope describes Belinda at her dressing table as if she were preparing for war: "This Nymph, to the Destruction of Mankind, / Nourished two Locks, which graceful hung behind." The effect of Belinda's beauty on the baron who admires her is of a corresponding aggressiveness and hostility: "Th' Adventurous Baron the bright Locks admir'd, / He saw, he wished, and to the Prize aspir'd: / Resolv'd to win, he meditates the way, / By force to ravish, or by Fraud betray." As in Shakespeare's sonnet, "Th' expense of spirit in a waste of shame / Is lust in action," where lust generates its own anger and is therefore "murd'rous, bloody, full of blame," here, too, we see an angry separation from the would-be loved one and a repression of the affection that normally should accompany sexual desire. The battle of the sexes, as Pope presents its comic surface in the rituals of societal manners, is only one step away from real violence and destruction in a world where sexual failure is displaced, hunger for hunger, into political cruelty: "The hungry Judges soon the Sentence sign, / And Wretches hang that Jury-men may Dine."

Belinda's chastity, her rejection of sexuality, is defended by Belinda and the sylphs as a consequence of Belinda's repression of the knowledge of death. Her fear of old age and mortality is displaced onto her fear of losing her chastity, and this displacement reinforces her narcissistic fascination with her own body. A structure of self-deception is thus established, but Pope exposes Belinda's essential confusion in his depiction of her unconscious motivations, her natural sexual instincts. As the baron sneaks up behind Belinda to cut off a lock of her hair with his scissors, Pope describes Belinda's ambivalence toward amorous advances in Ariel's disapproval, "anxious Ariel Sought / The close Recesses of the Virgin's Thought," and in the image of Belinda's unconscious fantasy, "An earthly Lover lurking at her Heart." Seeing sexual desire in Belinda's heart, Ariel is then "Resigned to Fate," although a fellow sylph interposes himself between the blades of the baron's shears: "Fate urg'd the Sheers, and cut the Sylph in twain, / (But Airy Substance soon unites again)." The wish relating inviolability to immortality is thus enacted in Belinda's mind, although Pope's narrator reminds us of what Belinda must learn and accept: "What Time would spare, from Steel receives its date, / And Monuments, like Men, submit to Fate . . . What wonder then, fair Nymph! thy Hairs should feel / The conqu'ring Force of unresisted Steel?"

Pope's depiction of Belinda's unconscious motives fills the poem in many forms: her dream at the poem's beginning that "caus'd her Cheek to glow"; the allegorical sylphs, gnomes, nymphs, and salamanders; the symbolic card game of sexual warfare, ombre; and especially the descent into the underworld, the "gloomy Cave of Spleen"—all reveal Belinda's archaic and adolescent sexual anxieties and confusions, in which: "Men prove with Child, as powerful Fancy works, / And Maids turn'd Bottels, call aloud for Corks." At this level of the unconscious mind, the difference in sexual function between men and women is obscured, and the desire for sexual intercourse is displaced with seeming innocence onto inanimate objects. The ruler of this dark palace of Spleen is a destructive goddess, the bad mother, whose poisonous gift to the world, in the place of nurturing milk, is a "swelling Bag" of foul winds from which the "Furies issued at the Vent." In the language of Belinda's dream, the bad mother gives birth to death rather than to life.

When Belinda awakes from her dream of the "World of Spleen," we see her in the arms of her attendant, Thalestris, who is the namesake of the queen of the warring Amazons and who is thus the conscious counterpart of the "wayward Queen" who reigns in the underworld. "Fierce Thalestris fans the rising Fire" of Belinda's hostility toward the baron so that "Belinda burns with more than mortal ire," and thus the potential passion of love and natural desire is perverted into the destructive fire of vengeance. Thalestris's obsession with Belinda's "Honor in a Whisper lost," because the baron has cut off her lock of hair, is revealed in the hypocrisy of Thalestris's selfish motivation: "Twill then be Infamy to seem your friend." Her slip of the tongue in choosing the word "seem" rather than "be" exposes her insincerity. Belinda, with extravagant self-pity, still indulging in her obsession with her own beauty, "Oh had I un-admired remain'd," curses this "detested Day, / Which snatched my best, my fav'rite Curl away!" Still blind to her own ambivalent motives, Belinda cries out to the baron, unaware of the implication of her own words: "Oh hadst thou, Cruel! been content to seize / Hairs less in sight, or any hairs but these!" Here Freud's "return of the repressed" receives its fullest comic expression.

In canto 5, the final section of the poem, Pope introduces the character Clarissa, who functions as the good mother in contrast to the queen of Spleen and Thalestris. Clarissa's gifts to Belinda are her "good sense" and, above all, her humor, as she lovingly and tenderly advises Belinda:

> "But since, alas! frail Beauty must decay,
> Curl'd or uncurl'd, since Locks will turn to grey,
> Since painted, or not painted, all shall fade,
> And she who scorns a Man must die a Maid;

> What then remains, but well our Pow'r to use,
> And keep good Humor still whate'er we lose?"

But good sense at such a conscious level still does not suffice; it has not yet become part of emotional conviction, and so, led on by Thalestris, Belinda must go to war with the baron. In the world of courtly flirtation and romance, of course, warfare is verbal and metaphorical, and no one really dies. Yet Pope insists, through innuendo, that breaking hearts is only once removed from actual destruction; the same emotions are involved. The element of play is also the element of safety, and so, too, Pope's humor is the protecting and redeeming aspect of his art. Pope exploits the double meaning of the verb "to die"—implying both physical death and sexual intercourse—in his parody of the battle between the sexes that ensues throughout the court:

> While thro' the Press enrag'd Thalestris flies,
> And scatters Deaths around from both her Eyes,
> A Beau and Whitling perish'd in the Throng,
> One dy'd in Metaphor, and one in Song.
> O cruel Nymph! a living Death I bear,
> Cry'd Dapperwit, and sunk beside his Chair.
> A mournful Glance Sir Fopling upwards cast,
> Those Eyes are made so killing—was his last:
> Thus on Meander's flowr'y Margin lies
> Th' expiring Swan, and as he sings he dies.

In the realm of play and poetry, events are once removed from real consequences, and herein lies the freedom of contemplation and laughter. Poetry and play are a kind of rehearsal for historical reality in which events cannot be changed once they are enacted. In her world of play, or foreplay, Belinda still has the opportunity to learn, just as Pope's readers have the opportunity to consider, the consequences of sexual hypocrisy and the repression of the reality of death.

When Belinda blows snuff in the baron's face, causing him to let out a magnificent sneeze, Pope's description makes clear that in the comic substitution of flirtation for real love, a sneeze can function as a surrogate orgasm. In effect, Pope of-

fers his readers an extravagant equation in which a sneeze is
to an orgasm as poetry is to reality. The connecting link, the
hiatus, is laughter:

> See fierce Belinda on the Baron flies,
> With more than usual Lightning in her Eyes;
> Nor fear'd the Chief th' unequal Fight to try,
> Who sought no more than on his Foe to die.
> But this bold Lord, with manly Strength indu'd,
> She with one Finger and a Thumb subdu'd:
> Just where the Breath of Life his Nostrils drew,
> A charge of Snuff the wily Virgin threw;
> The Gnomes direct, to ev'ry Atome just,
> The pungent Grains of titilating Dust.
> Sudden, with starting Tears each Eye o'erflows,
> And the high Dome re-ecchoes to his Nose.

The curative power of laughter, which Pope identifies with
the art of poetry, is intended to divest repression of its force,
and in doing so to enable Belinda to face the reality of death.
Full sexual pleasure is only possible when the limits of desire
are accepted on the analogy with death. This, indeed, is the
baron's recognition when, realizing that he has "fallen" for
Belinda, he chooses the fire of love over the fire of sexual anger whose innermost cause is the denial of mortality:

> Boast not my Fall (he cry'd) insulting Foe!
> Thou by some other shalt be laid as low.
> Nor think, to die dejects my lofty Mind;
> All that I dread, is leaving you behind!
> Rather than so, ah let me still survive,
> And burn in Cupid's flames, — but burn alive.

Even though the literal fact of death must be accepted, Belinda's wish for immortality can be granted by Pope as a metaphor in the realm of poetry by transfiguring her severed lock
of hair into a star. Thus reality and fantasy are brought into
their proper relationship in the spirit of play and laughter. Poetic illusion, therefore, can be given its own fictional status
as a visionary aspect of reality, so that Pope assures both Belinda and his readers that they can "trust the Muse." So, too,

Pope tells his readers that Belinda saw her transfigured lock of hair "upward rise, / Tho' marked by none but quick Poetic eyes." Only poetic immortality is possible to meet the need for consolation of human beings who choose not to deceive themselves. Recognizing the good sense of this fundamental (but difficult) knowledge of the reality of death, poetic triumph—the apotheosis of Belinda's lock of hair—may yet be achieved as the consummation of laughter and the reward that reality permits for the recognition of its limits.

The voice of Clarissa, who accepts both sexuality and death, merges at the end with the voice of the narrator—as if mother and father speak to Belinda together in loving unity: "Then cease, bright Nymph! to mourn thy ravish'd Hair / Which adds new glory to the shining Sphere!" In speaking to Belinda (who is really still a child at heart) with such controlling tenderness, the poem's narrator acknowledges the innermost truth of Belinda's serious distress beneath all the frivolity and parody of the poem: Belinda has been prematurely mourning her own death, and in holding herself back from death she has also held herself back from desire and the processes of living. Pope's ultimate paradox, then, is that only the consciousness of death, supported by irony and laughter —"For, after all the Murders of your Eye, / When, after Millions slain, your self shall die"—can free Belinda from the repressed death within her that emotionally murders her own life. With this freedom, Belinda could cease to be the rejecting La Belle Dame Sans Merci and achieve true innocence—innocence that comes from the acceptance of nature's requirement of mortality, and thus Belinda's future husband could have his love returned. This is what the narrator and Clarissa wish for in Belinda's behalf—as if they were her parents, contemplating the future happiness of their child.

V

For the poet, the acceptance of limits is not merely a philosophical option, but a principle of his very commitment to his art. To speak of poetic form is to reject the idea, as Stevens says, of "measureless measures," in favor of an idea of the vitality of constraints, such as the poetic line or the structural necessity of a meaningful beginning and an ending that accounts for what has gone before. Such limits for Stevens constitute what he calls "the vital boundary of the mind," and without these limits thought only can seek to escape itself, as when Keats attempts to follow his nightingale into eternity: "Thou wast not born for death, immortal Bird!" But Keats knows that such a flight of imagination finally is impossible; thought collapses under the attempt: "the fancy cannot cheat so well / As she is fam'd to do," Keats acknowledges to himself. He must return to the earth, the realm of what is thinkable, and to himself, "my sole self." Thought may be healed of a contradictory duality within itself when the mind is able to reject the outward separation between the self and an impossible desire for the infinite—either for eternity or for its counterpart in the dream of complete sexual satisfaction.

Yeats also seeks to heal an inner duality in "Sailing to Byzantium" where he describes his heart as being "sick with desire / And fastened to a dying animal," although at first he wishes to be embraced by eternity as if immortality could be depicted as a mother-lover. "Gather me / Into the artifice of eternity," Yeats implores in his poem, and in a letter he asserts: "We suck always at the eternal dugs." But after Yeats has transcended mortality in his fantasy, "Once out of nature I shall never take / My bodily form from any natural thing," and freed himself of mortal constraints, still he must return to himself in some finite form. The form he chooses is a work of art—a bird of "hammered gold and gold enamelling," and this form makes the thought of eternity possible, but only as an aspect of time, a way of meditating about inexorable change. As a bird on a "golden bough," Yeats is then able to sing about the theme of time, "Of what is past, or passing or to come," which earlier in the poem had caused such pain and prompted his desire to escape from nature. As with Keats, the work of art itself has provided the cure for the negating desire to escape thought; the poem, in fidelity to its own form, has affirmed thought in the unity of its metaphorical embodiment.

A successful metaphor can unite a perceived object with

the subjective feelings of the observer. Through metaphor the separation between outer and inner, between other and self, can be bridged. Metaphor is language that extends touching beyond physical touch and makes it possible for words, when necessary, to take the place of body. This power of metaphor, no doubt, explains why Frost declared that "I have wanted in late years to go further and further in making metaphor the whole of thinking." And so in his poem "The Silken Tent," Frost opens with a crucial distinction between metaphorical thinking and the use of simile that is merely a comparison: "She is as in a field a silken tent / At midday." The difficult but significant phrase here is "as in"—Frost does not say that she is *like* a silken tent—since the metaphor of the tent does not merely describe the "she" of the poem, but rather the tent, as a metaphor developed throughout the poem, conveys the narrator's feelings about the lady projected onto the lady herself. Fastened to the ground yet extending upward, the tent evokes an image of the two of them together, sharing both the desire for earth and physical pleasure and the "heavenward" wish for transcendence:

> She is as in a field a silken tent
> At midday when a sunny summer breeze
> Has dried the dew and all its ropes relent,
> So that in guys it gently sways at ease,
> And its supporting central cedar pole,
> That is its pinnacle to heavenward
> And signifies the sureness of the soul,
> Seems to owe naught to any single cord,
> But strictly held by none, is loosely bound
> By countless silken ties of love and thought
> To everything on earth the compass round,
> And only by one's going slightly taut
> In the capriciousness of summer air
> Is of the slightest bondage made aware.

The "she" of the poem may be an actual woman sitting in a field whom the speaker loves, a woman remembered, or both. She is as much an apparition as she is literal, and thus as the figure who inspires his imagination, she must be regarded as the speaker's muse as well as his lover. Frost's poem insists on her double reality, just as he defines metaphor as the "attempt to say matter in terms of spirit, or spirit in terms of matter, to make the final unity."

The metaphorical unity of Frost's poem can be seen and felt in several ways. Structurally, the poem is a single-sentence sonnet—as if the synthesis of movement and stillness when the tent "sways at ease" can be contained within a single breath, a single moment of thought, body, and mind as one. The potentially troubling antithesis of earth and heaven is resolved in the image of the tent as both tied to the ground and aspiring upward in its "cedar pole / That is its pinnacle to heavenward." Likewise, the antinomies of man and woman, body and soul, love and thought, are seen as unified in the poem's insistence on centrality: it is "midday," the pole is located as "central," and the lovers feel themselves to be at a mysterious spiritual center, measuring "everything on earth the compass round" by their own emotions. The repeating (four times) crucial verb of the poem, "is," which introduces the poem's first and last lines, insists that this is a moment of existential being that, nevertheless, is infused with a sense of the immanence of the soul. The presence of the poem's speaker, at one with the woman he watches, is made clear in his interpretive interjection that the cedar pole "signifies the sureness of the soul." To observe and to respond are a single action reflected in the speaker's mind.

The essential paradox of the poem that evokes the lady—not as fatally unattainable like La Belle Dame Sans Merci, but as there to be touched and loved, both in body and in thought—is the paradox of freedom within limits, of freedom resulting from the willed constraint imposed on the chooser by his own choice. If, in the ballads by Keats, Hardy, and Yeats, the mind is represented as a scene of separation between the lover and his desired beloved, with the implication that the beloved has unsuccessfully (but necessarily) replaced the lost mother, then Frost's poem represents the mind as a scene of union and reunion. As Wallace Stevens also declared in "Final Soliloquy of the Interior Paramour," depicting the loved woman as a muse speaking in his own mind: "Being there together is enough." In such an emotion, human longing comes momentarily to an end and achieves its necessarily temporary reward of rest and completion.

Frost's tent "is loosely bound / By countless silken ties of love and thought," so that even the fact of bondage cannot be exactly located. Bondage so diffused is barely experienced as a constraint; the lover does not wander from his choice. And when the wind of chance or temptation blows, as blow it must, "In the capriciousness of summer air," the lover experiences only the most delicate self-consciousness of his choice as he "Is of the slightest bondage made aware."

In Hardy's "The Aërolite" we see the mind divided against itself; we see the pain of consciousness as an affliction, and thus "normal unawareness" appears to be the only cure for thought—as if consciousness itself were nature's most insidious disease. Frost's vision of human love, and therefore of human thought, suggests a hopeful alternative: in a moment of amorous connection and happiness, thought almost dissolves in pleasure—*almost* dissolves, for if we should lose thought altogether, how could we savor the knowledge that such passion is a choice of limitation, accepting the necessity of the "bondage" of nature? In order to be truly free, one must know that one is free. Freedom, as Frost's poem celebrates its triumph, is bondage moving at "ease" in its chosen ties, touched by the mind's delicate spice of airy awareness.

That girls are raped, that two boys knife a third,
Were axioms to him, who'd never heard
Of any world where promises were kept
Or one could weep because another wept.
                    W. H. AUDEN, "The Shield of Achilles"

Generous tears filled Gabriel's eyes. He had never felt like
that himself towards any woman, but he knew that such a feeling must be love.
                    JAMES JOYCE, "The Dead"

TWELVE

The Tears of Art

❦

A
CCORDING to the Bible, the Lord made earth
and heaven and formed man from the dust of the
ground by breathing into his nostrils. Then he
planted a garden where man was placed, and in
the middle of Eden he set the tree of life and the tree of the
knowledge of good and evil. "There was a river flowing from
Eden to water the garden, and when it left the garden it
branched into four streams"—Pishon, Gihon, Tigris, and Eu-
phrates. And so the waters of fruitfulness were given to the
earth and to man before the Fall and before the knowledge of
evil and sorrow and death.

In canto 14 of the *Inferno*, Dante depicts this fallen landscape, derived from the image of Eden, as the old man of Crete
who is given figure as a mountain. In Dante's description, the
waters of edenic fruitfulness have been transformed into rivers of tears flowing from the old man. Natural sorrow is now
seen as the human condition; the metaphor of the stream of
time and history is characterized as the flowing of tears, the
continuity of grief. Virgil tells Dante:

"In mid-sea lies a waste land named Crete," he said then
"under whose king the world once was pure. A mountain

is there, once glad with leaves and waters, which was
called Ida; now it is deserted like a thing outworn. . . .
Within the mountain stands a great old man, . . . his
head is fashioned of fine gold, his breast and arms are
pure silver, then to the fork he is of brass, and from there
down all of choice iron except that the right foot is baked
clay, and he rests more on this than on the other. Every
part except the gold is cleft by a fissure that drips with
tears, which gather and force their way down through the
cavern there, then take their course from rock to rock
into this depth." (John D. Sinclair, trans.)

According to Ovid's *Metamorphosis*, gold, silver, and brass
represent the entropic ages of history, a progressive fall, and
the clay foot of the old man thus implies that he has almost
completely returned to the earth—the dust from which he
was originally created. The old man of Crete is an image of
the history of man's fall into evil and sorrow, and his tears are
the tears of the earth itself in the form of the rivers flowing
down the mountain. These rivers, once the four streams of
Eden, become the rivers of hell: Acheron, Styx, Phlegethon,
and Cocytus. Man's weeping expresses the sorrowful knowledge of the Fall, as Byron says: "Knowledge is sorrow," or in
Keats's words: "Where but to think is to be full of sorrow /
And leaden-eyed despairs."

II

Dylan Thomas is persuasive in identifying the artist with the
lovers, who have "their arms / Round the griefs of the ages,"
thus suggesting that the deepest functions of art are lamentation and celebration, mourning and praise. In bearing witness
to our fate, yet embracing it, the artist must lament what he
sees and knows; as lover, the artist must celebrate what is
precious to him. Witness and lover, both watching and involved, the artist possesses the knowledge of what he cherishes and inevitably must lose. The tears of art, then, are shed
for the human condition; they cannot merely be the tears of
one's own personal misfortune.

Robert Frost wrote (ca. April 19, 1932) to his biographer

and friend Sidney Cox, admonishing him: "To be too subjective with what an artist has managed to make objective is to
come on him presumptuously and render ungraceful what he
in pain of his life had faith he had made graceful." No biographer can reconstruct the leap an artist makes between his life
and his art. That particular transformation is the mystery,
the very essence of artistic freedom. The power to create
grace from disorder or personal sorrow derives from the culti-
vation of a discipline, the mastery of a craft, yet it also comes
from the empathetic power of being able to see oneself in
others. The grace of such connectedness derives from the inherent power of language that allows one to fictionalize oneself and thus to feel free, for the interim of art, of the limitation of being a singular individual bound by one's own life.

We do not invent language; we inherit it. Language has its
own genius, re-creating itself through our use of it, for we are
the means by which it grows and sustains itself. Like a god, it
speaks through us and survives us. Our thinking is made possible by the structure that language provides, just as our
bodies respond to that information which our senses are capable of receiving. And if, as artists and readers, we give ourselves to language, savoring the sounds of words, we take on
something of its grandeur and we receive its grace. Every
poem or story, by its very nature, is therefore a celebration of
its own means, its inheritance—the language—which is
never ours, though we partake of it.

The failure of art to use language as a communal medium
can be seen as another aspect of the fallen condition, as in
the story of the tower of Babel. Originally, "the whole earth
was of one language, and of one speech," but again in punishment for pride and ambition to exceed human limits, the
Lord punished mankind: "Let us go down, and there con-
found their language, that they may not understand one
another's speech." Wordsworth, in his "Appendix to Pref-
ace to Lyrical Ballads," retells the story of Babel when he
says:

> But the first poets . . . spake a language which, though
> unusual, was still the language of men. This circum-
> stance, however, was disregarded by their successors;

they found that they could please by easier means: they
became proud of modes of expression which they themselves had invented. . . . until, the taste of men becoming gradually perverted, this language was received as a
natural language. . . . this diction became daily more and
more corrupt, thrusting out of sight the plain humanities
of nature. . . .

Wordsworth's point is that man's unity with nature and with
humanity has been replaced by the assertion of the individualistic self. In *The Prelude*, praising his dear friend
Coleridge's "learning," his "gorgeous eloquence," his "subtle speculations," Wordsworth nevertheless condemns the
"self-created sustenance of [Coleridge's] mind / Debarred
from Nature's living images, / Compelled to be a life unto
herself." Coleridge's art had failed, for Wordsworth, because
it had become too personal, too self-invented. Yeats, more
bluntly, stated the same idea: "All that is personal soon rots."
The artist must express the ongoing life of his species rather
than his own uniqueness or peculiarity. His uniqueness,
from the perspective of time "stretching before and after," is
either an illusion or merely insignificant. And the rebellion
against death—the horror of the *idea* of death—may vanish
or at least diminish when we identify ourselves with our
species, or even, more generally, with existence itself.

I I I

In Gerard Manley Hopkins's poem "Spring and Fall: to a
young child," Hopkins moves from the image of a young girl
weeping at the falling of the leaves to an implied image of the
grown and knowledgeable woman:

> Márgarét, are you grieving
> Over Goldengrove unleaving?
> Leaves, like the things of man, you
> With your fresh thoughts care for, can you?
> Ah! as the heart grows older
> It will come to such sights colder
> By and by, nor spare a sigh
> Though worlds of wanwood leafmeal lie;

And yet you *will* weep and know why.
Now no matter, child, the name:
Sorrow's springs are the same.
Nor mouth had, no nor mind, expressed
What heart heard of, ghost guessed:
It is the blight man was born for,
It is Margaret you mourn for.

The first pronunciation of the girl's name is diminutive—
Márgarét (Hopkins's own stress markings)—but by the end of
the poem she will be called Margaret, her adult name. The
poem's narrator is watching the girl and thinking to himself;
he is not speaking to the child. A mature man, seeing a girl
crying because the leaves are falling, would not approach her
and tell her: "It is the blight man was born for, / It is Margaret
you mourn for." Surely, the poem takes place in the mind of
the speaker, for what he has to say to her in the isolation of his
own mind is precisely what he cannot articulate to her. Language is a barrier between them, not a means of connection.
This poem is about separation, about barriers: the leaves are
to Margaret what Margaret is to the speaker—both are watching images of a fall, yet they cannot share their similar
sorrows.

Hopkins invents the name "Goldengrove" because Margaret's childhood home is suggestive of the garden of Eden.
The poem's detached speaker is astonished that, unlike himself, Margaret is still so close to nature, that she can weep for
the falling leaves as if they were human presences, "the
things of man." The speaker no longer can weep, for nature
has become alien and hostile to him. He envisions what will
happen to her—she will become "blighted" because mourn-
fulness has already overtaken him: "Ah, as the heart grows
older / It will come to such sights colder." Fall will become
winter; Margaret's emotions will become frozen; she will be
estranged from others and from the natural world. Margaret,
when mature, will see the leaves crushed on the ground as
"leafmeal," but she will not respond to them as she does
now since she will not be sympathetic enough to weep for the
fallen leaves. The cause of her inability to weep will be a new

kind of personalized knowledge, pertaining not to the season-
al cycle of nature and the objects of the world, but merely to
herself and her own loss of innocence. Margaret, as the
speaker envisions, will become trapped in her own self, perceiving only "Sorrow's springs" and, therefore, seeing only
mortality in nature. Because Margaret will conceive of death
as the end of everything, she will define nature as if it had no
life apart from her own.

In projecting Margaret's future this way, however, the
speaker has forgotten the spring of the poem's title, "Spring
and Fall." Limited by his own morbid gloom and grief, the
speaker has depicted the seasons not as a cycle that outlasts
the life of an individual, but as a "fall" from spring to winter,
from life only to death. The phrase, "Sorrow's springs," as
misused by the narrator, with its implication of irremediable
tears, describes spring as flowing always toward decay, death,
and sorrow, and that movement is seen as nature's blight:
mortality is the disease of all existence. The corruption of the
Fall in each person seems absolute when viewed from this
dark perspective—the perspective of the self regarding itself.

The intervening spirit of the Holy Ghost, also misinter-
preted by the speaker, seems to lead Margaret to guess that
the Fall is irreversible and unmitigated by the sympathetic
human imagination, for we are sick unto death: "It is the
blight man was born for." The only force that the speaker sees
in nature and in man is blight, and, by this grim logic, the
only possible response is to mourn for one's personal death:
"It is Margaret you mourn for." Nevertheless, what is deeply
implied by the poem—and what the heartsick and self-indul-
gent narrator cannot see—is that winter always returns to
spring and that the cycle of nature is renewed. For Hopkins
the poet—unlike the speaker of this poem—the pattern of
nature, winter returning to spring, life going on, is an ana-
logue of the resurrection, the triumph over death. Or, for the
secular reader, the continuity of the seasons is a reminder
that there is always life that survives one's own and that we
must cultivate the generosity to identify with that ongoing
life. Like the fullness of the visionary imagination, the seasons unfold into infinity: they do not lead merely to death

without renewal, winter without spring. Behind the speaker of this poem resides the poet whose awareness is embodied in the poem itself as its repressed but recoverable knowledge. One might even argue that the poem is the poet's act of projected sympathy for the failed imagining of the speaker, who has doomed himself to confirm his own mourning.

Hopkins wrote in a letter to Robert Bridges that "this poem is not founded on any real incident." Hopkins has imagined the character-narrator of his poem as the most negative aspect of himself—the doubting self without faith, hope, or the ability to identify with the spiritual capacities of others. Yet the speaker possesses the potential for empathetic identification, as is portrayed in his initial response to Margaret. The poem, then, can be interpreted as a parable about the danger of despair that comes from a partial vision of nature and human mortality. That failed vision is the result of overemphasizing one's singular life rather than seeing one's life as part of a collective entity. But the self cannot sustain itself only as a self, for then its fate is death, final and absolute. It may be, however, that the death of the self is to the universe what the death of a cell is to the human body. Proper mourning, finally, requires perspective.

IV

For any serious literary artist, the impulse to write must derive, at least in part, from something seen or felt, something rooted in his own experience. Some element of that originating impulse will become manifest in the work of art, though it may be transformed significantly in the process of creation and revision. Yet the activity of artistic creation includes its own emotion that is independent of the particular subject with which the artist is working, whether the subject be sorrowful or joyous. Every good poem or story contains and expresses delight and satisfaction in its own creation, and thus its own creation is an implicit part of its subject along with its manifest theme. The poem, expressing the emotion of its own creation, possesses what Wallace Stevens calls the "gaiety of language" or what William Carlos Williams means

by "the precise counterpart of a cacophony of bird calls,"
the counterpart being the poet's transforming design of his
images and rhythms. Williams concludes his poem "The
Orchestra" by celebrating the imagination's power to celebrate the natural world: "The birds twitter now anew / but
a design / surmounts their twittering. / It is the design of a
man / that makes them twitter. / It is a design."

Williams's poem rejoices in itself as revealing the artist's
power to fabricate a design; therefore, the effect of the poem
differs radically from the emotion that the poem is about—
the fear of nuclear destruction: "Now that he can realize [his
innermost destructive wishes], he must either change them
or perish." No matter how sorrowful their subjects, all good
poems bring pleasure. No poetic attempt can be redeemed
from aesthetic failure by the poem's worthy subject or the
poet's personal sincerity. Because they make new designs,
poems often puzzle the reader at first and reveal their emotional force only upon contemplation. There may be passions
in them, but poems are not written at the instant of the actual
emotion. One does not write about death while attending
a funeral or about desire while making love. A human statement, written or spoken, may be directly and deeply moving,
but we do not value it as a poem, no matter how heartfelt it is,
unless it has the passion of poetic design as well as the passion appropriate to its own subject. Ultimately, we love
poems for being poems, though we demand that they be serious in the way they bear witness to human emotion and
behavior.

Let me illustrate my point by citing two passages from the
writings of Yeats on the subject of his friend and benefactor,
Lady Gregory, and her house where Yeats lived, and then
comparing them to the poem, "Coole Park, 1929," which
deals with the same material. The first passage is from
Yeats's *Autobiography*:

This morning I got a letter telling me of [Lady Gregory's]
illness. I did not recognize her son's writing at first, and
my mind wandered, I suppose because I was not well. I
thought my mother was ill and that my sister was asking

me to come at once: then I remembered that my mother
died years ago and that more than kin was at stake. She
has been to me mother, friend, sister and brother. I cannot realize the world without her—she brought to my
wavering thoughts steadfast nobility. All the day the
thought of losing her is like a conflagration in the rafters.
Friendship is all the house I have.

Every reader must be moved by this brief passage which flows
unmistakably from Yeats's heart. Yet this passionate and
vivid passage is not a poem, and we would not consider it to
be one. It does not offer us what Yeats's best poems do offer:
a design, fabricated from interrelated images, of thoughts and
feelings upon which we can *meditate*—a design that reveals
its full richness only through gradual awareness. Yeats's
poem "Coole Park, 1929" also is about Lady Gregory, her
house, the steadfastness she brought to Yeats's life, and
Yeats's fears about losing her, but it is doubtful that readers
could assimilate this poem on a first encounter as they could
the autobiographical passage.

> I meditate upon a swallow's flight,
> Upon an aged woman and her house,
> A sycamore and lime-tree lost in night
> Although that western cloud is luminous,
> Great works constructed there in nature's spite
> For scholars and for poets after us,
> Thoughts long knitted into a single thought,
> A dance-like glory that those walls begot.
>
> There Hyde before he had beaten into prose
> That noble blade the Muses buckled on,
> There one that ruffled in a manly pose
> For all his timid heart, there that slow man,
> That meditative man, John Synge, and those
> Impetuous men, Shawe-Taylor and Hugh Lane,
> Found pride established in humility,
> A scene well set and excellent company.
>
> They came like swallows and like swallows went,
> And yet a woman's powerful character
> Could keep a swallow to its first intent;

And half a dozen in formation there,
That seemed to whirl upon a compass-point,
Found certainty upon the dreaming air,
The intellectual sweetness of those lines
That cut through time or cross it withershins.

Here, traveller, scholar, poet, take your stand
When all those rooms and passages are gone,
When nettles wave upon a shapeless mound
And saplings root among the broken stone,
And dedicate—eyes bent upon the ground,
Back turned upon the brightness of the sun
And all the sensuality of the shade—
A moment's memory to that laurelled head.

What one sees in the poem that is absent in the autobiographical passage is the central, organizing image of the swallows, Yeats himself being one of them. As a "constructed" thing itself, the poem also is concerned with Lady Gregory's inspiring Yeats to produce "Great works constructed there in nature's spite," thus giving focus to Yeats's mind: "a woman's powerful character / Could keep a swallow to its first intent." We do not feel this poem fully until we experience it as a poem—that is, until we come to know it well enough to respond to the emotion inherent in its design, its construction. The poem, in celebration of its own creation, harmonizes with its overt theme—the lament for all natural things that are seen passing and in decay—and achieves "certainty upon the dreaming air"; as Yeats wrote in a letter of June 24, 1935, "I want to plunge myself into impersonal poetry to get rid of the bitterness." Thus, there are two poems here: the poem of autobiographical grieving for Lady Gregory and lamenting inevitable loss, "when all those passages and rooms are gone," and the poem of images and words in rhymed patterns that delights in itself and has the quality (to use Yeats's own phrase) of "intellectual sweetness of those lines." But the creation of design comes from a passion that, paradoxically, we must call impersonal—it is the passion to create art, an object with its own independent being, out of whatever emotional or thematic materials flow into the heart and mind. This is what Yeats calls "creative joy," and the craftsman's passion manifests itself in the intentional exercising of accumulated skills. Yeats describes this crafts-man's passion in another passage in his *Autobiography*: "Is it not certain that the Creator yawns in earthquake and thunder and other popular displays, but toils in rounding the delicate spiral of a shell?" With "eyes bent upon the ground," perhaps to hide his private tears, Yeats sets his imagination against the "shapeless mound" of nature in order to envision a "scene well set" and to picture the swallows in an ordered "formation." Lady Gregory herself is remembered for her "laurelled head," the laurel being an emblem of artistic disci-pline and her achievement of a cultured life, whereby per-sonal experience is made into a ceremonial ritual.

In Yeats's workbooks an entry reveals how Yeats toiled in preparing himself to write "Coole Park, 1929":

> Describe house in first stanza. Here Synge came, Hugh Lane, Shaw Taylor, many names. I too in my timid youth. Coming and going like migratory birds. Then ad-dress the swallows fluttering in their dream like circles. Speak of the rarity of the circumstances that bring to-gether such concords of men. Each man more than him-self through whom an unknown life speaks. A circle ever returning into itself.

The tone of this passage is detached and businesslike; it has the practicality of a shopping list. Compare the perfunctory "Describe house in first stanza" with the final outcry in the passage from the diary: "Friendship is all the house I have." These two passages seem to come from two different voices, two opposite psychologies, until we remind ourselves that a poet cares not only about the expression of what he feels and believes, but also about his composition of patterns of words and the sounds of words. To compose requires control—the deliberate making of choices. In "Coole Park, 1929," the per-sonal self that weeps and the artistic self that shops for words and makes decisions become one. The artist controls, like the actors in a play who must not "break up their lines to weep." This control, which transforms personal sorrow into artistic vision, is the goal Yeats leaves as his inheritance to the succeeding generations in "Under Ben Bulben": "Irish poets, learn your trade, / Sing whatever is well made." The tears of art must be as impersonal, though personally felt, as the composed and abstract beauty of a musical composition. As the tears of sympathy by which man "contemplates even his own death as if it were another's," ultimately they become the tears of transcending laughter, as in "The Cutting of an Agate":

> There is in the creative joy an acceptance of what life brings, because we have understood the beauty of what it brings, or a hatred of death for what it takes away, which arouses within us, through some sympathy perhaps with all other men, an energy so noble, so powerful, that we laugh aloud and mock, in the terror or the sweetness of our exaltation, at death and oblivion.

V

The profound sorrow of Tennyson's lyric "Tears, Idle Tears" finds its object in the general experience of memory and loss. In fact, memory is equated absolutely with this awareness of loss:

> Tears, idle tears, I know not what they mean,
> Tears from the depth of some divine despair
> Rise in the heart, and gather to the eyes,
> In looking on the happy autumn-fields,
> And thinking of the days that are no more.
>
> Fresh as the first beam glittering on a sail,
> That brings our friends up from the underworld,
> Sad as the last which reddens over one
> That sinks with all we love below the verge;
> So sad, so fresh, the days that are no more.
>
> Ah, sad and strange as in dark summer dawns
> The earliest pipe of half-awaken'd birds
> To dying ears, when unto dying eyes
> The casement slowly grows a glimmering square;
> So sad, so strange, the days that are no more.

Dear as remember'd kisses after death,
And sweet as those by hopeless fancy feign'd
On lips that are for others; deep as love,
Deep as first love, and wild with all regret;
O Death in Life, the days that are no more!

Nowhere in the poem does Tennyson locate a particular experience that defines the speaker as unique, and only in the
first line does the personal pronoun "I" appear when Tennyson says of his tears that "I know not what they mean."
These are everybody's tears; they originate from the collective "depth of some divine despair." Even an image of felic-
ity and beauty, such as the "happy autumn-fields," brings
forth these tears because happiness in the perspective of mortal transience also is a source of sorrow. The very strength
of our love for another is equally the potency of our grief
when they are gone, and memory "brings our friends up from
the underworld." Ironically, it is the memory of absence that
has a kind of permanence so that the pain of remembered
loss remains fresh: "So sad, so fresh, the days that are no
more."

The paradox of the inextricability of sorrow and love, or
grief and happiness, is one that Tennyson cannot completely
comprehend, and thus the essential quality of consciousness
itself is "So sad, so strange." In the final stanza of the poem
Tennyson extends the concept of memory as the awareness
of loss into the related concept of desire for the unobtainable:
they are twin sorrows. "Remember'd kisses after death" are
no less a source of tears than the "hopeless fancy" of kisses on
"lips that are for others." In effect, "first love," by its very
nature, desires an ideal and unobtainable object which is as
inaccessible as a loved one who has died. Grief and separation
have their roots in our very being. And for this grief, Tennyson, like everyman, is "wild with all regret." This is not
Tennyson's regret for any personal failure or any particular
sin; rather, this regret is the awareness of what immemorial-
ly has been called the fallen condition. The expression of this
collective regret is what Virgil describes as "tears for passing
things." These also are the representative tears of Dante's old

man of Crete. And these are the tears of what Wordsworth calls "natural sorrow." To weep these tears is simultaneously an acknowledgment of actual and inescapable grief and the soothing of that grief: sorrow made musical.

In Wordsworth's poem "The Solitary Reaper," which is suffused with "natural sorrow," a traveler—the speaker of the poem—stops to listen to a young woman who is reaping in a field and "singing by herself":

> Behold her, single in the field,
> Yon solitary Highland Lass!
> Reaping and singing by herself;
> Stop here, or gently pass!
> Alone she cuts and binds the grain,
> And sings a melancholy strain;
> O listen! for the Vale profound
> Is overflowing with the sound.
>
> No Nightingale did ever chaunt
> More welcome notes to weary bands
> Of travellers in some shady haunt,
> Among Arabian sands:
> A voice so thrilling ne'er was heard
> In spring-time from the Cuckoo-bird,
> Breaking the silence of the seas
> Among the farthest Hebrides.
>
> Will no one tell me what she sings?—
> Perhaps the plaintive numbers flow
> For old, unhappy, far-off things,
> And battles long ago:
> Or is it some more humble lay,
> Familiar matter of to-day?
> Some natural sorrow, loss, or pain,
> That has been, and may be again?
>
> Whate'er the theme, the Maiden sang
> As if her song could have no ending;
> I saw her singing at her work,
> And o'er the sickle bending;—
> I listened, motionless and still;

> And, as I mounted up the hill,
> The music in my heart I bore,
> Long after it was heard no more.

The words "single" and "alone" give heavy emphasis to the
title, and the speaker's stressing of her isolation is embodied in his impression of her song as a "melancholy strain."
The very landscape seems to contain this song, as if the
maiden's melancholy is an extension of the earth's voice itself: "O listen! for the Vale profound / Is overflowing with
the sound." Despite the speaker's intense awareness of the
maiden's melancholy, with which he identifies, her song is
greeted by him as having a desired and needed effect: "No
Nightingale did ever chaunt / More welcome notes to weary
bands / Of travellers." The speaker has been mystically presented with an actual image to verify the hope of Psalm 126:
"They that sow in tears shall reap in joy." The speaker cannot
identify the source of this song, although he speculates that it
lies deep in the remote and barely remembered past: "Perhaps the plaintive numbers flow / For old, unhappy, far-off
things, / And battles long ago." Whatever its origin, the
maiden's song is interpreted by the speaker as the expression
of "natural sorrow, loss, or pain"—the fundamental experience of all human beings suffering their own mortality.

Although the poem appears to be set in the present, beginning with the speaker's injunction to himself (or to the reader
as companion-traveler), the final stanza reorients the readers
and makes them realize that this entire experience has taken
place some time ago: "Whate'er the theme, the Maiden *sang*"
(italics mine). And yet this past has remained so aesthetically
powerful in the speaker's memory that he has continued to
experience it, and, indeed, he is still experiencing it now. In
the stillness of the speaker's body as he listens to the
maiden's song, pausing in his life's journey from the vale "up
the hill," time also seems to stop and be contained in this
visionary interval in which "I saw her singing at her work."
In his mind her image has become eternalized—a prototype
of human sorrow transformed to music. The speaker's own
isolation and its attendant melancholy is mitigated by his

identification with the maiden; her song is now recognized as an ongoing part of his own life: "The music in my heart I bore, / Long after it was heard no more." In effect, the speaker has reaped the maiden's song, and in doing so, natural sorrow, through empathy, has been converted into joy.

Wordsworth acknowledged that he had gotten the idea for "The Solitary Reaper" from the manuscript of his friend Thomas Wilkinson, *Tours to the British Mountains*, which reads: "Passed a female who was reaping alone: she sung in Erse as she bended over her sickle; the sweetest voice I ever heard: her strains were tenderly melancholy, and felt delicious, long after they were heard no more." Wordsworth's poem is written in the first person, creating the illusion that he is literally describing an event that he has experienced. Yet, the concept of an experience being one's own because it actually happened to one is modified both by the poem and by the circumstance of its genesis. In the poem, the speaker shares and identifies with the maiden's melancholy. In fact, Wordsworth has taken Wilkinson's experience and rendered it as his own. Even though Wordsworth has reworked Wilkinson's language into musical form, Wordsworth varied Wilkinson's line only slightly to "long after it was heard no more," as the final line of his poem. Wordsworth recognized in Wilkinson's scene an experience of shared melancholy that his imagination seized as belonging to everyone. And this experience of shared "natural sorrow"—the paradox that transfigures suffering into pleasure—became the very center of Wordsworth's art; it clarifies, for example, what Wordsworth meant by "primal sympathy" in "Ode: Intimations of Immortality" and by "the soothing thoughts that spring / Out of human suffering." Even more fundamental than unavoidable sorrow, pain, and loss for Wordsworth was the capacity for transforming that sorrow through identification with nature and other human beings.

Just as Tennyson's "Tears, Idle Tears" had the benevolent mark of Wordsworthian influence (it was composed at Tintern Abbey), the model of empathetic and sympathetic identification for Wordsworth is to be found in Milton. By the end of book 9 of *Paradise Lost*, the marital bond of being "one

flesh" has been broken by Adam and Eve, and we see them
arguing without hope of resolution: "Thus they in mutual
accusation spent / The fruitless hours." Milton's profound
irony is that for Adam and Eve, having eaten the forbidden
fruit and violated their covenant with God, time itself has
lost its meaning and has become "fruitless." Milton's view of
human communication is that empathy cannot be achieved
through physical touch alone and that only language can
complete what the body initiates. Thus Milton had earlier, in
book 4, depicted our first parents at the utmost of happy
harmony in conversation with each other: Eve says to Adam,
"With thee conversing, I forget all time, / All seasons, and
their change, all please alike. / Sweet is the breath of morn,
her rising sweet, / With charm of earliest birds." In harmony
with Adam and with nature, Eve is also in harmony with
time, and thus time is not felt to be a burden or a curse. Everything has the quality of sweetness, like the taste of ripe and
nourishing fruit, and language possesses the musical richness
of poetry as suggested by the pun in the word "conversing."
Body and mind, man and woman, human consciousness and
nature—all are one in their rhythmic expression.

The breach between Adam and Eve seems absolute until
Eve "with tears that ceased not flowing, / And tresses all dis-
ordered, at his feet / Fell humble." This is the precise moment of the poem when the Fall begins to be reversed through
Eve's action of humility. By kneeling down—a gesture that
acknowledges the foregone fact of their Fall—Eve makes possible the restoration of their relationship through the reestablishment of mutual compassion. Eve's weeping, testifying to
her own remorse, "in Adam wrought / Commiseration," and
Adam is then able to respond gently to her, both in gesture
and in speech: "And thus with peaceful words upraised her
soon." The movement upward both in body and in spirit has
begun.

Eve's gesture of kneeling before Adam becomes the model
that inspires Adam to kneel humbly before God, and Adam
invites Eve to join him in this mutual supplication:

> "What better can we do, than to the place
> Repairing where he judged us, prostrate fall

> Before him reverent, and there confess
> Humbly our faults, and pardon beg, with tears
> Watering the ground, and with our sighs the air
> Frequenting, sent from hearts contrite, in sign
> Of sorrow unfeigned, and humiliation meek."

Once again the Fall is reenacted and acknowledged in a bodily gesture, and in doing so, in judging themselves, Adam and Eve are in harmony with God's judgment of them. The harmony of mutually accepting their mortal limits begins the process of "repairing" their Fall. They must go back ("repair") in place and in time in order to restore what has been lost, and once again become a wedded couple; they must re-pair. Their tears are now fruitful, "Watering the ground," so that their harmony with nature also is reestablished, and the expression of "sorrow unfeigned" is a cathartic source of relief, rather than an extension of pain and guilt. At this point another curative event takes place: the voice of Milton, the narrator, enters in, echoing and ritualizing Adam's words:

> So spake our father penitent, nor Eve
> Felt less remorse: they forthwith to the place
> Repairing where he judged them prostrate fell
> Before him reverent, and both confessed
> Humbly their faults, and pardon begged, with tears
> Watering the ground, and with their sighs the air
> Frequenting, sent from hearts contrite, in sign
> Of sorrow unfeigned, and humiliation meek.

Here Milton identifies himself with his father, Adam (just as God the Father and God the Son also are one), embracing Adam's sin, and seeing in the Fall the bond of sorrow among everyone. One language speaks for the history of humanity, and it is the triumph of Milton's art for him to have found this collective voice. *Paradise Lost* ends by returning (repairing) to the beginning of mortal time when Adam and Eve are being led out of Eden to make their way in the world through their own labor. Milton says, "Some natural tears they dropped, but wiped them soon." Since Adam and Eve are now in nature as we know it, they must express the sorrow inherent in nature, and yet, together again in sympathy, "hand in hand," they have a resource that is deeper than tears; tears can be wiped away. So, too, Milton guides his reader beyond weeping through the grace of his art.

V I

Weeping enables grief to be exorcised and mourning brought to an end. Paradoxically, we shed tears so that we may stop shedding tears. The perverse corollary of this process occurs in the repression of grief and weeping; the effect of such repression is to prolong mourning—indeed, to eternalize it. By refusing to give expression to grief, one sustains its brooding energy which breeds upon itself, and grief is extended into generalized anger, hatred of the conditions of life, and finally rejection of the self. In his essay "Mourning and Melancholia," Freud defines this state of introjected grieving in which the individual suffers "painful dejection, abrogation of interest in the outside world, loss of the capacity to love, inhibition of all activity, and a lowering of the self-regarding feelings." In such an emotional state, for example, the wife in Frost's "Home Burial" seeks to preserve grief for her dead child so that grieving will not, as she says to her husband, lead "back to life / And living people":

> 'No, from the time when one is sick to death,
> One is alone, and he dies more alone.
> Friends make pretense of following to the grave,
> But before one is in it, their minds are turned
> And making the best of their way back to life
> And living people, and things they understand.
> But the world's evil. I won't have grief so
> If I can change it. Oh, I won't, I won't!'

Repressive anger has replaced her tears. She wants grief to last forever and desires darkly that the living should remain fixated entirely upon death. She envisions the world as an evil place where everyone is doomed to psychological isolation.

In Keats's letter to George and Georgiana Keats of May 3, 1819, meditating on King Lear's line describing man as a "poor, bare, forked animal," Keats remarks: "Do you not see how necessary a World of Pains and troubles is to school an Intelligence and make it a Soul? A Place where the heart must feel and suffer in a thousand diverse ways!" This is exactly how Lear's intelligence must be schooled, and Lear's soul will emerge through a process that enables him, first, to feel compassion for others and, then, in identification with all suffering creatures, to be able to weep for himself as well. Banished into the storm with Kent, Edgar, and the Fool, Lear insists, in exalted diction, that first they take shelter in the hovel on the heath:

> Poor naked wretches, whereso'er you are,
> That bide the pelting of this pitiless storm,
> How shall your houseless heads and unfed sides,
> Your looped and window'd raggedness, defend you
> From seasons such as these? O! I have ta'en
> Too little care of this. Take physic, pomp;
> Expose thyself to feel what wretches feel,
> That thou mayst shake the superflux to them,
> And show the heavens more just.

Lear, however, will not allow his generosity toward all "naked wretches" to extend to himself, even though by now he is one of them. His earlier refusal to weep persists as a form of self-punishment: "You think I'll weep? / No, I'll not weep. / I have full cause of weeping, but this heart / Shall break into a hundred thousand flaws / Or ere I'll weep." And until Lear can weep, his soul will remain locked in anger and self-pity; his ability to love still will be fettered.

Only when Lear is rescued by Cordelia can he permit himself to weep redeeming tears. So tormented and yet so powerful is Lear's relief that he believes he has been resurrected from the grave and that Cordelia has come to him from heaven, although he himself is still bound in earthly—even infernal—punishment:

> You do me wrong to take me out o' the grave.
> Thou art a soul in bliss; but I am bound
> Upon a wheel of fire, that mine own tears
> Do scald like molten lead.

Nonetheless, his tears have a healing effect, and Lear is able to address himself to Cordelia's sorrow which is mixed with her joy at their reunion. "Be your tears wet?" Lear asks; "Yes, faith. I pray, weep not." After this extreme moment of sympathy, Lear is able to say to Cordelia, "Pray you now, forget and forgive," so that Lear's vision of the world as a place where *love is possible* carries him beyond weeping. In act 5, when Lear and Cordelia are about to be led away to prison, Lear's vision of possible love is brought to its consummation when he implores Cordelia to "Wipe thine eyes. / The good years shall devour them, flesh and fell, / Ere they shall make us weep." The wheel of fate, however, turns again, and Lear lives to witness the death of his daughter, but before Lear, too, dies and is released from the "rack of this tough world," he imagines that Cordelia is still alive. Holding a feather to her lips, Lear thinks that her breath stirs the feather, and he cries, "If it be so, / It is a chance which does redeem all sorrows / That ever I have felt." Lear is not blessed to have this chance be true in actuality, and yet the emotion of what he has envisioned is true. Beyond tears, although replete with weeping, Lear has seen what he could not see before his soul was created through his suffering. Earlier in the play, Kent had told him, "See better, Lear," and finally Lear has come to see and experience the possibility of sympathetic love.

VII

Saul Bellow's novel *Seize the Day* begins, "When it came to concealing his troubles, Tommy Wilhelm was not less capable than the next fellow." Like Lear, he sees his world collapsing, and he feels that he is drowning in his life. Wilhelm's troubles include enduring the breakup of his marriage, separating from his children, losing the last of his money in the stock market, and arguing with his old father who will neither loan him money nor offer him sympathy. Wilhelm cannot control his journey that leads to his destiny: thus his ironic name, Will-helm. He has renamed himself, hoping to separate himself from the sins of his father, Dr. Adler, whose name suggests Adam, the fallen father of us all, "Adler being

in his mind the title of the species." Even though Wilhelm
knows that "there's very little that a man can change at will,"
he struggles to set right the circumstances of his life and to
"conceal" or deny the inescapable sorrow of his condition.
When he was talking to his father (who blames Wilhelm for
his failures), "tears approached his eyes but he didn't let them
out." Yet Wilhelm also possesses a countersense of himself
and his fate. He suspects that, perhaps, instead of opposing
sorrow, he should embrace it, acknowledge it as the meaning
of his life: "Maybe the making of mistakes expressed the very
purpose of his life and the essence of his being here. Maybe he
was supposed to make them and suffer from them on this
earth." Still, he continues to set himself apart from his own
suffering and to repress the tears that are gathering within
him: "he was afraid that he would cry. But he hardened himself. The hardening effort made a violent, vertical pain go
through his chest. . . . And yet his unshed tears rose and rose
and he looked like a man about to drown."

At the end of the novel, Wilhelm instinctively follows a
procession of people into the chapel of a funeral parlor where
a service is being held for a man he has never known. Finally,
the tears come: "Standing a little apart, Wilhelm began to
cry. He cried at first softly and from sentiment, but soon from
deeper feeling. He sobbed loudly and his face grew distorted
and hot, and the tears stung his skin. A man—another human
creature, was what first went through his thoughts." Beyond
his will, yet with his acceptance, the tears of some mysterious primal sympathy flowed forth as he "gave in utterly and
held his face and wept. He cried with all his heart." In his
tears Wilhelm finds his destiny and his reward; in these tears
he both loses and finds himself in the central, collective emotion of mankind; and in these tears he moves, as Bellow says,
"deeper than sorrow": "heavy sea-like music came up to his
ears. It poured into him where he had hidden himself in the
center of a crowd by the great and happy oblivion of tears. He
heard it and sank deeper than sorrow, through torn sobs and
cries toward the consummation of his heart's ultimate
need." In celebration and lament, the tears of Bellow's art return us to the originating sea, resounding with the rhythmic

music of creation and destruction, and identifying each of us
with the collective heart of humankind.

V I I I

Having been rescued from the sea (where it had been prophe-
sied that eventually he will die), Odysseus is invited by the
king Alkínoös to attend the games and the feast that are to be
held in his honor. The culmination of the ceremonies comes
when Alkínoös asks his minstrel to sing the story of the fall
of Troy: "The minstrel stirred, murmuring to the god, and
soon / clear words and notes came one by one." As the minstrel recounts the fated destruction, "For Troy must perish,
as ordained, that day / she harbored the great horse of tim-
ber," Odysseus draws back into his own memories:

> And Odysseus
> let the bright molten tears run down his cheeks,
> weeping the way a wife mourns for her lord
> on the lost field where he has gone down fighting
> the day of wrath that came upon his children.
> At sight of the man panting and dying there,
> she slips down to enfold him, crying out;
> then feels the spears, prodding her back and shoulders,
> and goes bound into slavery and grief.
> Piteous weeping wears away her cheeks:
> but no more piteous than Odysseus' tears,
> cloaked as they were, now, from the company.

It is the song itself that releases Odysseus's tears, freeing him
to suffer the grief of the war's victims, freeing him to weep
for himself and for all mankind. Alkínoös, who alone has
heard Odysseus's sobbing, shares his sorrow when he says,
"since our fine poet sang, / our guest has never left off weeping. Grief / seems fixed upon his heart," and commands that
the song be interrupted: "Break off the song!" Alkínoös
knows, however, that the song will be resumed, for it is the
gift of the gods that enables men to endure their lives: "That
was all the gods' work," Alkínoös declares, "weaving ruin
there / so it should make a song for men to come."

When Odysseus returns home, having been reunited with his son Telémakhos, and begins to take vengeance on the suitors, the minstrel, Terpis Phêmios, confronts Odysseus's wrath. Phêmios's immediate instinct is to "flee that way to the courtyard altar," but a value deeper than his own life determines his next amazing action:

> But first to save
> his murmuring instrument he laid it down
> carefully between the winebowl and a chair,
> then he betook himself to Lord Odysseus,
> clung hard to his knees, and said: "Mercy,
> mercy on a suppliant, Odysseus!
> My gift is song for men and for the gods undying."

At Telémakhos's urging, Odysseus spares the minstrel, sharing the minstrel's knowledge that the gift of song offers grace to our lives. Having returned home, Odysseus knows that the happy tears of such song—art that both imitates and affirms the limits of our mortal condition—must be cherished and protected.

Index

Acknowledgment is made to publishers and individuals who have granted permission to quote from material under copyright.

"Lapis Lazuli," "The Man and the Echo," "John Kinsella's Lament," "The Three Bushes," © 1940 by Georgie Yeats, renewed 1968 by Bertha Georgie Yeats, Michael Butler Yeats, and Anne Yeats; "Father and Child," "Three Things," "A Dialogue of Self and Soul," "Cap and Bells," and "Coole Park, 1929," © 1933 by Macmillan Publishing Company, renewed 1961 by Bertha Georgie Yeats. From *The Collected Poems of W. B. Yeats*, ed. Richard J. Finneran. Reprinted with permission of Macmillan Publishing Company, and Michael B. Yeats, and Macmillan London, Ltd.

"The Aërolite" from *The Complete Poems* by Thomas Hardy, ed. James Gibson. Copyright renewed 1953 by Lloyds Bank, Ltd. Reprinted with permission of Macmillan Publishing Company.

"During a Solar Eclipse" from *Sentences* by Howard Nemerov (University of Chicago Press, 1980). Reprinted by permission of the author.

"The Snow Man," "Life is Motion," "Final Soliloquy of the Interior Paramour," "Autumn Refrain," "The Plain Sense of Things," "The Woman in Sunshine," and excerpts from "Sunday Morning," "The Owl in the Sarcophagus," "An Ordinary Evening in New Haven," and "The Auroras of Autumn" from *The Collected Poems of Wallace Stevens*. © 1923, 1931, 1935, 1936, 1937, 1942, 1943, 1944, 1945, 1946, 1947, 1948, 1949, 1950, 1951, 1952, 1954 by Wallace Stevens. Reprinted by permission of Alfred A. Knopf, Inc.

"The Sea Elephant" from William Carlos Williams, *Collected Earlier Poems*. © 1938 by New Directions Publishing Corporation; "The Orchestra" from William Carlos Williams, *Pictures from Brueghel*. © 1954 by William Carlos Williams. Reprinted by permission of New Directions Publishing Corporation.

Selections from *The Poetry of Robert Frost*, ed. Edward Connery Lathem. © 1916, 1928, 1930, 1939, 1969 by Holt, Rinehart and Winston; © 1942, 1944, 1956, 1958, 1962 by Robert Frost; © 1967, 1970 by Lesley Frost Ballantine. Reprinted by permission of Holt, Rinehart and Winston, Publishers, Jonathan Cape, Ltd., the Estate of Robert Frost, and Edward Connery Lathem.

"My Papa's Waltz," © 1942 by The Hearst Magazine, Inc. from *The Collected Poems of Theodore Roethke* by Theodore Roethke. Reprinted by permission of Doubleday & Company, Inc., and Faber and Faber Ltd.